Prisoners Among Us

DAVID T. STANLEY

Prisoners Among Us
The Problem of Parole

THE BROOKINGS INSTITUTION
Washington, D.C.

Copyright © 1976 by
THE BROOKINGS INSTITUTION
1775 Massachusetts Avenue, N.W., Washington, D.C. 20036

Library of Congress Cataloging in Publication Data:
Stanley, David T
    Prisoners among us.

    Bibliography: p.
    Includes index.
    1. Parole—United States.   2. Parole officers—
United States.   3. Community-based corrections—
United States.   I. Title.
HV9304.S7   364.6′2′0973   75-44506
ISBN 0-8157-8106-7
ISBN 0-8157-8105-9 pbk.

1 2 3 4 5 6 7 8 9

THE BROOKINGS INSTITUTION is an independent organization devoted to nonpartisan research, education, and publication in economics, government, foreign policy, and the social sciences generally. Its principal purposes are to aid in the development of sound public policies and to promote public understanding of issues of national importance.

The Institution was founded on December 8, 1927, to merge the activities of the Institute for Government Research, founded in 1916, the Institute of Economics, founded in 1922, and the Robert Brookings Graduate School of Economics and Government, founded in 1924.

The Board of Trustees is responsible for the general administration of the Institution, while the immediate direction of the policies, program, and staff is vested in the President, assisted by an advisory committee of the officers and staff. The by-laws of the Institution state: "It is the function of the Trustees to make possible the conduct of scientific research, and publication, under the most favorable conditions, and to safeguard the independence of the research staff in the pursuit of their studies and in the publication of the results of such studies. It is not a part of their function to determine, control, or influence the conduct of particular investigations or the conclusions reached."

The President bears final responsibility for the decision to publish a manuscript as a Brookings book. In reaching his judgment on the competence, accuracy, and objectivity of each study, the President is advised by the director of the appropriate research program and weighs the views of a panel of expert outside readers who report to him in confidence on the quality of the work. Publication of a work signifies that it is deemed a competent treatment worthy of public consideration but does not imply endorsement of conclusions or recommendations.

The Institution maintains its position of neutrality on issues of public policy in order to safeguard the intellectual freedom of the staff. Hence interpretations or conclusions in Brookings publications should be understood to be solely those of the authors and should not be attributed to the Institution, to its trustees, officers, or other staff members, or to the organizations that support its research.

To Helen, David, Mimi, and Betsy

Foreword

DIFFICULT and important policy choices originating in the criminal justice system now confront the American people. The crime problem is ever before our eyes, and the financial and human costs of attempts to deal with it are the focus of much attention in the media. Political leaders, no less than ordinary citizens, are concerned about the hardship and jeopardy that prison life inflicts on criminal offenders, yet they are justifiably fearful of the consequences for society if criminals are not incarcerated. This ambivalence pervades the central question that the parole system seeks to answer: How can prisoners be released to supervised living in the community without endangering society?

The officials who administer the parole system have varied qualifications. They are organized in different patterns in the fifty states and the federal government, and they work under divergent laws and other guidelines. Yet they all share the desire to protect society from crime while fostering the reform of criminal offenders.

The importance, complexity, and persistence of the parole problem led the Brookings Institution to undertake this inquiry into the purposes and performance of parole systems in the United States. The study was carried out by David T. Stanley, at the time a senior fellow in the Brookings Governmental Studies program. Mr. Stanley, who has also been an advisor to the federal Law Enforcement Assistance Administration on setting goals and evaluating programs, made an extensive review of the literature and statistics of corrections generally, and of parole in particular, and consulted with leading analysts and practitioners in these fields. He studied the parole operations of the federal government, the District of Columbia, and four states—California, Colorado, Georgia, and Wisconsin.

He finds much uncertainty of purpose and practice in the decision-making of parole boards, waste motion in supervision of parolees, injustice in methods of revoking parole, and inadequacy in the provision of community rehabilitative assistance. He proposes an alternative system

ix

that is likely to encounter formidable political obstacles, one that would end indeterminate sentencing, eliminate parole release and supervision, and upgrade community help to exoffenders.

In most of his research, Mr. Stanley was assisted by Douglas C. Person, a graduate student in the sociology department of Howard University, who did much of the library work and some of the interviewing and observation of parole operations in the federal system, the District of Columbia, and Georgia. After Mr. Person's return to full-time university work, the author was assisted by Joy Silver of the Brookings staff, who edited an early draft of the manuscript and compiled the bibliography. Gloria Jiménez was secretary for the project. The manuscript was prepared for publication by Ellen A. Ash; the index was prepared by Florence Robinson.

The interpretations and conclusions in this volume are solely those of the author and should not be ascribed to the trustees, officers, or other staff members of the Brookings Institution.

GILBERT Y. STEINER
Acting President

May 1976
Washington, D.C.

Author's Acknowledgments

I AM GRATEFUL for the assistance of the many persons who patiently and cooperatively explained to me the concepts and operational details of their parole systems. In the governments studied, I am especially indebted to the following officials:

U.S. Government. Chairman Maurice H. Sigler and other members and staff of the U.S. Board of Parole, especially Peter B. Hoffman and Lucille DeGosten of the Research Unit; Bureau of Prisons Director Norman A. Carlson and Director of Research Howard Kitchener; Donald L. Chamlee, William A. Cohan, Jr., and James McCafferty of the Probation Division of the Administrative Office of the U.S. Courts, and their field staffs; and the Bureau of Intergovernmental Personnel Programs of the U.S. Civil Service Commission.

District of Columbia. The Reverend H. Albion Ferrell, his fellow members, and the staff of the District of Columbia Parole Board; Director of Corrections Kenneth Hardy, his successor Delbert C. Jackson, and the corrections and parole staffs; and Benjamin Renshaw and his associates at the Office of Criminal Justice Plans and Analysis.

California. Former Chairman Henry W. Kerr, Administrative Officer Joseph A. Spangler, and the staff of the Adult Authority; former Corrections Director Raymond K. Procunier; the staff of the Parole and Community Services Division, especially William Sidell; and Lawrence Bennett, Director of Research.

Colorado. Chairman Gordon W. Heggie and other members of the State Board of Parole; Robert Trujillo, former Corrections Director and later Acting Director of Parole; and parole and corrections staff members.

Georgia. Chairman Cecil C. McCall of the State Board of Pardons and Paroles, other members of the board, and their staff; Commissioner of Offender Rehabilitation Allen L. Ault; and correctional and parole staff members.

Wisconsin. Former Vice Chairman William D. Dawson and other members of the Parole Board; former Corrections Administrator Sanger B. Powers; and members of the correctional and parole staffs.

I also acknowledge with gratitude the assistance of the following scholars and other authorities, who provided valuable information and helpful criticism:

Gerald Caplan, Walter R. Burkhart, and Stuart Adams of the Nation Institute of Law Enforcement and Criminal Justice of the Law Enforcement Assistance Administration of the U.S. Department of Justice; Morton Goren, librarian of the LEAA; Seymour Brandwein and William Throckmorton of the Manpower Administration of the U.S. Department of Labor; Donald P. Smith of the U.S. Office of Management and Budget; Harry Scarr of the Office of Justice Policy and Planning of the U.S. Department of Justice; and the Washington staff of the International Personnel Management Association.

Alvin J. Bronstein and staff of the National Prison Project of the American Civil Liberties Union; David Rudenstine and Diana Gordon of the Citizens' Inquiry on Parole and Criminal Justice; Daniel I. Skoler, Melvin T. Axilbund, and other staff members of the Commission on Correctional Facilities and Services of the American Bar Association; E. Preston Sharp, Anthony P. Travisono, Leon Leiberg, and William Parker of the American Correctional Association; and Vincent O'Leary and Fred Cohen of the School of Criminal Justice of the State University of New York at Albany.

James V. Bennett, former Director of the U.S. Bureau of Prisons; the late F. Lovell Bixby, a former federal and New Jersey correction official; Donald D. Brewer of the Institute of Government of the Unviersity of Georgia; John P. Conrad of the Academy for Contemporary Problems; Jameson W. Doig of the Woodrow Wilson School of Public and International Affairs at Princeton University; Howard Eglit of the Roger Baldwin Foundation of the American Civil Liberties Union; Daniel Glaser of the University of Southern California; and David Greenberg of New York University.

Keith Hawkins of Wolfson College, Oxford; Donald L. Horowitz of the Brookings Institution; Robert H. Hughes of the University of Colorado at Colorado Springs; Richard A. McGee, President of the American Justice Institute; Robert Martinson of the City University of New York; Sheldon I. Messinger, Dean of the School of Criminology of the University of California at Berkeley; Marcus A. Neithercutt of the National

Council on Crime and Delinquency; and E. K. Nelson, Dean of the School of Public Administration of the University of Southern California.

James O. Robison of Criminological Research Associates; Howard R. Sacks of the University of Connecticut Law School; Charles E. Silberman of the Study of Law and Justice; Alexander B. Smith of the John Jay College of Criminal Justice of the City University of New York; Gilbert Y. Steiner of the Brookings Institution; Elliot Studt of the University of California at Los Angeles; Andrew von Hirsch of the Committee for the Study of Incarceration; and David A. Ward of the University of Minnesota.

D.T.S.

Contents

1. The Idea of Parole   1
   Theories and Purposes of Parole 1
   The Functions of Parole 3
   This Study 5

2. The Decision to Imprison   7
   Theories of Punishment 7
   Sentencing and Its Preliminaries 20

3. The Board and the Prisoner   26
   Parole Board Organization 26
   Board Members and Their Selection 28
   Who Hears the Prisoner? 33
   The Hearing: What Goes On 34
   Appraising the Hearings 41
   Making the Decision and Notifying the Prisoner 44

4. The Decision to Release   47
   Guides for the Board 47
   Data about the Offender 48
   Prediction 50
   How Parole Boards Decide 57
   Legal Fairness and Due Process 70
   Evaluation and Alternatives 76

5. The Parolee under Supervision   81
   The Parole Agreement 82
   Assignment to a Parole Officer 84
   Organization of Parole Staffs 86
   The Parole Officer and His Job 89
   The Routine of Surveillance 95
   The Parole Relationship 101

6. The Parolee in Trouble   104
   The Road to Revocation 105
   Arrests and Weapons 111

The Formal Revocation Process 112
Reparole after Revocation 118
Discharge from Parole 120
Mandatory Releasees 122
Parolees from Other States 122
Can the Parole Officer Do It? 124
Time Studies 125
The Parole Officer's Performance and Attitudes 129
Evaluation and Alternatives 132

7. Helping the Parolee in the Community   135
Prerelease Indoctrination 136
Community Reentry 137
Community Services for Offenders Not Yet on Parole 139
The Money Problem 145
Employment 149
Concentrated Assistance Projects 163
Volunteer Aid 167
Evaluation and Alternatives 168

8. How Good Is Parole?   171
What to Evaluate? 171
Measures and Methods for Evaluation 172
Parole Evaluation Studies 178
Should Parole Continue? 184

Selected Bibliography   192

Index   199

Tables

4-1. Parole Success Rates of New York State Male Parolees
Released in 1964–66, by Number of Previous Arrests and History
of Excessive Drug or Alcohol Use   51

4-2. Parole Success Rates of New York State Male Parolees
Released in 1964–66, by Crime of Conviction and History
of Excessive Drug or Alcohol Use   52

4-3. Success and Failure Rates of 1,367 Federal Adult Offenders
Released in 1970, by Number of Prison Punishments   55

4-4. Criteria for Parole Deferral, by Their Critical Use and Stated
Influence, New York State, 1968   61

5-1. Qualifications and Monthly Salaries for Parole Officers, 1975   90

6-1. Distribution of Federal Probation Officers' Working Time,
by Type of Activity   125

7-1. Difficulties Experienced during First Year of Parole, by Number of
     Visitors Received While in Prison and Amount of Release Money   148

7-2. Employment Status of Male Federal Parolees and Mandatory
     Releasees and the National Male Civilian Labor Force, June 1964   150

7-3. Parole Success and Characteristics of Employment,
     Two Samples of Massachusetts Parolees, 1959   151

7-4. Parole Performance of Federal Offenders and Longest Time
     on a Job after Release, 1970   152

8-1. Prison and Parole Costs, Selected States and Years   182

CHAPTER ONE

The Idea of Parole

EVERY YEAR more than 60,000 felons are released from prison and permitted to live, under supervision, among the rest of us while they readjust to life in the free community. The parole system generally works quietly, attracting little attention except when well-known figures like the Fathers Berrigan or the Watergate criminals are paroled, when a parolee commits a crime, when scandal is alleged, or when parole laws are drastically changed. Yet inherent in the operation of parole systems is a difficult dilemma: how can the requirements of individual freedom, justice, and public safety best be balanced? The ways in which the various components of the parole system strike this balance is explored in this book.

Theories and Purposes of Parole

The theoretical underpinning of the parole system includes three basic concepts of what happens when a prisoner is paroled: (1) grace or privilege—the idea that the offender could be kept in prison for his full sentence but the government extends him the privilege of release; (2) contract or consent—the idea that the government makes a deal with the offender, letting him out in return for his promise to abide by certain conditions; and (3) custody—the idea that the parolee, even though free, is in the keeping of the government. As the parole process is examined in detail in the succeeding chapters, it will become clear how far reality deviates from these rationales.

Parole is thought of as performing both a helping and a shielding function: it is "aimed at helping the parolee and supervising his adjustment to society, while at the same time protecting society."[2] Some writers empha-

1. See Michael Gottesman and Lewis J. Hecker, "Parole: A Critique of Its Legal Foundations and Conditions," *New York University Law Review*, vol. 38 (June 1963), pp. 703–07.
2. William Parker, *Parole: Origins, Development, Current Practices and Statutes,*

1

size the helping aspect: it should "achieve the rehabilitation of the parolee and his reintegration into society by the time of the termination of his parole."[3] Others emphasize protection: "The purpose of parole is to protect the public. First, it releases a prisoner only to circumstances that are the best available for maximizing his chances of achieving a noncriminal life; second, it permits his return to prison for all or part of the balance of his sentence if he fails to comply with the rules of parole behavior believed conducive to the prevention of felonies."[4]

So parole involves hard decisions for high stakes. They are hard because there is a conflict in public attitudes, reflected in law, between the wish to give a human being in trouble a chance to succeed and the wish to keep a possibly dangerous person locked up. The dilemma this conflict poses for decision making confronts parole officials every day. This book inquires how, and to what extent, this conflict is resolved by parole boards and parole officers, organized in widely differing patterns, in the fifty states and the federal government.

If one were to construct a composite explanation of the goals of parole offered by the scores of officials interviewed during work on this book, it would take the following form: We are trying to find reasons to release the prisoner, to find noninstitutional remedies that will get him out of a life of crime, that will build a feeling of responsibility in attaining his goals—and trying to do all this in a way that will be congruent with the attitudes of the community. In a similar vein, the National Advisory Commission on Criminal Justice Standards and Goals identified the basic purpose of parole as reduction of recidivism (return to criminal behavior) but noted three other "core sets of concerns": (1) fairness to the criminal offender in decisions and supervision; (2) the appropriateness of criminal punishment in relation to the expectations of the public; and (3) maintenance of the criminal justice system, that is, management of parole selection and supervision in ways that will be supportive of the efforts of police and prison officials.[5]

American Correctional Association, Parole Corrections Project Resource Document no. 1 (College Park, Md., 1975), p. 26. See also similar definition in *International Encyclopedia of the Social Sciences* (Macmillan, 1968), vol. 11, p. 518.

3. "Comment: The Parole System," *University of Pennsylvania Law Review*, vol. 120 (December 1971), p. 284.

4. Daniel Glaser, *The Effectiveness of a Prison and Parole System* (Bobbs-Merrill, 1969), p. 13.

5. National Advisory Commission on Criminal Justice Standards and Goals, *Corrections* (Government Printing Office, 1973), pp. 393–95. For other quasi-official statements of goals and standards for parole, see the following cited in Parker, *Parole,*

This last concern is connected to another goal of parole organizations: to survive and be well regarded. Parole boards and parole staff, like other government bodies, work under a political spotlight. They must please chief executives and legislators, compete successfully for funds, and demonstrate diligence and competence (if not success) in working toward their goals. The spotlight is intense because citizens are afraid of criminals who threaten violence or invade their homes. When parole officials release an offender who then commits a new crime, the social and political repercussions are severe. Thus a major goal of parole boards and officials becomes avoidance of error—or at least of frightening, obvious, publicized error.

Entwined with parole in this political environment are the other elements of the criminal justice system: police, courts, prisons, and, in recent years, organizations responsible for planning, coordination, statistics, research, and grants management. These agencies form a system in the sense that criminals (actual or alleged) pass through the hands of several different organizations, and some communication and coordination among them are necessary. Many an observer has labeled it a "nonsystem" because the organizations sometimes work at crosspurposes, communicate poorly, and maintain incompatible records. Yet this failure in coordination may also have beneficial effects. The various parts of the criminal justice system are brakes on or correctives for one another. If the police arrest an innocent person, the prosecutor, the grand jury, or the court may free him; conversely, the prosecutor or grand jury may find an important development inadequately investigated by the police. If a prisoner is unjustly punished for a breach of discipline, a court may overrule the decision. If some particular data on local crime rates are unavailable from police statistics, a criminal justice planning agency may be able to do the necessary study.

The Functions of Parole

Parole is thus embedded in this partly useful, partly ineffective system of checks and balances. Parole board members and parole officers must work daily with prison administrators, judges, prosecutors, and police. Dif-

---

pp. 208–15: "Declaration of Principles," from *Proceedings*, National Parole Conference, 1939 (app. D); President's Commission on Law Enforcement and Administration of Justice, "Standards for Parole and Aftercare" (app. E); "Essential Elements of an Adequate Parole System," from American Correctional Association, *Manual of Correctional Standards* (1966) (app. F).

ferences in judgment on decisions and priorities must be reconciled; detailed complexities in processing have to be adjusted. Hence, boundary lines are not clear, and one criminal justice agency gets involved in the work of another. Parole actually serves a complex of functions and is related to decisions made by other parts of the criminal justice system.

• Parole is sentencing. Boards decide how long criminals stay in prison. Hence parole is also a way of controlling prisoners: well-behaved inmates are more likely to be released.

• Parole is policing. Some parole officers make searches and have power to arrest.

• Parole is attempted rehabilitation. Parole officers offer counseling, referral, and job-finding services.

• Parole is reimprisonment. Parole officers may propose and boards approve action to put back in a prison a parolee who has violated his agreement.

These decisions are reflected in the process of parole:

1. *Eligibility.* An offender serving a prison sentence approaches a time when under the law he is eligible for parole—often after he has served a third of his maximum sentence.

2. *Decision.* A parole board (though it may have some other name) considers his past record, his offense, his prison record, the recommendations of his prison officers, and his plans for parole and decides whether to grant, delay, or refuse parole. In most states the prisoner is interviewed in person.

3. *Supervision and assistance.* If the board grants parole, the offender is released under the terms of a written agreement. A parole officer supervises him to ensure that he lives up to those terms and helps him with problems of working and living in the free community.

4. *Revocation.* If the parolee commits a crime or violates his agreement he may be sent back to prison after a formal revocation proceeding.

5. *Discharge.* The parolee is discharged from parole when the time of his maximum sentence has expired, or sooner if the law permits discharge for good performance on parole.

A prisoner who has completed his maximum sentence, less time off for good prison behavior, is also released under supervision in some states until he completes that maximum. He is said to be on "conditional release" or "mandatory release" but is treated like a parolee.

This Study

An extensive literature both on parole itself and on other issues in criminal justice that impinge on it has been produced by criminologists and by other behavioral scientists, correctional officials, and attorneys. The literature is sometimes scholarly, sometimes opinionated, sometimes anecdotal; but invariably its authors have preexisting positions on crime, punishment, and deterrence. This book represents an effort at a different—albeit not unique—approach to the study of an urgent problem in public policy. I undertook the inquiry unhampered by prior judgments on the effectiveness of any prison or parole system, but with the advantage of having assisted the federal Law Enforcement Assistance Administration on problems of goal setting and program evaluation. My intent was to convey to a wide audience the understanding gained in the course of my research of what the decision to parole involves, how it is made, and how it is implemented.

The findings in this volume are based on review of the literature, on consultations with authorities and other researchers in the field, on examination of operating statistics, and on interviews and analyses of documents in six jurisdictions—the District of Columbia, California, the federal government, Colorado, Wisconsin, and Georgia (studied in that order). These six parole systems were selected for their variety in location, size and composition of population, and size and method of appointment of parole boards. All six made liberal use of parole, as compared with other means of release.

In each of the six governments, my research assistant and I conducted interviews with parole board members, correctional officials, parole officers, parolees, prison caseworkers, research and statistical staff, administrative officers, and local researchers, academic and nonacademic—a total of 226 interviews. We also accompanied parole boards to prisons and attended parole hearings and deliberations concerning 166 prisoners or parolees, almost all of them adult male felons. Policy statements, decision guidelines, budgets, statistical reports, and evaluative studies were obtained and analyzed.

While this is not a book on theories of crime or the problems of prisons, it cannot ignore these subjects. The treatment of parole decision making (chapters 3 and 4) is thus necessarily preceded by some discussion of why we incarcerate people and what happens to them as a result (chapter 2). The discussion moves then to parole supervision (chapters 5 and 6), covering issues involved in both surveillance and revocation. Chapter 7 examines ways in which parolees are helped to get along in the community. Chapter 8 contains a general evaluation of parole and an appraisal of some possible alternatives.

The conclusion reached in this book can be stated bluntly at the outset: *parole authorities simply are not sure of what they are doing when they decide to release an offender from prison and deal with him in the free community.* The succeeding chapters tell a story of uncertainty of purpose and practice in decision making, waste motion in supervision, injustice in revocation, and inadequacies in rehabilitative assistance. As will be shown, however, there are feasible (though politically difficult) alternatives to the parole systems that have produced these conditions.

CHAPTER TWO

The Decision to Imprison

A PAROLE board's decision on when to release a prisoner comes late in a long chain of events in the offender's relationship with the criminal justice system. There have been previous decisions: to arrest, to charge, to prosecute, to sentence, to classify, and to assign to a prison. The parole board is concerned with the results of all these earlier decisions, particularly the sentence. Both the sentencing judge and the parole board are concerned with the "why" of imprisonment—the theories that underlie our system of punishment.

Theories of Punishment

Judges and parole boards are the heirs of centuries of painful, controversial thought about why we punish, particularly by incarceration. Theories of punishment have their roots in equally diverse and conflicting theories of crime and its causes, for there are no real "laws" of criminology as there are laws of physics. The most frequently encountered simplifica-

1. For helpful discussions of crime causation theory, see Daniel Glaser, "Criminality Theories and Behavioral Images," *American Journal of Sociology*, vol. 61 (March 1956), pp. 433–44; Gresham Sykes, *Crime and Society* (Random House, 1967), pp. 109–37; Arthur P. Miles, "Social Theory, Civil Rights, and Crime," *Crime and Delinquency*, vol. 19 (July 1973), pp. 394–405; Richard D. Knudten, *Crime in a Complex Society* (Dorsey Press, 1970); and James Q. Wilson, "Crime and the Criminologists," *Commentary*, vol. 58 (July 1974), pp. 47–53. For theoretical discussions emphasizing economic factors, see Gary Becker, "Crime and Punishment: An Economic Approach," *Journal of Political Economy*, vol. 76 (March–April 1968), pp. 169–217; Simon Rottenberg, ed., *The Economics of Crime and Punishment* (Washington, D.C.: American Enterprise Institute for Public Policy Research, 1973); Billy L. Wayson, "Correctional Myths and Economic Realities," in American Correctional Association, *Proceedings: Second National Workshop on Corrections and Parole Administration*, Resource Document no. 4 (San Antonio, 1974), pp. 25–34; and David M. Gordon, "Class and the Economics of Crime," *The Review of Radical Political Economics*, vol. 3 (Summer 1971), pp. 51–75.

tion of the rationales for punishment divides them into four categories: retribution, incapacitation, deterrence, and rehabilitation.

Retribution

This school of thought, stemming from the philosophy of Kant and Hegel, holds that a criminal, presumed to be rational, commits an offense and must pay the penalty provided by society. In practice it is essentially a schedule of punishment: do something *this* bad, and you will be punished *that* much. Seen as revenge, this concept can be made to look evil—punishment for the sake of punishment, or to put it more gently, proven criminals getting their "commensurate deserts."[2]

While the idea of retribution has overtones of hostility[3] that seem offensive to citizens who profess to love their fellow humans,[4] its alternative is also unpalatable. Life in a society without punishment produces feelings of despairing normlessness or anomie:[5] if a man bribes a jury, maims a child, or burns down a cathedral and nothing happens to him, people ask "what sort of a society *is* this?" More than that, upright citizens, conformists to the law, become demoralized when the collective conscience is defied.[6] Thus retribution is more acceptable if it is seen as a means of maintaining ethical standards and of distributing penalties for their violation rather than as a justification for inflicting pain.

Society, under this theory, expects offenders to be punished, and the

2. Andrew von Hirsch, *Doing Justice: A Rationale for Criminal Sentencing*, Report of the Committee for the Study of Incarceration (Hill and Wang, 1976), esp. pp. 66–76. For other defenses of retributive theory, see J. D. Mabbott, "Punishment," in Frederick A. Olafson, ed., *Justice and Social Policy* (Prentice-Hall, 1961), pp. 39–54; K. E. Armstrong, "The Retributive Hits Back," *Mind*, vol. 70 (October 1961), pp. 471–90; and Jackson Toby, "Is Punishment Necessary?" *Journal of Criminal Law, Criminology, and Police Science*, vol. 55 (September 1964), pp. 332–37.

3. George H. Mead, "The Psychology of Punitive Justice," in Talcott Parsons and others, eds., *Theories of Society*, II (Free Press of Glencoe, 1969), pp. 876–86; Herbert L. Packer, *The Limits of the Criminal Sanction* (Stanford University Press, 1968), pp. 37–38.

4. A happier way to look at retribution is revealed in a story told at the 1973 convention of the American Correctional Association. A man being released from prison insisted that the warden give him a receipt for the time he had served. The warden was not unwilling but wanted to know why. "Well," said the inmate, "when the time comes for me to enter the gates of heaven and St. Peter asks me 'Have you paid for your sins?' I don't want to chase all over hell to find you to verify it."

5. Robert K. Merton, *Social Theory and Social Structure* (Free Press of Glencoe, 1957), pp. 135–36.

6. Toby, "Is Punishment Necessary?" p. 334.

framers of legal codes struggle to make the punishment fit the crime. So do judges and, later, parole boards, in asking themselves how much punishment is right in a given case.[7]

Deterrence

It is a very short step from the idea that retribution maintains community standards to the idea that punishment deters crime. The latter goes back to the philosophy of Jeremy Bentham and Cesare Beccaria. They believed that man acted

to maximize the amount of pleasure and to reduce pain. . . . They argued that, if would-be criminals knew ahead of time that a definite punishment would swiftly and surely follow the commission of a crime, many of them would be deterred from breaking the law in the first place; still others would be deterred by the punishments of those who actually committed crimes in spite of the warnings; and that sentences to prison were admirably fitted to accomplish this deterrent function.[8]

This philosophy, referred to as "utilitarian," is attacked by those who hold the psychological or psychiatric viewpoint that people act because of deep-seated drives or impulses and are restrained by equally internalized norms.[9] However, research psychologists find that punishment generally *is* effective in modifying behavior. On the other hand, behavior can also be changed by nonpunitive stimuli, and one major effect of punishment can be efforts to escape the punishment, rather than efforts to improve conduct.[10]

7. One would think that the amount of retributive imprisonment would grow with the amount of crime, but some recent research suggests that this is not necessarily so. Regardless of fluctuations in official crime rates, the number of persons imprisoned annually per 100,000 population remains stable. Researchers speculate that this is the result of more lenient penalties for victimless crimes. Alfred Blumstein and Jacqueline Cohen, "A Theory of the Stability of Punishment," *Journal of Criminal Law and Criminology*, vol. 64 (June 1973), pp. 198–207.

8. Elliot Studt, "Time, Punishment, and Parole" (University of California at Los Angeles, 1973; processed). See also comparable summary interpretations in Packer, *Limits of the Criminal Sanction*, pp. 39–48; Edmund L. Pincoffs, *The Rationale of Legal Punishment* (Humanities Press, 1966), pp. 17–23; and Johannes Andenaes, "Does Punishment Deter Crime?" *The Criminal Law Quarterly*, vol. 11 (November 1968), p. 79.

9. Packer, *Limits of the Criminal Sanction*, pp. 40–42; Andenaes, "Does Punishment Deter Crime?"

10. For a review of research on punishment done by psychologists, see James M. Johnston, "Punishment of Human Behavior," *American Psychologist*, vol. 27 (November 1972), pp. 1033–54.

Like many other commonsense ideas, the notion that punishment deters wrongdoing is oversimple. Often it does, of course. We all know (or are) citizens who obey speed limits in patrolled areas or who mail in honest tax returns because of the fear of being caught and punished. But rhetoric about punishment as deterrence can sometimes go too far, as in the case of publicized statements by a governor of New York,[11] a President of the United States,[12] and a president of the International Association of Chiefs of Police.[13]

Contrary to these simplistic assertions, some recent research demonstrates that the greater the severity of punishment for a crime, the less certain it is to be used;[14] and that severity of the sentence alone has no deterrent effect but that certainty of its use *does* have such an effect.[15] Other researchers demonstrate that the combination of certainty *and* severity of punishment reduces crime.[16] One sociologist advances the seemingly sensible hypothesis that deterrence depends on the type of crime and criminal: "instrumental" crimes (shoplifting, parking violations, larceny) are more likely to be deterred by punishment than "expressive" crimes (drug-related crimes, some murders). He suggests, too, that punishment is more of a deterrent to persons who have a low commitment

11. In January 1973, Governor Nelson Rockefeller proposed longer prison terms and more limited opportunities for probation and parole for persons convicted of selling drugs. A softened version of his proposal was enacted and became effective September 1, 1973. M. A. Faber, *New York Times*, Aug. 31, 1973.

12. In a 1973 message to Congress, President Richard M. Nixon recommended reenactment of the death penalty for specified crimes and lengthened prison sentences for persons convicted of trafficking in heroin or morphine. Those trafficking in more than four ounces would receive mandatory life imprisonment without parole. *Federal System of Criminal Justice: Message from the President of the United States*, H. Doc. 93-60, 93:1 (GPO, 1973), pp. 6–7, 9.

13. Francis B. Looney, "Let's Put the Death Penalty in Proper Focus," *The Police Chief* (January 1974), p. 8, in an editorial arguing that the death penalty should be used for specified crimes because the number of homicides rose sharply during the years in which executions declined in number and then stopped.

14. William C. Bailey and Ronald W. Smith, "Punishment: Its Severity and Certainty," *Journal of Criminal Law, Criminology, and Police Science*, vol. 63 (December 1972), pp. 530–39.

15. George Antunes and A. Lee Hunt, "The Deterrent Impact of Criminal Sanctions: Some Implications for Criminal Justice Policy," *Journal of Urban Law*, vol. 51 (November 1973), pp. 145–61; and Richard G. Salem and William J. Bowers, "Severity of Formal Sanctions as a Deterrent to Deviant Behavior," *Law and Society Review*, vol. 5 (August 1970), pp. 21–40.

16. Llad Phillips, "Crime Control: The Case for Deterrence," in Rottenberg, ed., *Economics of Crime and Punishment*, pp. 82–83; and Solomon Kobrin and others, *The Deterrent Effectiveness of Criminal Justice Sanction Strategies* (University of Southern California Public Systems Research Institute, September 1972), p. 46.

to crime as a way of life than to those with a high commitment.[17] Another researcher suggests more testing of the proposition that "punishment leads to the extinction of learned behavior most effectively if alternatives to the punished behavior are reinforced."[18]

On these and many other significant matters there is little conclusive research evidence: "In spite of a very few quite limited studies, there has been no adequate empirically based examination of the general problem of deterrence which takes into account the effects of different kinds of penalties, the speed, the certainty, and the circumstances of their application, the behavior for which they are applied, and the kinds of persons to whom they are applied."[19]

Even if the research data were better, even if they proved that particular sanctions prevented particular crimes, that would not mean that a court should necessarily use such penalties. Hanging, for example, might well deter parking violations, but could hardly be considered a punishment fitting to the crime.[20]

All things considered, when a judge prepares to sentence an offender he does not really know whether a heavy sentence will deter others from committing a similar crime or a light one encourage them. A parole board considering an inmate's release is even more unsure (and, as chapter 4 indicates, boards tend to be more concerned with other factors anyway).

Incapacitation

\The concept of incapacitation is simple: a person cannot commit crimes while he is in prison—at least crimes against people outside of

17. "Persons with a high commitment perceive group support, conceive of themselves as criminal, and pattern their way of life around their involvement in criminality." William J. Chambliss, "Types of Deviance and the Effectiveness of Legal Sanctions," *Wisconsin Law Review* (1967), pp. 712–19.

18. Daniel Glaser, "Maximizing the Impact of Evaluative Research on Corrections," in Emilio Viano, ed., *Criminal Justice Research* (D. C. Heath, 1975), p. 160.

19. Albert Morris, *Correctional Reform: Illusion and Reality*, Massachusetts Correctional Association Bulletin no. 22 (Boston, November 1972), p. 6. For comparable expressions of research needs, see Franklin E. Zimring and Gordon J. Hawkins, *Deterrence: The Legal Threat in Crime Control* (University of Chicago Press, 1973); Charles R. Tittle and Charles H. Logan, "Sanctions and Deviance: Evidence and Remaining Questions," *Law and Society Review*, vol. 7 (Spring 1973), pp. 371–92; and "Questions and Answers," *Crime and Delinquency Literature*, vol. 6 (December 1974), pp. 524–25.

20. Letter to the author from David Greenberg, Dec. 23, 1974; also Gordon Tullock, "Does Punishment Deter Crime?" *The Public Interest*, no. 36 (Summer 1974), p. 108.

prison. This thought is comforting to those who, like most citizens, fear the presence of dangerous criminals in the community: it boils down to "lock them up and throw away the key." The nation's big-city police chiefs in a recommendation to the attorney general of the United States said: "Society, and members of the criminal justice community, should recognize that some offenders cannot be rehabilitated and should be permanently separated from society."[21] "Permanently" is a long time, but incapacitative imprisonment has some justification in crime-by-age statistics. People outgrow propensities for certain crimes: "More burglaries, larcenies, and auto thefts are committed by young people, ages 15 to 17 years, than by any other group. . . . For crimes of violence, those from 18 to 20 are the most responsible, with the second largest group in the 21 to 24 age range."[22] And a leading criminologist comments ironically: "Virtually all criminals can have their subsequent violent crime dramatically reduced by detaining them in prison until their fiftieth birthday."[23]

This idea of protecting the public from violence was emphasized also by the National Council on Crime and Delinquency (NCCD), which recommended as a policy that "all paroling authorities should deny parole only when there is a compelling reason to believe that release would endanger the public safety,"[24] thus making incapacitation of the "dangerous" the sole rationale for continued incarceration. The NCCD was soon attacked by a law professor who argued that the public is entitled to greater protection and that the relative rights of the offender and the public should be weighed.

The defendants' legal rights change significantly immediately upon a conviction and . . . at that point (if not sooner, at the point of arrest and bail decisions) the pendulum swings in favor of public protection. If one accepts this, the answer is clear: the presumption must be against the convicted person as to his future good conduct *until he adequately supports the contrary*. The comparatively more law-abiding public has the right to be protected by virtue of

21. *New York Times*, Oct. 14, 1974.

22. LaMar T. Empey, "Juvenile Justice Reform: Diversion, Due Process, and Deinstitutionalization," in Lloyd E. Ohlin, ed., *Prisoners in America* (Prentice-Hall, 1973), p. 15.

23. Norval Morris, *The Future of Imprisonment* (University of Chicago Press, 1974), p. 80.

24. Board of Directors, National Council on Crime and Delinquency, "Parole Decisions: A Policy Statement," *Crime and Delinquency*, vol. 19 (April 1973), p. 137; followed by "The Nondangerous Offender Should Not Be Imprisoned," ibid., vol. 19 (October 1973), pp. 449–56.

the diminution of the offender's right to liberty *as a result of his own consti-tutionally proven bad conduct.*[25]

The other side of this argument starts with the fact that prediction is very difficult, as chapter 4 will show. Judges and parole boards can find out how many convicted burglars out of a thousand are likely to repeat their crime, but they cannot know which ones. So when they incarcerate burglars primarily to keep them from repeating their crime, they are lock-ing up some who will never burglarize again. If such former burglars were in the community they would be presumed innocent unless convicted of another crime; the incapacitative argument would presume them danger-ous unless they prove otherwise. Prisons, unfortunately, are dubious en-vironments for demonstrating satisfactory proof of rectitude. Moreover, it can be argued that our collective morality includes an "understanding of how important it is to give even the most dubious human being the benefit of the doubt."[26] This value obviously conflicts with the theory of incapaci-tation.

Another difficulty with incapacitative imprisonment is that it may have little effect on crime rates. One researcher estimates that even if 100,000 of the 200,000 inmates of federal and state prisons were released, the in-crease in "index crimes" (those covered by the FBI's uniform crime re-ports) would be only between 0.6 and 4.0 percent.[27] Such research is at an early stage and is based in part on unvalidated assumptions. But the point is that many future crimes will be committed by persons not now in prison.

Finally, incapacitation is not indefinite. Fewer than 0.5 percent of fed-eral and state inmates die in prison.[28] Most people eventually get out able, though not necessarily willing and ready, to return to crime.

Despite the shortcomings of incapacitation as a rationale, it is a power-ful factor in the minds of parole board members. They devote much atten-tion to the question "will he commit another crime?"

Rehabilitation

Prisons are sometimes regarded as institutions that "cure" inmates of their criminal tendencies and train them for law-abiding lives. The sen-

25. Raymond I. Parnas, letter to the editor, *Crime and Delinquency*, vol. 19 (October 1973), pp. 551–52 (emphasis in original).

26. Kingman Brewster, "A Ray of Sunshine," *New York Times*, Sept. 6, 1973.

27. David F. Greenberg, "The Incapacitative Effect of Imprisonment," *Law and Society Review*, vol. 9 (Summer 1975), pp. 541–80. See also Greenberg, "Deterrence

tencing judge must consider whether prison will prepare the offender for life in the free community. Later on the parole board must decide whether the offender has in fact been rehabilitated.

DO PRISONS REHABILITATE? Originally proposed as alternatives to the gallows, the stocks, and other harsh measures, prisons have long been the object of reform efforts themselves. Public criticism of the inhumanity and ineffectiveness of prisons has been increasingly insistent in recent years. The Attica disaster in 1971 focused public attention more than ever before on the miseries of inmates. There were federal court decisions in Arkansas, Virginia, and elsewhere holding that practices within state prisons were cruel and unusual punishment and hence unconstitutional. Influential journalists blasted correctional systems,[30] and the pained writings of inmates reached a large audience.[31]

Meanwhile federal and state correctional officials continued to run their institutions, trying to avoid riots, escapes, and epidemics *and* trying to motivate and train prisoners despite inadequate resources and lack of public support. All the prisons visited in the course of the present study had the avowed objective of rehabilitating inmates. They all, in varying degrees, provided for high school education, at least a few college-level courses, vocational training, libraries, and individual or group therapeutic counseling. Prisons without such objectives and some of these facilities are rare.

Yet experts in criminology doubt that rehabilitation is brought about by what happens in prisons. The former director of the U.S. Bureau of Prisons, a respected consultant and author in penology, says: "Broadly speaking, our so-called correctional system does not correct."[32] The report of a survey of prisons sponsored by the American Foundation concludes: "The prison is not a satisfactory setting in which to rehabilitate, and,

---

Research Methodology," in Stuart Nagel, ed., *Modeling the Criminal Justice System* (Sage, forthcoming).

28. Computed from "National Prisoner Statistics," *Statistical Abstract of the United States*, 1974, p. 164.

29. In Arkansas, *Holt* v. *Sarver*, 309 F. Supp. 362 (Ark. 1970); in Virginia, *Landman* v. *Royster*, 333 F. Supp. 621 (E.D. Va. 1972).

30. For example, Jessica Mitford, *Kind and Usual Punishment* (Random House, 1973); and Tom Wicker, *A Time to Die* (Quadrangle, 1975).

31. George Jackson, *Soledad Brother: The Prison Letters of George Jackson* (Bantam, 1970); Robert J. Minton, Jr., ed., *Inside: Prison American Style* (Random House, 1971).

32. James V. Bennett, "Reform of the Penal System" (n.d.; processed), p. 1.

what is worse, it seems to degenerate."[33] A professor of sociology contends
that the "dangerous myth" of rehabilitation is the main obstacle to progress in dealing with crime.[34] He and two colleagues made a massive review
of research conducted from 1945 through 1967 to evaluate correctional
treatment programs and found "very little evidence . . . that any prevailing
mode of correctional treatment has a decisive effect in reducing the recidivism of convicted offenders."[35]

This "nothing works" viewpoint is itself under attack as being over-
simplified in its approach and inadequately based on theory;[36] certainly
there is a need for more elaborate and specific research on correctional programs. Meanwhile it is difficult to be optimistic about rehabilitation in
prisons. Some prison-keepers, however, disagree. They say that rehabilitation within institutions has not really been tried, or not tried well enough.

I completely reject the notion [says the former head of Wisconsin's division of
corrections] that correctional institutions cannot correct . . . they have helped
countless thousands of offenders who have gone through them over the
years. . . . There will always be some offender who can best be helped in the
controlled environment afforded by a good correctional institution. Indeed
such confinement and the wealth of resources which can be brought to bear on
the problems of the incarcerated offender may well serve not only the public
interest but that of the offender as well.[37]

It is this kind of thinking that leads professional penologists and national
study commissions to join the prison-keepers in urging more enlightened

33. William G. Nagel, *The New Red Barn: A Critical Look at the Modern American Prison* (Walker and Co., 1973), p. 180.

34. Robert Martinson, "The Paradox of Prison Reform," *New Republic* (April 1,
1972), pp. 23–25; (April 8, 1972), pp. 13–15; (April 15, 1972), pp. 17–19; (April 29,
1972), pp. 21–23.

35. Douglas Lipton, Robert Martinson, and Judith Wilks, *The Effectiveness of
Correctional Treatment: A Survey of Treatment Evaluation Studies* (Praeger, 1975).
Quotation is from a statement by Martinson in Gene Kassebaum, David A. Ward, and
Daniel M. Wilner, *Prison Treatment and Parole Survival: An Empirical Assessment*
(Wiley, 1971), p. 309. This book presents further evidence of the ineffectiveness of
prison treatment. See also Martinson, "What Works? Questions and Answers About
Prison Reform," *Public Interest*, no. 35 (Spring 1974), pp. 22–54; and Morgan V.
Lewis, *Prison Education and Rehabilitation: Illusion or Reality?* (Pennsylvania State
University, Institute for Research on Human Resources, 1973).

36. See Glaser, "Maximizing the Impact of Evaluative Research," esp. pp. 157–60;
also Glaser, *Routinizing Evaluation: Getting Feedback on Effectiveness of Crime and
Delinquency Programs* (National Institute of Mental Health, 1973).

37. Sanger B. Powers, "Wisconsin's Mutual Agreement Program," in American
Correctional Association, *Proceedings* (1974), p. 11. For other spirited defenses of
rehabilitation within the walls, see Michael S. Serrill, "Is Rehabilitation Dead?" *Corrections Magazine*, vol. 1 (May–June 1975), pp. 3–7, 10–12, 21–32.

policies, increased resources, better designed facilities, changed internal organization, and more ambitious rehabilitative programs.[38] It is hard to disagree, but there will never be enough resources for all these purposes, and doubt remains that prisons can change people.

SHOULD WE EXPECT PRISONS TO REHABILITATE? Sociologists say that prison life is an ugly distortion of life in society. Here is Erving Goffman commenting on "total institutions":

A basic social arrangement in modern society is that the individual tends to sleep, play, and work in different places, with different co-participants, under different authorities, and without an over-all rational plan. The central feature of total institutions can be described as a breakdown of the barriers ordinarily separating these three spheres of life. First, all aspects of life are conducted in the same place and under the same single authority. Second, each phase of the member's daily activity is carried on in the immediate company of a large batch of others, all of whom are treated alike and required to do the same thing together. Third, all phases of the day's activities are tightly scheduled, with one activity leading at a prearranged time into the next, the whole sequence of activities being imposed from above by a system of explicit formal rulings and a body of officials. Finally, the various enforced activities are brought together into a single rational plan purportedly designed to fulfill the official aims of the institution.[39]

Total institutions disrupt or defile precisely those actions that in civil society have the role of attesting to the actor and those in his presence that he has some command over his world—that he is a person with "adult" self-determination, autonomy, and freedom of action. A failure to retain this kind of adult executive competency, or at least the symbols of it, can produce in the inmate the terror of feeling radically demoted.[40]

Another scholar puts this more colloquially: "The inmate is placed in a 'double-bind,' that is, he is punished for irresponsibility while being denied the opportunity to be responsible."[41]

Goffman writes further of "a milieu of personal failure in which one's fall from grace is continuously pressed home" and "a strong feeling that time spent in the establishment is time wasted or destroyed or taken from

38. Gerald O'Connor, "Toward a New Policy in Adult Corrections," *Social Service Review*, vol. 46 (December 1972), pp. 581–96; National Advisory Commission on Criminal Justice Standards and Goals, *Corrections* (GPO, 1973), pp. 357–88.

39. Erving Goffman, *Asylums: Essays on the Social Situation of Mental Patients and Other Inmates* (Doubleday, 1961), pp. 5–6. "Total institutions" include not only prisons, but also such other confining places as orphan homes, mental hospitals, army camps, and cloisters of strict religious orders.

40. Ibid., p. 43.

41. Ronald J. Scott, "Correctional Treatment: A 'Double-Bind' Problem," in American Correctional Association, *Proceedings* (1974), p. 76.

one's life."[42] Other experts express similar judgments.[43] How can we expect such institutions to rehabilitate?

EFFORT TO REHABILITATE. Nonetheless, prison staffs, in this discouraging setting, do try to rehabilitate prisoners. If they did not they would be mere cage minders. Doubtless there are numerous cases of men trained in prison to weld, to repair fenders, to keep records, to lay bricks, or to read and write who have used these skills in jobs outside the walls; but because of inadequate records and follow-up studies, little is known about how often this occurs.

Certainly the working conditions in prison (whether vocational training or labor in prison industries) do little to prepare inmates for productive life in the free community. The wages are atrociously low (measured in cents per hour), so the inmate cannot save money. The work itself is likely to be assigned without reference to the workers' aptitudes, performed on obsolete equipment, not well planned for effective productivity, and carried on in an atmosphere of coercion and poor morale.[44] A study of federal offenders found that vocational training programs "have little effect on released prisoners, as indicated by the negligible differences in employment rates between those who did and those who did not have vocational training . . . Over half of those releasees who allegedly received vocational training were employed at unskilled or semi-skilled jobs upon release . . . Further . . . less than one-third of those who received training utilized training in post release jobs."[45]

The odds are all against rehabilitative success—partly because of the generally destructive effect of imprisonment, partly because of a variety of institutional priorities, contingencies, and administrative errors. The warden in charge must give priority to custodial and maintenance necessities. He cannot have escapes, murders, riots, or epidemics; prisoners

---

42. Goffman, *Asylums*, p. 67.

43. Good examples include Gresham M. Sykes, *The Society of Captives: A Study of a Maximum Security Prison* (Princeton University Press, 1958); David J. Rothman, "Prisons, Asylums, and Other Decaying Institutions," *The Public Interest*, no. 26 (Winter 1972), pp. 3–17; Richard G. Singer, "Privacy, Autonomy, and Dignity in the Prison: A Preliminary Inquiry concerning Constitutional Aspects of the Degradation Process in Our Prisons," *Buffalo Law Review*, vol. 21 (Spring 1972), pp. 669–716; and Charles W. Thomas, "The Correctional Institution as an Enemy of Corrections," *Federal Probation*, vol. 37 (March 1973), pp. 8–12.

44. Neil M. Singer, "Incentives and the Use of Prison Labor," *Crime and Delinquency*, vol. 19 (April 1973), pp. 200–11.

45. George A. Pownall, "Employment Problems of Released Offenders," Report to the U.S. Department of Labor (1969; processed), pp. 12–13.

must be fed, clothed, sheltered. Programs of education or assistance take lower priority, or are used to control inmates. One criminologist, after intensive research at a prison specializing in vocational training, concludes:

It seems fair on balance to suggest that at [this institution], at any rate, treatment programs, broadly conceived, were pressed to operate as strategies of control. On the one hand they were pressed to function as "baby sitters," a complaint persistently made by treatment personnel. Programs were exploited for their capacity to keep inmates busy, thus to reduce the chances, it was hoped, that they would band together to violate rules or, perhaps mutiny.

There is persistent pressure on treatment programs to preserve the structure of power in the prisons; those who run them are surely not encouraged to change it.[46]

The failures of rehabilitation are revealed in many smaller ways, as these illustrations from the present research show:

—Prisoners were trained to operate looms, machine tools, and printing presses of types now obsolete in private industry.

—Up-to-date equipment was available to train inmates in small gasoline engine repairs, but there was a four-month gap in filling a vacancy on the instruction staff.

—A convict was trained on the job to be a meatcutter good enough for a prison kitchen but not good enough for employment in community supermarkets.

—A supervisory correctional officer refused to release a very competent inmate clerk from his office duties to attend a training course.

—Prisoners could not attend therapy sessions because they worked conflicting shifts in the mess hall or laundry.

—Inmates chose to work in a prison industry that does not train them for jobs in the labor market because it pays better than does participation in vocational training.

—High school courses (with inmate instructors) degenerated into bull sessions, crap games, and criminal indoctrination classes.

Prison staffs maintain that such problems are inevitable given their limited budgets and manpower and that meaningful rehabilitation requires more resources. More money, more staff, more equipment would certainly make prison life more bearable and might even make better tests of the rehabilitation theory possible. Yet resources could be doubled without real assurance of success. As far as we can tell now prisons do not rehabilitate primarily because of the structural and psychological prob-

46. Sheldon L. Messinger, *Strategies of Control* (Ph.D. dissertation, University of California at Los Angeles; microfilm, 1969), pp. 285–86.

lems discussed above. It is significant that the federal Bureau of Prisons is moving toward abandonment of the rehabilitative rationale for imprisonment, although not reducing its efforts to make prison life "humane."[47]

What Citizens Think

To summarize, research suggests that: (1) imprisonment probably deters crime, but little is known about which persons are deterred from which crime by which penalties; (2) incapacitation is essentially preventive detention—jailing more for what may be done than for what has been done; and (3) rehabilitation is unlikely to be effected by what happens in prisons. This leaves punishment for breaking society's rules—or retribution—as the most clearly valid basis for imprisonment. But public opinion on this matter is mixed.

All classes of citizens covered by one poll said they would be much more likely to vote for a candidate who advocated tougher sentences for law breakers:[48]

Opinion	Percent
More likely to vote for such a candidate	79
Less likely	10
No opinion	11

There was no indication, however, why tougher sentences were favored. Clearer views emerge from a comparison of answers to two questions in a 1970 Harris poll. The first asked, "Do you think the main emphasis in most prisons is on punishing the individual convicted of a crime, trying to rehabilitate the individual so he might return to society as a productive citizen, or putting him in prison to protect society from future crimes he might commit?" The second asked what the main emphasis *should be* rather than *is*. The replies:

Prison emphasis	Is (percent)	Should be (percent)
Protect society [incapacitation]	36	12
Punish the crime [retribution]	27	8
Rehabilitate	25	73
Not sure	12	7

47. Lawrence Meyer, *Washington Post*, April 13, 1975.
48. Michael J. Hindelang, "Public Opinion Regarding Crime, Criminal Justice, and Related Topics," *Crime and Delinquency Literature*, vol. 6 (December 1974), p. 510.

Other poll results show a clear preference for rehabilitative rather than punitive purposes:[49]

	Emphasis should be (percent)		
Poll	Punish	Rehabilitate	No opinion
Gallup, 1955	16	78	5
Harris, 1966	11	77	12
Minnesota, 1972	20	71	9

So the public wants prisons to rehabilitate, unsuccessful in and ill-adapted to this purpose as they are. This reinforces the need for a continuing search for other facilities as alternatives or sequels to prisons to help offenders who want to stop criminal activities.

This, then, is the background, in theory, practice, and public opinion, to the decisions on imprisonment that must be made by the sentencing judges and, later, parole boards.

Sentencing and Its Preliminaries

Much has already happened before a criminal stands before a judge to be sentenced. Most commonly the offender has pleaded guilty after a process of negotiation between his attorney and the prosecutor; this happens in 90 percent of the convictions in many courts.[50] Typically the defendant has been charged with a greater offense (say armed robbery) and has pleaded guilty to a lesser (possession of a dangerous weapon). Plea bargaining is a controversial practice that should not be evaluated here,[51] but it is relevant to parole later on because the parole board considers not only the offense to which the criminal pleaded but also the offense with which he was charged.

In deciding on a sentence the judge normally considers a presentence investigation report, prepared by a professional probation officer, as well as the conviction and plea. This usually covers the circumstances of the offense and the offender's background and may include a recommendation as well.

49. All from Hazel Erskine, "The Polls: Control of Violence and Crime," *Public Opinion Quarterly*, vol. 38 (Fall 1974), pp. 498–500. (To facilitate comparison, the wording in these examples has been simplified.)

50. National Advisory Commission on Criminal Justice Standards and Goals, *Courts* (GPO, 1973), p. 42.

51. Ibid., pp. 42–69.

The Indeterminate Sentence

The judge is guided in his decision by his jurisdiction's criminal code, and particularly by the extent to which determinate or indeterminate sentences are used. An indeterminate sentence is one in which the judge sets a maximum term and then a minimum term, or even no minimum at all, that must be served before the offender can be released (for example, one to ten years or zero to ten years for armed robbery). A determinate sentence sets only a maximum term (for example, nine years for robbery). The distinction is important for parole because a convict will be considered for parole much sooner under an indeterminate sentencing law. The difference is really one of degree, however. All states, even those using determinate sentences, make some use of parole, so that the prisoner can be released before he has served his maximum sentence.[52] An indeterminate sentence usually means that the offender is legally eligible for release sooner and that the area left to the discretion of the parole board is much wider—as, for instance, in sentences of one to twenty or zero to ten years for some crimes in California. But if a parole board is tough the offender may actually serve more time under an indeterminate than a determinate sentence. Indeterminate sentences are the general rule; only eight states have determinate sentencing statutes.[53]

In its purest form the indeterminate sentence was conceived by reformers who believed that criminal tendencies were like illnesses and that a convict should stay in prison until his keepers or other officials decide he is "cured" or rehabilitated.[54] Legislatures have often limited this kind of discretion because of doubts about the ability of prisons to reform criminals and because of reluctance to surrender so much control of punishment to the nonlegislative, nonjudicial parole boards.

The judge's decision is also complicated by laws governing "good time" —days deducted from the prisoner's sentence for staying out of trouble. Some states make the inmate serve his entire minimum sentence before he is eligible for parole, while others make him eligible at the minimum

52. Richard C. Hand and Richard G. Singer, *Sentencing Computation Laws and Practice: A Preliminary Survey* (Washington, D.C.: American Bar Association, Resource Center on Correctional Law and Legal Services, January 1974), p. 7.

53. James W. Gresens, "The Indeterminate Sentence: Judicial Intervention in the Correctional Process," *Buffalo Law Review*, vol. 21 (Spring 1972), pp. 936–40.

54. Hand and Singer, *Sentencing Computation Laws*, p. 7.

(or even less than the minimum) minus good time.[55] In the latter states, parole eligibility is delayed when a prisoner loses good time because of an attempted escape, an assault, or other misconduct.

The Judge's Options

The sentencing judge has a wide range of options to consider on the basis of what he knows about the crime and the criminal. He may suspend sentence. He may impose probation, usually supervised, sometimes not. If he chooses to imprison the offender he knows how much time must be served before parole is possible. He may in unusual cases impose a sentence from which no parole is possible.

In making his decision the judge usually is not guided by any general statutory exposition of the goals of criminal sentencing. He draws upon his own theories of crime and punishment, precedents in his own and other courts, the circumstances of the offense, and his knowledge of the offender's record, personal characteristics, and attitude. This wide discretion in administering justice naturally leads to impressive disparities in sentencing—among jurisdictions, among courts, among judges in the same court, and among different cases decided by the same judge. For example:

Jack Greenberg took $15 from a post office; last May in Federal Court in Manhattan he drew six months in jail. Howard Lazell "misapplied" $150,000 from a bank; in the same month in the same courthouse he drew probation.

"There's no question about it," says Paul J. Regan, chairman of New York State's Board of Parole, whose job entails seeing hundreds of sentences from all across the state. "In the city of New York a man may get four years, and for the same crime upstate he may get 10 years."[56]

The average sentence [for all federal offenses] in Northern Oklahoma is 44 months longer than in Eastern Oklahoma.

Actual figures show the average Eastern Illinois sentence [for auto theft] to be 47.0 months compared to 23.1 months in Eastern Wisconsin.[57]

A careful scrutiny of fifty judges' decisions in identical cases in one federal

55. William Parker, *Parole: Origins, Development, Current Practices and Statutes,* American Correctional Association, Parole Corrections Project, Resource Document no. 1 (College Park, Md., 1975), p. 60. For a summary analysis of good-time provisions, see Hand and Singer, *Sentencing Computation Laws,* pp. 30–37.

56. Lesley Oelsner, *New York Times,* Sept. 27, 1972. These quotations are taken from one of six articles on sentencing published September 26–October 2, 1972.

57. William James Zumwalt, "The Anarchy of Sentencing in the Federal Courts," *Judicature,* vol. 57 (October 1973), p. 97.

circuit found "substantial disparity in sentences . . . [and] large differences in lengths of prison terms imposed in the same case. In 16 of the 20 cases there was no unanimity on whether any incarceration was appropriate."[58]

Such variations have led to considerable criticism of sentencing in criminal justice literature. Critics, led by Federal Judge Marvin E. Frankel,[59] have called sentencing outrageously unjust because judges generally do not use or follow guidelines, do not try to impose sentences congruent with those of their associates, are not required to give reasons for their sentences, and are only infrequently reviewed in this respect.[60]

Some of the variation is to be expected because a judge's decisions necessarily reflect his philosophy of punishment. Moreover, they may reflect his personality—his essential punitiveness or mercy, his bias for or against certain groups, his anger at or tolerance of certain crimes. These human variations are part of the price we pay for an independent judiciary.

Two other factors, both controversial, add to the difficulty of achieving even-handed sentencing. One already mentioned is plea bargaining, where the judge accepts a guilty plea to a lesser offense than that with which the defendant was originally charged. This may or may not lead to a more appropriate penalty or to more disparate sentences. The second is sentencing by juries, used in thirteen states, including (of those in this study)

58. Anthony Partridge and William B. Eldridge, *The Second Circuit Sentencing Study: A Report to the Judges of the Second Circuit* (Federal Judicial Center, August 1974), p. iii.

59. Marvin E. Frankel, *Criminal Sentences: Law without Order* (Hill and Wang, 1973). See also Willard Gaylin, *Partial Justice: A Study of Bias in Sentencing* (Knopf, 1974); Zumwalt, "The Anarchy of Sentencing"; Association of the Bar of the City of New York, "Report on Sentencing Practices in the Federal Courts in New York City" (June 11, 1973; processed); Nigel Walker, *Sentencing in a Rational Society* (Basic Books, 1971); U.S. District Attorney, Southern District of New York, "1972 Sentencing Study, Southern District of New York" (1972; processed) (frequently cited as Seymour Report); U.S. Department of Justice, Law Enforcement Assistance Administration, National Institute of Law Enforcement and Criminal Justice, "Report on the Institute Study of Sentencing in the Federal District Courts," in *Reform of the Federal Criminal Laws*, Hearing before the Subcommittee on Criminal Laws and Procedures of the Senate Committee on the Judiciary, 92:2 (GPO, 1972), pp. 3896–912; James Q. Wilson, "If Every Criminal Knew He Would Be Punished if Caught," *New York Times Magazine* (Jan. 28, 1973), pp. 9, 44, 52–56; and Leonard Cargan and Mary A. Coates, "The Indeterminate Sentence and Judicial Bias," *Crime and Delinquency*, vol. 20 (April 1974), pp. 144–56.

60. For somewhat less critical analyses, see William L. Martin, "Note: The Collective Sentencing Decision in Judicial and Administrative Contexts. A Comparative Analysis of Two Approaches to Correctional Disparity," *American Criminal Law Review*, vol. 11 (Spring 1973), pp. 695–720; and Joseph S. Mattina, "Sentencing: A Judge's Inherent Responsibility," *Judicature*, vol. 57 (October 1973), pp. 105–10.

Georgia.[61] This introduces one more source of variation in the setting of penalties because judges are normally permitted by law to change juries' recommendations. Evaluation of both complications is, however, beyond the scope of this book.[62]

Toward Improvement of Sentencing

For these difficulties critics of sentencing offer several categories of solutions, most of which require legislative action. First, they urge that the legislature concerned define the objectives of criminal sentencing—what results are expected.[63] They call, second, for better organized, more rational codifications and gradations of criminal penalties.[64] Third, some critics ask that indeterminate sentences be eliminated, used less, or be accompanied by statements of justification when they are used.[65] Fourth, sentencing judges should be provided with standards, guidelines, and information on precedents.[66] Fifth, judges might be required to state the reasons for the sentences they impose and the results expected.[67] Sixth,

61. As of the time of the field research for this study in 1973. Sentencing responsibility was transferred from juries to judges in Georgia effective July 1, 1974. Letter to the author from the chairman, State Board of Pardons and Paroles, Jan. 3, 1975.

62. But see National Advisory Commission on Criminal Justice Standards and Goals, *Corrections*, pp. 168–69 (on plea bargaining) and 148–49 (on jury sentencing). See also H. Joo Shin, "Do Lesser Pleas Pay? Accommodations in the Sentencing and Parole Processes," *Journal of Criminal Justice*, vol. 1 (March 1973), pp. 27–42; and, for a strong defense of jury sentencing, "Statement of Robert F. Horan, Jr., Commonwealth's Attorney in Fairfax County before the Senate Courts of Justice Committee [Virginia Legislature]" (Feb. 20, 1974; processed).

63. Frankel, *Criminal Sentences*, p. 108.

64. American Law Institute, "Model Penal Code" (preliminary official draft, May 1962) (see excerpts in *Judicature*, vol. 57 [October 1973], pp. 106–07); and Council of Judges, National Council on Crime and Delinquency, "Model Sentencing Act, Second Edition," *Crime and Delinquency*, vol. 181 (October 1972), pp. 335–70.

65. Frankel, *Criminal Sentences*, pp. 98, 110–11; Wilson, "If Every Criminal *Knew* He Would Be Punished," p. 53; F. Lovell Bixby, letter to the editor, *Judicature*, vol. 57 (October 1973), p. 128; and Constance Baker Motley, " 'Law and Order' and the Criminal Justice System," *Journal of Criminal Law and Criminology*, vol. 64, (September 1973), p. 268.

66. Association of the Bar of the City of New York, "Report on Sentencing Practices," p. 14; Frankel, *Criminal Sentences*, p. 113; Zumwalt, "The Anarchy of Sentencing," p. 104; Wilson, "If Every Criminal *Knew* He Would Be Punished," p. 55; Peter B. Hoffman and Lucille K. DeGostin, "An Argument for Self-Imposed Explicit Judical Sentencing Standards," *Journal of Criminal Justice*, vol. 3 (Fall 1975), pp. 195–206.

67. Association of the Bar of the City of New York, "Report on Sentencing Practices," pp. 16–17.

some writers urge collegial judgments—sentencing by councils or panels of judges.[68] Seventh, others want sentences reviewed by courts of appeal.[69] Finally, judges should attend seminars, conferences, or institutes on sentencing—a remedy already tried without signal success, but perhaps not tried hard enough.[70]

Such changes would be efforts to answer the questions, What purposes are served by sentencing offenders to prison? How can sentencing decisions be more consistently related to the purposes?[71] More basic questions, which are also more relevant to parole, are, How much discretion should public officials (judges included) be given to punish offenders? Who should exercise it and at what points?[72] The division of responsibility between judges and parole boards is an especially crucial problem. Is it sound and desirable for the parole board to reach a later, separate judgment from that already rendered by the judge? Before dealing with these questions we must discuss the nature of the parole board, how it gets the information it uses, and how it makes its decisions.

68. Ibid., p. 14; Walker, *Sentencing*, p. 159; National Advisory Commission on Criminal Justice Standards and Goals, *A National Strategy to Reduce Crime* (GPO, 1973), pp. 117–18.

69. Zumwalt, "The Anarchy of Sentencing," p. 104; Richard A. McGee, "A New Look at Sentencing: Part I," *Federal Probation*, vol. 38 (June 1974), pp. 3–8; and "Part II" (September 1974), pp. 3–11; National Advisory Commission on Criminal Justice Standards and Goals, *A National Strategy to Reduce Crime*, pp. 117–18.

70. Ibid., pp. 21–22; Seymour Report, pp. 17–18.

71. These issues are compactly summarized in Roy Moreland, "Model Penal Code: Sentencing, Probation and Parole," *Kentucky Law Journal*, vol. 57 (Fall 1968–69), pp. 51–82. See also the recommendations in *A Program for Prison Reform*, Final Report of the Annual Chief Justice Earl Warren Conference on Advocacy in the United States (Cambridge, Mass.: Roscoe Pound–American Trial Lawyers Foundation, 1972).

72. Again, see Motley, " 'Law and Order'," pp. 259–69.

CHAPTER THREE

The Board and the Prisoner

THE FIRST critical phase of parole itself is the decision whether to release an inmate to supervision in the community now or keep him in prison longer—a process sometimes called parole selection. The nature of the parole board and its confrontation with the prisoner are considered in this chapter, while chapter 4 describes and analyzes the board's decision making.

Parole Board Organization

It is standard practice to use a parole board to make release decisions about adult prisoners, but this is not the only way to handle parole decisions. In some juvenile facilities and institutions for the criminally insane it is the keepers who decide when the inmate is ready to leave. This approach has been rejected in order to avoid letting the needs of the prison influence the decision unduly.

Overcrowding, the desire to get rid of a problem case, enforcement of a relatively petty rule, or some other concern of institutional management can very easily become the basis for decision-making. Institutional decision-making also lends itself to so much informality and lack of visibility that its capacity for fairness—or what may be as important, the appearance of fairness—may be called into question. A good deal of reform has been associated with transferring parole decisions from institutional control to an independent releasing authority. No adult parole authority now includes among its membership the operating staffs of penal institutions.[1]

A parole board independent of the correctional institutions has also been criticized on the grounds that it is insensitive to institutional programs, that it may do a cursory and hence incorrect job of decision making,

1. Vincent O'Leary and Joan Nuffield, *The Organization of Parole Systems in the United States* (Hackensack, N.J.: National Council on Crime and Delinquency, 1972), p. xiv.

and that it may utilize persons with little experience or training in corrections.[2] Nevertheless, independent parole boards are the general rule.

There has been an increasing tendency in recent years, however, to
locate the parole board organizationally in the corrections department, or
in a multifunction department that may include law enforcement, welfare, or health as well as corrections. Such a board has independent decision-making powers but is presumed to be more sensitive to institutional
concerns. According to the 1972 survey made for the National Council on
Crime and Delinquency (NCCD), twenty-one boards are autonomous,
twenty are within the corrections department, and eleven are in a larger
state agency.[3] A 1966 study, covering only the fifty states, showed forty
autonomous boards and only ten within either corrections departments or
larger state agencies.[4]

There are no studies showing whether state parole boards perform differently in different organizational situations. Field observations in the
present study suggest that it makes little difference. Boards studied decided as they pleased without direction from the department in which
they are located; this is true even in Wisconsin, where the department
head is officially the parole authority.[5] Under all patterns of organization,
however, the boards rely heavily on information and recommendations
from the prison staffs and put strong emphasis on the inmate's institutional
performance. Board and prison have an interest in collaboration; both look
bad if a parolee commits a publicized crime, and they will work together
whether or not they are in the same department. A parole board is not
necessarily more sensitive to institutional concerns because it is within
the same large organization.

On the federal level, there are strong arguments against the location of
the U.S. Board of Parole in the Department of Justice. Although Justice
both prosecutes alleged offenders (through the U.S. attorneys) and has
custody of prisoners (in the Bureau of Prisons), these functions operate so
separately that the parole board's independence cannot fairly be said to be
compromised. It is more significant that the attorney general controls the
budget and administration of the parole board and has on occasion altered

2. Ibid.
3. Includes federal government, District of Columbia, and parole boards for adult
males of fifty states. Ibid., pp. xix–xxi.
4. Ibid., p. xv.
5. Of the state systems studied here, the Georgia and District of Columbia boards
are autonomous; the California Adult Authority is in the department of corrections;
and the Colorado and Wisconsin boards are in large, multifunction departments.

the board's judgments.[6] A study made for the Administrative Conference
of the United States has recommended that the board be removed from
the department in order to reduce its political vulnerability.[7] New legislation creating a U.S. Parole Commission "as an independent establishment
in the Department of Justice" is a step in this direction.[8]

Board Members and Their Selection

A state parole board is likely to have either three or five members,
though there are several that have more. In 1975 fifteen states had three-
member boards and twenty-three had five-member boards—the median
number.[9]

Selection Standards

The experience and attitudes of all these board members are of crucial
importance to offenders and to society in general, and of considerable interest to political leaders. There are two main criteria in choosing board
members—expertness and community responsiveness.[10] These traits could
be in conflict, as when the board member's professional wisdom tells him
that a felon is ready for parole but his political sense tells him that all hell
will break loose if the inmate comes out. Decisions reflect both kinds of
judgments, or perhaps uneasy compromises between them. Nevertheless,
board members should obviously be as knowledgeable as possible, so there
is merit in the recommendations of the National Advisory Commission on
Criminal Justice Standards and Goals that parole board members "should
possess academic training in fields such as criminology, education, psychology, psychiatry, law, social work, or sociology [and] . . . a high degree
of skill in comprehending legal issues and statistical information and an

6. See statements of former board member Charlotte Reese in *Corrections: Federal
and State Parole Systems*, Hearings before Subcommittee No. 3 of the House Committee on the Judiciary, 92:2 (GPO, 1972), pt. VII-A, pp. 411–36, 744–58.

7. Phillip E. Johnson, "Report in Support of Recommendation 72-3, Federal Parole
Procedures," in *Recommendations and Reports of the Administrative Conference of
the United States, July 1, 1970–December 31, 1972* (GPO, 1973), pp. 739–41.

8. P.L. 94-233, March 15, 1976. (The new "commission" is the old "board.")

9. The District of Columbia has three and the U.S. Parole Board, eight. William
Parker, *Parole: Origins, Development, Current Practices and Statutes*, American Correctional Association Resource Document no. 1 (1975), pp. 49–50.

10. O'Leary and Nuffield, *Organization of Parole Systems*, pp. xxii–xxiii.

ability to develop and promulgate policy."[11] Earlier standards published by the American Correctional Association (ACA) agree but add other important qualifications: members should have ". . . such integrity, intelligence, and good judgment as to command respect and public confidence . . . be forthright, courageous, and independent . . . [and] have an intimate knowledge of common situations and problems confronting offenders."[12]

State laws have a long way to go in catching up with all these standards. The NCCD study of fifty-four boards showed that "twenty-four jurisdictions have no statutory requirements for parole board members responsible for the release of felony offenders. One state makes generalized references to character, twenty-one states refer broadly to experience or training."[13] That leaves only eight with more specific requirements. What the law requires, however, may not be enough. West Virginia law ordains that "each member shall have had experience in the fields of social science or administration of penal institutions,"[14] but its board chairman (according to a tongue-in-cheek reporter) "claims proudly to be a farmer with a good dairy herd that is established on his farm at Lewisburg. But farming has been his interest since 1962, after he studied European history and graduated from Princeton University. He worked in a trust department in a Philadelphia bank after graduation, then sold tooth paste for a while in New York."[15]

One of the ACA's selection standards seems out of date: "He should be appointed without reference to creed, color, or political affiliation."[16] There is a growing tendency to select members *because* of their color or ethnic background to give at least a symbolic degree of representativeness. The California Adult Authority has a black and a Spanish-surnamed member; so does the Colorado Board of Parole. The District of Columbia board has two black members out of three; the U.S. Parole Board includes one black and (a category not mentioned in the standard) one woman. Political affiliation is also considered in many governments. Says the NCCD report: "Many appointments have stemmed from political patron-

11. National Advisory Commission on Criminal Justice Standards and Goals, *Corrections* (GPO, 1973), p. 420.

12. American Correctional Association, *Manual of Correctional Standards* (Washington, D.C.: ACA, 1969), p. 119.

13. O'Leary and Nuffield, *Organization of Parole Systems*, p. xxiii. This survey includes the District of Columbia, the federal government, two boards in California, two in Indiana, and one each in the remaining forty-eight states.

14. Parker, *Parole*, p. 185.

15. Fanny Seiler, *Charleston Gazette*, May 31, 1974.

16. American Correctional Association, *Manual* (1969), p. 119.

age, an especially dangerous criterion for positions which involve great discretion, human freedom in its most basic forms, and difficult moral, legal, and scientific issues."[17]

Whether the primary motive is patronage or the selection of a well-qualified person, parole board appointments are politically important enough to require high-level attention. Members are chosen by the chief executive in forty out of fifty-three jurisdictions; in thirty-one of the forty confirmation by at least one house of the legislature (or by a council) is required. Only two states select board members from civil service lists.[18]

Do Qualifications Matter?

There is no solid evidence that a parole board member with a certain type of background will make decisions that differ significantly from those of a member with a different background. Hawkins has demonstrated that fairly "liberal" and "conservative" patterns of decisions can be identified, but he did not relate them to members' qualifications.[19] One can speculate on a commonsense basis that a psychologist or sociologist would have a more constructive and informed attitude toward offenders than a druggist chosen for patronage purposes by the governor's political apparatus. A board member who has been a correctional officer, a prison caseworker, or a parole officer certainly has a realistic understanding of offenders' attitudes and problems. Such board members may, however, take an unduly punitive or harassing line with offenders.

Since performance cannot be predicted from backgrounds, about all that can be done is to stress both qualifications and representativeness, as the Standards and Goals Commission does: "Members should be appointed by the governor for six-year terms from a panel of nominees selected by an advisory group broadly representative of the community. Besides being representative of relevant professional organizations, the advisory group should include all important ethnic and socio-economic groups."[20]

17. O'Leary and Nuffield, *Organization of Parole Systems*, p. xxiii.

18. Parker, *Parole*, pp. 47–49. There are several variations and exceptions, however. The study covered the federal government, the District of Columbia, two boards in California, and one each in the other forty-nine states. It also included Canada, which is not represented in the data extracted here.

19. Keith Owen Hawkins, "Parole Selection: The American Experience" (Ph.D. dissertation, University of Cambridge, 1971), pp. 293–95.

20. National Advisory Commission, *Corrections*, p. 420.

Full-Time or Part-Time?

Parole board membership used to be a hobby for public-spirited citizens, and still is to some extent. There has been a growing trend, however, toward use of full-time boards. The NCCD report shows the following distribution for state boards:[21]

Board members	1966	1972	1975
Full-time	22	26	27
Part-time	25	18	19
Some of each	3	6	4

Normally a member will do a more energetic and conscientious job if board service is his primary occupation rather than a secondary interest, and the Standards and Goals Commission has recommended that all boards be full time.[22] Nevertheless, a part-time member could give excellent service, and a full-time member could be a hack.

How Long a Term?

Governments have given widely differing answers to this question. The terms of board members range from "at the pleasure of the governor" and "two years" to "life." Seventeen states have six-year terms, as do the District of Columbia and the U.S. Parole Board. Another seventeen states have four-year terms.[23]

Longer terms are presumed to assure more competent performance and greater independence from outside influences. This may be so, but not necessarily. After nearly a year of meeting with parole boards, it is clear to me that a new member can get on top of the job in about six months—can learn the process and relationships, the biases of his fellow members, the tactics of inmates and prison staff, and the weighing of the factors that enter into his own decisions. As to independence, he may have more of it in his second year than in his sixth. As time goes on his brain may be washed paler and paler by institutional officials, by manipulative prisoners, by his colleagues, or by statehouse politicians. There is no one answer: the optimum term depends on the individual and the setting.

21. 1966 and 1972 data from O'Leary and Nuffield, *Organization of Parole Systems*, p. xvii; 1975 data from Parker, *Parole*, pp. 53–54. The District of Columbia and U.S. parole boards both have full-time members.

22. National Advisory Commission, *Corrections*, p. 420.

23. Parker, *Parole*, pp. 51–52.

How Much Pay?

The salaries paid for all these responsibilities and qualifications are, like everything else in this field, widely divergent. The ACA survey, based on 1975 data, shows these figures for board chairmen and associate members required by law to be full time.[24]

Position	Salary (dollars)	Position	Salary (dollars)
Chairman		Associate member	
Top salary (New York)	43,050	Top salary (New York)	36,100
Low salary (West Virginia)	13,500	Low salary (Louisiana)	12,000
Median salary (between Tennessee and New Jersey)	24,667	Median salary (between New Jersey and Alabama)	21,280

Supporting Staff

Parole board professional staffs do three main types of work.

Administrative: an executive officer or administrative assistant handles budget, personnel, equipment, supplies, space, and other such necessities and works with his counterparts in the board's parent department, if any.

Case monitoring: one or more analysts and clerks (many more in the big parole systems) prepare dockets, check parole eligibility dates, see that files get to board members on time, ensure that decisions are properly recorded, notify persons concerned of decisions, work with prison staff and field staff on records, answer inquiries from offenders' relatives and attorneys, and prepare reports. These duties go far beyond routine clerical processing both because of their importance to the offender and because of their complexity. An error in an eligibility date, in forwarding a decision, in including all pertinent documents, can result in a serious grievance, litigation, or damaging publicity. So the board staff (and also the members) become experts on the procedural aspects of the criminal statutes and masters at computing "good time," "street time," "jail time," and other figures. They learn, sometimes painfully, that a convict and his attorney are also experts.

Hearing cases: a few boards use staff members as well as board members to hold hearings.

24. Extracted and computed from ibid., pp. 55–57. The California Women's Authority is excluded because the present study deals primarily with adult male felons.

Who Hears the Prisoner?

The prisoner who is eligible for parole is sure of getting a hearing every-where but in Texas and Georgia, and sometimes in the latter.[25] About half of the boards that hold hearings have the full board membership present for that purpose; these tend to be in the less populous states with smaller parole caseloads. The rest use two- or three-member panels or, in a few instances, hearing examiners[26] instead of board members. A survey of fifty-four paroling jurisdictions conducted for the National Council on Crime and Delinquency in 1972 showed:[27]

Composition of hearing body	Number of jurisdictions
No hearings	3
Full board	23
Two or three members	22
One member	2
Varies	4

The delegation of hearing authority to panels or to hearing examiners permits a greater volume of cases to be heard at less expense per case, but with the danger that the impressions and judgments of the panel or examiners may differ from those of the full board.

25. The Georgia board interviews certain categories of prisoners at five of the penal institutions. Also, beginning in March 1974, a panel of two board members interviews each inmate shortly before his second parole consideration (letter to the author from the chairman of the Georgia State Board of Pardons and Paroles, Jan. 13, 1975). The Wisconsin board also holds interviews of prisoners rather than hearings. This is be-cause the paroling authority, or decisionmaker, is not the board but the secretary of the Department of Health and Social Services to whom the board makes recommenda-tions. In fact, the board's recommendations are almost never changed (in only four cases in twenty-five years, according to the senior member of the board), and the inter-views are similar to the hearings observed in other jurisdictions.

26. The District of Columbia has hearing officers to hold some types of preliminary hearings and recommend a decision to the board. California uses representatives inter-changeably with board members to hear inmates, but they can only recommend deci-sions. The U.S. board uses hearing examiners to make almost all decisions, with board members deciding appeals.

27. O'Leary and Nuffield, *Organization of Parole Systems*, p. xxx. The fifty-four jurisdictions are the U.S. Parole Board, the District of Columbia, the California Adult Authority (for men), the California Women's Authority, Indiana (men), Indiana (women), and one each in the other forty-eight states. Of the three states listed as having no hearings, two—Hawaii and Georgia—have since begun holding them.

The Hearing: What Goes On

"We have this terrible power; we sit up here playing God," said the chairman of the U.S. Board of Parole after a day's hearings that were reported in detail in a magazine article.[28] The power may seem godlike, but the premises and proceedings are on a decidedly lower level. The typical parole hearing takes place in a small, plain room inside the prison. In a hall outside half a dozen prisoners wait their turn under the eye of a guard. Inside the room the panel of two or three board members or hearing examiners[29] sits behind a table holding a stack of files and a tape recorder. Sitting nearby is a prison caseworker who maintains the docket, calls prisoners in to be heard, and records the decisions.

The Dialogue

When the prisoner enters, often visibly tense or sullen, he is greeted by the member who will question him. It is customary to take turns interviewing and for one to talk to the prisoner while the others review files of prisoners scheduled next and pay partial attention to the hearing.

Normally the questioner gives the others a chance to ask a question when he is finished. About half of the time they do, generally only a single question or piece of advice. Wisconsin board members, however, all of whom are educated as social workers, were more likely to participate in hearings they do not conduct themselves, and at much greater length, than members in the other governments studied.

The prisoner is greeted by name—usually his first name—and an effort is made to put him at ease. The tone adopted is normally friendly, but in a majority of hearings observed in the present study it became patronizing and sometimes demeaning: "Well, John, have you been behaving yourself lately?" "What can we do with you now, Bill?" (In fairness to parole board members it must be acknowledged that the stakes in this proceeding are very high, that the situation is tense, and that anything the member says can be objected to by a rubbed-raw prisoner or a critical observer.) The conversation usually centers on one or more of three subjects: the inmate's prison record, his parole plans, and the circumstances of his crime.

28. Robert Wool, "The New Parole and the Case of Mr. Simms," *New York Times Magazine* (July 29, 1973), pp. 14–16, 18–20, 24–25, 30.
29. Those who conduct the hearing will be called "members" whether they are actually board members or employees.

Whatever the topic, the members are watching for indications of the inmate's willingness to face his problems, both past and future.

PRISON RECORD. Referring to the inmate's file, the board member moves quickly to discussion of disciplinary infractions, assigned duties, and training. Talking about discipline is usually not productive. The prisoner caught fighting, talking back to a correctional officer, or possessing weapons, drugs, or excess food has already been dealt with by a prison disciplinary board. He may simply acknowledge his offense to the parole board and say he will do better in the future. Sometimes he will claim that he was unfairly treated or argue about the specifics ("I was just carrying those pills to Robinson; he had forgotten them," or "I didn't do it; they wrote up the wrong man"). Infrequently there is an outburst, as when one hearing examiner kept criticizing the prisoner for disciplinary failures recorded in the file and the inmate angrily said, "When I come to the Board you never talk to me. You talk to my jacket [file]. That's not me. You should tell me how much progress I must make."

Board members whom we observed usually did tell prisoners what they expected of them in terms of improved behavior or participation in therapy or training. There was occasional resistance: "If I learn a trade I won't use it." "That group therapy—man, all they do is hassle you." Normally, however, prisoners try to sound cooperative: "Yeah, I been going to AA [Alcoholics Anonymous]." "Expect to get my high school certificate." Humor may appear:

PAROLE BOARD MEMBER: "Why did you have that knife, Jim?"
INMATE (in very impressive manner): "Why *did* I have that knife, Mr. J——? Well, you might say it was for social purposes."

PAROLE PLANS. This is another natural topic. Even though the board member has studied a report showing what the inmate expects to do when he gets out, he asks the prisoner to tell him about his job prospects and living arrangements. In the governments studied here the prisoner was not pressed for a specific job with a specific employer if his prospects seemed reasonable considering his qualifications ("I'll work with graders and bulldozers in the Tampa area").

A recent survey of fifty parole boards showed that thirty-eight of them require that an offender have a job or "satisfactory other resources, which could include a place to stay where the person would be taken care of until he could find a job, a social security check, personal financial resources, a training slot, and the like" before he can be released on parole.[30]

30. Parker, *Parole*, p. 217.

The inmate is also questioned about whom he will live with, what his relationship with that person has been, and whether he will have problems with transportation to work. Parole boards naturally object to a prospective parolee's living with someone who seems to have led him or driven him to crime in the past (though autocratic parents seem to be an exception to this). If he plans to go to school he will be asked about his expected income and residence.

This sort of questioning can be constructive. The board gets an understanding of how realistically and sensibly the inmate is facing the future (if he is being candid). The inmate, in turn, may benefit from the board members' reactions. The discussion will also be useful in cases where the board has conflicting recommendations in the file. It is not unusual, for example, for the prison staff to endorse the prisoner's wish to be paroled to San Diego, but for a parole officer in that area to recommend against it. In some cases, the board may defer decision until a satisfactory parole plan is agreed upon. In others, they may grant parole anyway, feeling that the prisoner is "ready," even if he has no job lined up and is headed for an unwholesome neighborhood.

The constructive tone was shattered in some hearings when the member abruptly and harshly asked something like "How do we know you can stay out of trouble there?" "What makes you think you can stay on the wagon?" Such questions are hard on a scared inmate, who feels that anything he replies will seem wrong. The more confident, experienced convicts handled them easily: "I've learned my lesson, sir. Nothing like that will ever happen again, sir."

"RETRYING THE CASE." The board member has "played God" in both of the above types of questioning. He does so also when he questions the prisoner about his crime. He "plays prosecutor," too. The prisoner may be interrogated in some detail about the facts of the crime: "What got you started on this?" "Who drove the car? How did you break in?" "Why didn't you go home sooner?" If the prisoner's answers do not match the reports in the file he is cross-examined. Some prisoners respond openly and penitently, others become defensive or evasive. We heard numerous arguments about locations, times, actions. The manner of the board member may be firm and objective, or sternly prosecutorial, or even morbidly interested. Some board members keep after inmates about sex crimes, others on drug-related cases. Their interests differ, and their motives are not always apparent. What appears to be pointless harassment may be an effort to get the inmate to face up to his responsibility for the crime. The effort is not always successful, as in the case of one convicted rapist who just kept saying that he had been drunk and the victim was willing.

Many of the offenders who come before parole boards have been imprisoned after plea bargaining. In the cases we observed the board's questioning clearly assumed guilt of the major crime: armed robbery instead of possession of a dangerous weapon, burglary instead of possession of burglar's tools, murder instead of neglect resulting in death of a child. Such a course of questioning is defended by parole board members on the grounds that they are trying to find out more about the inmate—how dangerous a person is he? The opposing argument is that it is unfair to the prisoner to grill him about a crime other than the one for which he is in prison. It would be interesting to know (if one could find out) how frequently prosecutors accept plea bargains knowing that the parole board will take into account the greater crime and may therefore decide to deny parole for a few more months, or even longer.

Such retrials in general are pointless. They may contribute something to the board's understanding of the inmate by testing his attitude toward his crime and his intentions for the future. But how much does it mean for an inmate to look the board in the eye and say something contrite? It is not hard for a prisoner to be sincere when he tells the board that he regrets the crime that brought him to prison.

COUNSELING EFFORTS. In all the jurisdictions we visited, particularly Colorado and Wisconsin, the hearings were used for counseling as well as inquisition. Inmates were advised to "get their heads together," that is, to make up their minds to stay out of trouble. More specifically they were told to quit fighting, to attend alcohol or drug therapy sessions, to work for their high school equivalency certificates, or to learn a trade. Inmates usually respond cooperatively but sometimes explain why it is difficult to take part: they can't leave their work; there are no vacancies in the class; even "the therapist turns me off."

Some counseling efforts are decidedly inexpert and unhelpful, like these observations from members of one board:

You are small in stature. Do you feel inadequate?
You have a fear syndrome.
You have made a career of avoidance and underachieving.
Tony, when are you going to stop acting like a juvenile delinquent?
It's just a matter of time before you are a rumdum again, walking down the street with a stolen eight-dollar radio under your arm.

How Long It Lasts

To the convict the hearing is a big moment—which is about how long it seems. He has only a few minutes to present his case for a crucial decision. Jessica Mitford writes that the California Adult Authority averages a little less than seventeen minutes per prisoner, but she was told by one prisoner, "In my experience, five to seven minutes is more like it."[31] Both statements are probably right.

The average numbers of hearings per day conducted by parole boards in fifty-one jurisdictions, according to the National Council on Crime and Delinquency survey, are as follows:[32]

Average number of cases per day	Number of jurisdictions
1–19	11
20–29	15
30–39	14
40 and over	11

The national median based on these figures is twenty-nine cases a day. Field observations for this study show a far lower number: board members and hearing examiners thought they were doing "well" if they got through more than fourteen or fifteen cases in a day.

First of all, a board panel probably spends only six hours a day in actual sessions, hearing and deciding cases. Why not eight hours? Because they use some time in the morning traveling to the institution, then conducting necessary business with the warden or members of his staff. An hour must be subtracted for lunch, coffee breaks, other discussions with prison staff, and rest periods And they cannot run late in the afternoon because prisoners may have a 4:30 P.M. "count" in their cells or a 5:00 P.M. evening meal. Of the six hours left in the day our field observations suggest that two-thirds is spent hearing cases and one-third deciding them and dictating or noting the decision. So four hours are available for hearing prisoners.

This means that at ten cases a day, each prisoner gets twenty-four minutes; at fifteen cases a day, fifteen minutes; at twenty cases, twelve minutes; at twenty-six cases, nine minutes; at thirty-five cases, seven minutes; at forty cases, six minutes. Fifteen cases a day was our own observa-

31. Jessica Mitford, "Kind and Usual Punishment in California," *Atlantic Monthly*, vol. 227 (March 1971), p. 49.

31. Jessica Mitford, "Kind and Usual Punishment in California," *Atlantic Monthly*, vol. 227 (March 1971), p. 49.

32. O'Leary and Nuffield, *Organization of Parole Systems*, p. xxx. Data exclude Georgia, Hawaii, and Texas, where no hearings were conducted at the time.

tion; twenty is the maximum recommended by the National Advisory Commission on Criminal Justice Standards and Goals;[33] and twenty-nine is the median of the boards surveyed by NCCD.[34] Six minutes was the average time per prisoner in New York State hearings, "including the time for reading the inmate's file and deliberation," according to the commission that investigated the Attica prison disaster.[35] A later New York study showed a range of four to twenty-five minutes, with the majority between six and twelve.[36]

Prisoners are plainly right when they say, in effect, that any of these periods is a short time to get acquainted with a man and size him up for a decision that will affect his liberty for months or years. Parole boards would reply that the hearing is only a part of what they base their decision on. They have test results, prison caseworkers' reports, recommendations of psychologists, comments on the parole plan, and other data to consider. They could add that prisoners are bitterly and understandably critical of any process that does not result in their prompt release.

Attorneys, Witnesses, Records

Brief as the hearings are, informal as they are, there must still be some procedural protections of the parolees' rights. Due process in the usual legal meaning of that term does not as yet apply to parole release hearings,[37] but some states have taken modest steps in that direction. The NCCD survey in 1972 showed that twenty-one out of fifty-one boards allowed inmates to have counsel present but that the prisoners rarely did so because they were unable to pay for attorneys.[38] Seventeen boards permitted the inmate to present witnesses, "but in no instance are witnesses permitted when counsel is not."[39]

33. National Advisory Commission, *Corrections*, p. 422.

34. O'Leary and Nuffield, *Organization of Parole Systems*, p. xxx.

35. New York State Special Commission on Attica, *Attica* (Bantam Books, 1972), p. 96.

36. Citizens' Inquiry on Parole and Criminal Justice, *Prison without Walls: Report on New York Parole* (Praeger, 1975), p. 49.

37. See below, pp. 70–75, for discussion of due process in parole release decisions and later (pp. 112–18) in revocation decisions, where procedural protections are more firmly established by case law. For a brief general introduction see David Gilman, "Developments in Correctional Law," *Crime and Delinquency*, vol. 21 (April 1975), pp. 163, 167–68.

38. O'Leary and Nuffield, *Organization of Parole Systems*, p. xxxiv.

39. Ibid., pp. xxxiv, xxxvi.

The prisoner may need a lawyer in a parole hearing, but not in the same way that he needs one in a court trial. Parole is not an adversary proceeding, and courtroom rules of evidence are not applicable. Nevertheless the typical prisoner needs a better advocate than himself. Some inmates are indeed articulate, forceful "jailhouse lawyers," but most have limited analytical powers and verbal facility; they do not have the skill to "sell" their readiness for parole. Nor are the witnesses they call—wives, other relatives, former employers—likely to be better. Any reasonably competent attorney (or for that matter law student or even lay volunteer) could help them present themselves more effectively, by putting adverse material in perspective and by emphasizing the inmate's progress in gaining responsibility and skills. But the inmate rarely has an advocate of any kind to assist him.

Hearings were recorded verbatim in twenty of the fifty-one boards surveyed by the NCCD[40] and in four of the six covered in the present study. The normal practice is not to transcribe the proceedings but to save the tapes, disks, or belts for replay if there are later inquiries or challenges. In some cases this can be helpful to the prisoner (or the board) if the record shows that certain factors were or were not considered in the hearing.

The Prison Caseworker's Role

The prison caseworker (variously called social worker, counselor, classification and parole officer, or by some other title) present at the hearings does more than hand records to the board and make sure its decisions are recorded. He may be called upon to solve a problem about eligibility dates, clarify some discussion of a training assignment or a disciplinary problem, or supply other information needed by the board. He may even help an inarticulate prisoner make a point to the board.

Caseworkers sometimes feel they can offer their own judgments about inmates' readiness for release: "If there are grounds for parole, sir, they are community based psychiatric program [sic] in his home state. He needs very intensive individual psychotherapy. He won't recover in a state institution. He *might* in a community-based program."[41] Another example comes from the present study. We heard one caseworker turn to the board member after the prisoner had left the room and say, "That son of a bitch will never make it on parole." Another one said after another

40. Ibid., p. xxxiv.
41. Wool, "The New Parole," pp. 15–16.

hearing, "I think he can probably make it this time." Such comments may or may not be valid, but two points should be made about them. First, they amplify the influence that information from prison authorities already has on the presumably independent parole board.[42] Second, as a matter of fairness in this important proceeding, adverse comments should be made in the presence of the inmate or his attorney. (One board we observed prohibited such "late shots" from prison personnel.)

Appraising the Hearings

Members of parole boards interviewed for this study do not question the need for hearings; they take it for granted that a prisoner must be heard before a decision is made. Board members differ in their confidence in their own ability to appraise prisoners, but most of them believe they can tell when the inmate is trying to con them, whether his attitude toward crime has changed, and whether he has violent propensities. Sometimes they predict well, sometimes poorly (see chapter 4 for more discussion of this). Mainly, however, board members wanted to talk to us about the rigors of their hearing work—days away from home, hours spent in automobiles, excessive caseloads of inmates to see, and the tensions involved in making wise, safe decisions under the hostile scrutiny of inmates, prison officers, judges, and the press.

The Prisoner's View

The hearing is a highly traumatic experience for the inmate, according to board members, prison officials, and the prisoners themselves. A statement by a prisoner in one of the states we studied is particularly vivid. He describes on tape what it is like to anticipate and take part in a hearing.

Sat down by myself and started thinking really heavy on what the parole board was going to say to me and what I was going to say to them. God, I really caught a drag.

I was sort of expecting the parole board to be loud and more or less belligerent and tell me where I messed up at and get on my case over bad things I had done and I spent all that night up thinking about what I was going to say and what I was going to do. I did sleep that night for about two hours but woke up when the doors opened and I was bright-eyed, I was ready to go and meet that parole board.

42. See pp. 49–50 below on the prison's control of data about the inmate.

I went to breakfast, came back and thought a little more about what I was going to say—their questions, my answers—and they called me that afternoon, it wasn't till afternoon and they called me down about 2:15, I think it was, and I sat down to wait for the parole board and I started thinking and thinking hard. I started pacing back and forth and then I walked back to my house [cell] and got sick, vomited. It was just something. All of a sudden my mind was a blur. I couldn't think, I couldn't talk or nothing. Then they came to the door and told me to come in and I walked to the door and sort of stood there for a second or so and looked the room over. The man in the middle was the guy that really struck me. I felt as though he knew what he was talking about just by looking at him. The other two I didn't think too highly of. They looked like second-rate people types. I walked over, I sat down and said my hellos more or less and I was still feeling upset over being sick and my mind really wasn't working at all. The first question that guy asked me took me a long time to answer. The first big question. He asked me what I was trying to prove to the world and all the questions that ran through my mind the night before and all that day that wasn't one of them that I thought about. That question I just didn't have an answer for and I just couldn't rap to this guy and I couldn't tell him what it was. I couldn't speak right. I was nervous and shaky and my hands were twitching.

I wanted to look around the room and see who else was there. You know, I just couldn't move my head. I couldn't take my eyes off this guy because I was afraid he was going to throw something under the table. You know a question under the table I wasn't ready for and I wanted to be ready for it. I waited for the other two guys to start firing you know saying you should have done this or you shouldn't have done that or why didn't you do that and they never said a word, not once. I got uptight because nobody yelled at me. No one yelled and no one said you should have done this or you should have done that. Nobody got on my case. It upset me.[43]

This reaction is typical of prisoners' feelings about parole hearings, though milder perhaps than some in the literature.[44]

The Value of Hearings

Parole hearings need to be evaluated both in themselves and as part of the criminal justice decision-making process. To begin with the most important point, they are of little use in finding out whether the inmate is likely to succeed on parole. The authors of a large-scale research project on parole point out that "evidence that interviews are useful in parole prediction . . . has been preponderantly negative; repeatedly, comparisons have

43. Remarks of a state reformatory inmate taped by a parole officer; tape loaned to the author.

44. See Robert J. Minton, Jr., ed., *Inside: Prison American Style* (Random House, 1971), pp. 176–93.

shown that statistical prediction devices are more valid.... Interviewer judgments disagree notoriously with one another and have little to do with parole outcome."[45]

A strong case can be made for abolishing hearings on commonsense grounds alone. In cases where the information in the file and the board's own precedents plainly show that parole must surely be granted or denied, the hearing is a charade. In cases where the outcome is not so obvious it is a proceeding in which the inmate is at a great disadvantage and in which he has reason to say anything that will help his chances for parole. The atmosphere at such a hearing is full of tension and latent hostility. Under these circumstances the hearing is an ineffective way to elicit information, evaluate character traits, and give advice, all of which parole boards try to do. Hearings entail expense for travel, recording equipment, and paperwork that would otherwise be unnecessary. Prison routine is disrupted; inmates must be excused from classes or tasks; guards and caseworkers must be diverted from other duties. Board members are fatigued and strained; prisoners are upset. So why have hearings at all?

Given the present parole system, hearings are necessary as an expression of our national tradition and culture. A man has his day in court before he is convicted and sentenced. In all sorts of situations we feel outraged if a person is not even confronted with the evidence before something adverse is done to him. In the hearing the prisoner is at least given a chance to state his case, correct erroneous statements, and impress the board with his determination (real or alleged) to reform. Board members feel that they have at least a chance to learn more about the prisoner. His

employment history, relations with his family, feelings about authority, his disappointments and his expectations, all are frequent topics. The interview may reveal something of his abilities and interests, his sexual attitudes or defenses against anxiety, his values, and his plans.... [It] may suggest a further treatment plan (on parole or in prison), particular areas of weakness to be guarded against, and special potentials to favorable adjustment in certain situations.[46]

Nice work if the board members can get all this out of an overpowered and resentful individual in nine, eleven, or even fifteen minutes!

Nevertheless, as a matter of apparent fairness and decency the prisoner has to be interviewed, and the information gained is believed by the board

45. Don M. Gottfredson, Leslie T. Wilkins, and Peter B. Hoffman, *Summarizing Experience for Parole Decision-Making,* National Council on Crime and Delinquency, Research Center, Report no. 5 (Davis, Calif.: 1972), p. 8.

46. Ibid., pp. 8–9.

to be useful. The prisoners themselves believe they must be heard, although they denounce any hearing with an adverse outcome. Board members feel frustrated and guilty if they make decisions about a person who is only a name, a number, and a collection of data in a file. Hearings are called for by the standards recommended by the American Correctional Association[47] and by the National Advisory Commission on Criminal Justice Standards and Goals.[48] So as long as there are parole decisions there will be hearings.

Making the Decision and Notifying the Prisoner

As soon as the inmate leaves the hearing room the parole board or panel makes its decision.[49] (What matters are considered and how they are weighed are subjects explored in detail in chapter 4.) These are complex and difficult problems, but the board usually decides quickly. The member who led the questioning of the prisoner generally states his view, which may be phrased in figures, initials, or abbreviations unintelligible to an uninitiated observer, or even conveyed by a wink or a gesture. Examples of the most common decisions are:

—To grant parole effective in six months and recommend a work-release assignment (to prepare for parole) as soon as possible.
—To continue in prison and reconsider parole at a future time, such as in three, six, twelve, eighteen, or twenty-four months (some state laws require reconsideration every year).
—To continue imprisonment until expiration of the prisoner's maximum term.

The other one or two members present agreed with the decision in most cases observed. In a few there was discussion of a condition of parole, such as the need for drug therapy or an injunction to stay away from certain people or places. Strong disagreement over whether or when to parole the man was rare. In a three-person board or panel this is resolved by a vote.

47. American Correctional Association, *Manual of Correctional Standards* (1965), p. 116.
48. National Advisory Commission, *Corrections*, p. 422.
49. Although this statement is a fair generalization it is oversimple. The boards that hold hearings differ widely in number of members, use of panels, delegation to nonmember examiners, and voting procedure. See O'Leary and Nuffield, *Organization of Parole Systems*, pp. xix–xxxi, xxxii–xxxiii, and, in much greater detail, 1–167.

When two are present one gives way, probably the member with the milder personality.

There may be no decision, only a recommendation at this stage. A panel may refer its recommendation for later decision by the full board, as in some cases of famous or notorious persons, or a panel may have a disagreement that needs to be resolved by the full board. When hearings are held by examiners or representatives without power to parole they also record their recommendations at this time. The usual practice in the hearings observed was for the member who led the discussion with the prisoner to dictate or write the decision, giving reasons for the decision in those systems that followed this practice (only eleven of the fifty-one boards in the NCCD survey recorded reasons).[50]

The prisoner, tense and anxious after his ordeal and, indeed, about his whole future, may get his answer right away or may have to wait weeks for it. The typical inmate can predict whether his parole will be granted or denied from the way the board has questioned him. The members do not conceal their reactions to the inmate's progress, behavior, and attitude. They may state, or hint, their conclusions as to whether he has been punished enough or whether he can safely be returned to the community. In any event he wants to know, and know soon, what the decision is.

In twenty-two of the fifty-one governments where hearings are held, the prisoner gets the news at once in person from whoever conducted the hearing.[51] In the others, as in those that do not hold hearings, the inmate is notified by mail or by prison staff (usually his caseworker) after the prison receives the board's decision. Getting the word in writing varies from "immediately" (Maine) and "same day" (Kentucky) to "4–6 weeks" (South Carolina).[52] For news of such importance a short time is a long time, and a long time unbearable. The intensity of a prisoner's feeling when parole is deferred, even when the wait for notification is brief, is suggested by more of the taped observations of the inmate quoted earlier.[53] (In this case he did not predict the board's decision correctly.)

It was about 1:00. I just came back from lunch and they shut my door. I heard them call work lines out and I knew they weren't going to open my door because you know I was going to find out if I was going home or find out if I

50. Ibid., p. xxxiv. The prisoner's "right" to be given reasons for parole denial is discussed in Chapter 4 below.
51. Ibid., p. xxxi.
52. Ibid., pp. 1–167 passim.
53. See n. 43 above.

got a set-back. Everybody left and on the way they stopped and said what did you get. I told them I hadn't got it yet and about five minutes later it was really quiet. It was nice and easy, no disturbance, my radio was off and I heard the footsteps coming up from the house. I knew who was coming down. I sat down on my bed. He sort of knocked on my door and gave me a big smile and he said "here you go," and he slipped it under the door. I just brooded. I sat there for a minute or so and I flashed back on the parole board before I picked it up. You know, I flashed on them not yelling at me. I flashed on them just talking about my home town, my wife and so on and how they had talked real good to me. I thought there was a good possibility I'll go home and I stood up and the paper was face down, the writing was down, and reached over and picked it up. I didn't look at it right away. I walked over to my desk and sat down. I flipped the paper up and started reading from the top. It had my name and the date and started running it down. I got to the bottom where it said I had been deferred parole by a unanimous vote and that part really didn't bother me because I was really sort of expecting that but it said I would meet the board again in July. When I seen the July part I counted the months on my fingers and just said well fuck it. That's a fucking six and dropped the paper down and sort of leaned back and started thinking well let's see, let's make sure. That's February, March, April, May, June, July. God damn, that's a fucking six. They just gave it to me just like that. Well shit! I got up and paced around and walked back over to my desk and put the paper in my hand and looked at it and set it back down and made sure the name was mine on there. Walked over to my door and sort of knocked on it and asked them to let me out. I was getting upset and I didn't want to be in my house. I walked back and sat down on my bed. I was feeling like I was going to be sick for a minute so I took the cover off my shitter and was getting already in case I did get sick. Then I flashed back on the parole board again and thought what a bunch of bastards. Those guys are really fucking pricks. To slap a six on me the way they did and talk to me the way they did, as good as they did. It was a trip.

This prisoner was told the board's decision fairly soon, but the message was impersonal and gave no reasons.

Prompt personal notification by the board is obviously most desirable: the anxious period is shortened, and the inmate hears just what they have decided and why, in some of the states. Mail notification has the advantage of official clarity, but it is a chilling way to convey bad news. When the prisoner is notified by prison staff there is an opportunity for discussion and for ventilation of feelings. The caseworker or other staff member may be able to explain the board's policy or to make some constructive suggestions.

CHAPTER FOUR

The Decision to Release

BEHIND the board's decision is a complex array of laws, policies, beliefs, reactions, and pressures. Even further behind it are the varying understandings and applications of the concepts of imprisonment held by the board members. Each member seems, like a computer, to be capable of nearly instantaneous processing of all this material according to a program of his own into a simplified output statement like one of these: "He seems dangerous to me; let's see him next year." "We can't let him out this soon for a crime like *that*." "I'm for a mid-November [parole] date with drug clinic supervision."

Guides for the Board

The most authoritative and often briefest source of guidance is the governing statute, whose policy directive may be as brief as:

If it appears to the [U.S.] Board of Parole from a report by the proper institutional officers or upon application by a prisoner eligible for release on parole, that *there is a reasonable probability that such prisoner will live and remain at liberty without violating the laws,* and if in the opinion of the Board *such release is not incompatible with the welfare of society,* the Board may in its discretion authorize the release of such prisoner on parole.[1]

Another example:

No prisoner shall be . . . placed on parole until and unless the [Georgia] Board shall find that *there is reasonable probability that, if he is so released, he will live and conduct himself as a respectable and law-abiding person, and that his release will be compatible with his own welfare and the welfare of society.*[2]

These are both examples of conservatively stated guides; that is, the inmate should be let out only if his success on parole can be foreseen. This

1. 18 U.S.C. 4203 (a) (emphasis added).
2. Georgia State Board of Pardons and Paroles, *Constitutional and Statutory Provisions: Policies, Rules, and Regulations* (1971), p. 8 (emphasis added).

is the predominant thinking behind parole statutes.[3] The American Law Institute's Model Penal Code approaches the matter from the opposite point of view: it recommends that a prisoner considered for his first parole *shall* be released unless the board believes:

(a) there is substantial risk that he will not conform to the conditions of parole [the idea of incapacitation];

(b) his release at that time would depreciate the seriousness of his crime or promote disrespect for law [retribution and deterrence];

(c) his release would have a substantially adverse effect on institutional discipline [parole as a means of inmate control];

(d) his continued correctional treatment, medical care or vocational or other training in the institution will substantially enhance his capacity to lead a law-abiding life when released at a later date [rehabilitation].[4]

The recently enacted federal parole law has now shifted to a similar, more positive, policy.[5]

Whichever way the policy leans, the boards need far more specific guides, or at least a list of more specific factors to be considered. Specific factors are included in the statute in Georgia, but this is unusual. They are more likely to have the standing of officially promulgated guidelines, as for the U.S. Board of Parole, or an informal listing, such as the Wisconsin board gives to persons who inquire about parole criteria.

Data about the Offender

The raw data that the board considers are in the prisoner's file, typically including:[6]

1. An account of the offense for which the prisoner is serving time, starting with the arrest report and interviews with police and with the offender when first arrested. Enough detail is included so that the board

3. Robert O. Dawson, "The Decision to Grant or Deny Parole: A Study of Parole Criteria in Law and Practice," *Washington University Law Quarterly* (June 1966), pp. 255–95. Also Keith Owen Hawkins, "Parole Selection: The American Experience" (Ph.D. dissertation, University of Cambridge, 1971), pp. 137–40.

4. American Law Institute, "Model Penal Code" (preliminary official draft, May 1962), sec. 305.9 (1). Bracketed words show how the model code provisions relate to theories presented in chapter 2 of this book or, in the case of subsec. (c), to an idea discussed in this chapter.

5. P.L. 94-233, March 15, 1976.

6. For a more detailed account of such a dossier, see Citizens' Inquiry on Parole and Criminal Justice, *Prison without Walls: Report on New York Parole* (Praeger, 1975), pp. 33–40.

can consider motivation, provocation, use of weapons or violence, and other significant circumstances.

2. The offender's personal background: type of upbringing, education, intelligence level, work history, and health and medical data. The typical inmate whose hearing we attended or whose records we saw was young, from a broken or badly troubled home, had part of a high school education, an I.Q. a little above 100, a very unsettled employment record with several periods of unemployment, and generally good physical and mental health.

3. His criminal record: arrests and the disposition of each one, previous convictions and penalties, and performance on probation or on earlier periods of parole.[7]

4. His institutional record: type of work assignment and quality of work; academic or vocational training courses taken and performance in each; disciplinary charges and action taken on each; reports by psychiatrists or psychologists; participation in therapeutic programs; health record; participation in athletics, entertainment, and prisoners' organizations; comments by caseworkers, instructors, therapists, and other prison staff. Usually found in the front of the file is information about the date he began his sentence; time previously served in jail (while awaiting trial or sentencing for this offense); the sentence imposed, minimum and maximum; and date eligible for discharge.

5. The parole plan: where the offender will live, in what sort of housing and with whom; what employment is assured or expected and at what rate of pay; any special conditions of parole recommended by the prison staff (participation in an alcoholism clinic, staying away from former partners in crime); and any indications of possible adverse community reaction to the inmate's release. In some states the prosecutor and judge responsible for the conviction are given an opportunity to comment on the desirability of paroling this person.

6. A recommendation (or comments tantamount to a recommendation) by the prison staff on the prisoner's readiness for parole. This may

7. The record may show in a few cases that another government has a detainer against the prisoner. This is a writ asking that the inmate be held because the other government wants to charge him, try him, or return him to complete a prison sentence. The board may decide to "parole him to the detainer," meaning that he is released to the custody of the other government, rather than to that of the field parole staff. The presence of a detainer may be a factor influencing the board to deny parole. If the board thinks the offender should not be in prison at all it may ask the other government to drop the detainer.

include observations on his apparent sense of responsibility, his ability to relate to others, his propensity to relapse into misconduct, his employability, and the effect on institutional discipline of a decision to grant or defer parole for this particular inmate.

All this information is prepared, and hence controlled, by staff of agencies other than the parole board: the police, probation officers, and particularly the prison staff. To a major extent, therefore, these people influence the board's decisions. Unfortunately, as one criminologist points out, prison staff members who "feel they know the inmates best (and in my own early research who the inmates feel do know them best) —the cell block guards and the immediate work crew supervisors—are rarely asked to submit reports to the board about the prospective parolee."[8]

Prediction

With all this documented information about the prisoner, plus personal impressions of him from the interview, board members move toward a prediction, however impressionistic or ill formed, of how likely he is to stay out of crime. The better-trained members know something of the copious literature of prediction. Behavioral scientists have been making statistical studies for more than four decades of the extent to which various characteristics of prisoners are associated with recidivism. The studies demonstrate some things that would seem obvious to anyone: for instance, that people who drink heavily or who have many previous convictions are more likely to return to prison than are offenders who do not have such histories. Some findings might be more unexpected: murderers are less likely to return to crime than are burglars or bad-check writers. Surprising or not, prediction studies, on the basis of thousands of offenders, their backgrounds, and their crimes, enable the construction of experience tables that show the frequency with which persons with certain qualities or experiences have been returned to prison either for new crimes or for parole violations.[9]

8. Letter to the Brookings Institution from Prof. David A. Ward, Department of Criminal Justice Studies, University of Minnesota, July 28, 1975.

9. For a convenient introduction to the subject, see several articles in Robert M. Carter and Leslie T. Wilkins, eds., *Probation and Parole: Selected Readings* (Wiley, 1970): Hermann Mannheim and Leslie T. Wilkins, "The Requirements of Prediction," pp. 573–79; Lloyd E. Ohlin, "Predicting Parole Behavior," pp. 580–95; Wilkins and P. Macnaughton-Smith, "New Prediction and Classification Methods in Criminol-

Illustrative Prediction Research

Some specific figures from prediction studies will illustrate what they can tell us. Table 4-1 shows that in New York State the parole success[10] rate was higher for men who had had fewer arrests and who had not used

Table 4-1. *Parole Success Rates of New York State Male Parolees Released in 1964–66, by Number of Previous Arrests and History of Excessive Drug or Alcohol Use*

Percent

| | History of excessive drug or alcohol use | |
Number of known previous arrests	Absent	Present
None	78	74
One	71	69
Two or three	63	58
Four or more	60	46
Total	66	52

Source: John M. Stanton, "Success Rates of Male Parolees" (State of New York, Division of Parole, Bureau of Research and Statistics, 1970; processed), p. 3.

drugs or alcohol to excess. Parole success is also more likely for men who are older at time of release (though these data are for men with no previous arrest record and no history of excessive use of alcohol or of drug dependence):[11]

Age at time of release	Success rate (percent)
20 and under	71
21–25	78
26–30	84
31–40	89
Over 40	97

The data by type of crime given in table 4-2 show that men convicted of homicide make more successful parolees than forgers do, whether or not they have been dependent on drugs or alcohol. Other research in New York has demonstrated that parolees with a history of drug addiction (pri-

ogy," pp. 596–614; Victor H. Evjen, "Current Thinking on Parole Prediction Tables," pp. 615–25; and Norman S. Hayner, "Why Do Parole Boards Lag in the Use of Prediction Scores?" pp. 626–32.

10. Defined as "the absence of an effective delinquency during the year of release and during the two calendar years following release." John M. Stanton, *Success Rates of Male Parolees* (State of New York, Division of Parole, Bureau of Research and Statistics, 1970; processed), p. 2.

11. Ibid., p. 4.

Table 4-2. *Parole Success Rates of New York State Male Parolees Released in 1964–66, by Crime of Conviction and History of Excessive Drug or Alcohol Use*

Percent

	History of excessive drug or alcohol use		
Crime of conviction	Absent	Present	All cases
Forgery	52	36	44
Larceny	59	42	52
Burglary	60	45	52
Possession or sale of drugs	78	52	54
Robbery	65	50	58
Assault	71	62	67
Murder or manslaughter	82	68	75
Sex offenses	79	73	77
All crimes	66	52	59

Source: Same as table 4-1, p. 7.

marily those who started drug use at a late age) are more likely to succeed on parole if they support themselves than if they are supported by others or are on welfare.[12]

A California research study affirms some of the factors already mentioned: "the absence of excessive drinking; the presence of a spouse, legitimate or common-law; along with conviction for crimes against persons [as contrasted with crimes against property]; are the factors which are associated with [parole] success. . . ."[13] California research also shows that inmates receiving more visitors while in prison tended to experience less difficulty on parole.[14]

PREDICTING DANGEROUSNESS. Many research projects find no relationship between parole performance and the variables being tested. It is especially difficult to predict dangerousness in individual cases, as these summary results from a Massachusetts study suggest.

This is a report of a ten-year study involving 592 male convicted offenders. Most of the crimes that brought these offenders to our notice were sex offenses. Several were compounded by extreme violence including murder, man-

12. James A. Inciardi, "The Use of Parole Prediction with Institutionalized Narcotic Addicts," *Journal of Research in Crime and Delinquency*, vol. 8 (January 1971), p. 69.

13. James A. Painter, "Factors Influencing Parole Success" (unpublished manuscript, 1969), p. 9.

14. Norman Holt and Donald Miller, *Explorations in Inmate-Family Relationships*, California Department of Corrections, Research Division, Report no. 46 (Sacramento, January 1972), pp. 42–43.

slaughter, assault with intent to kill, and assault with a dangerous weapon. The staff's initial diagnosis indicated that 304 of these persons were not dangerous, and they were released into the community after completing their sentences. Twenty-six (8.6 percent) subsequently committed serious assaultive (dangerous) crimes.

The courts concurred in our diagnosis of dangerous in 226 cases and committed these offenders to our special "treatment" facility for an indeterminate period of one day to life. Following treatment for an average period of forty-three months, eighty-two patients were discharged on recommendation of the clinical staff. Of these, five (6.1 percent) subsequently committed serious assaultive crimes, including one murder.

Forty-nine of the originally committed patients were released by court order against the advice of the clinical staff. Of these, seventeen (34.7 percent) subsequently committed serious assaultive crimes, including two murders.

Criteria of dangerousness and guidelines for its prediction were elaborated. *No tests or psychiatric examinations can dependably predict a probability of dangerous behavior in the absence of an actual history of a seriously violent assault on another person.*[15]

A California research effort on violence also "failed to yield a practicable prediction instrument that would warrant implementation in actual preventive or correctional practice."[16] These and other studies strongly suggest that parole board members who think they can identify which prisoners will be dangerous persons in the future are mistaken.

PRISON PERFORMANCE AS A PREDICTOR. Is good behavior in prison a reliable omen of good behavior in the free community? Parole boards certainly use institutional behavior as an important indication of readiness for parole, according to our field observations and to research by Hawkins in New York State, who found that "an inmate's behavior in prison is the factor most frequently taken into account by the board members when they make parole decisions."[17]

The same emphasis on prison behavior is shown in results of the National Council on Crime and Delinquency (NCCD) research in California, but it has little predictive value:

15. Harry L. Kozol, Richard J. Boucher, and Ralph F. Garofalo, "The Diagnosis and Treatment of Dangerousness," *Crime and Delinquency*, vol. 18 (October 1972), pp. 371–72 (emphasis added).

16. Ernst A. Wenk, James O. Robison, and Gerald W. Smith, "Can Violence Be Predicted?" *Crime and Delinquency*, vol. 18 (October 1972), p. 393. See also similar discussion in Daniel Glaser, Donald Kenefick, and Vincent O'Leary, *The Violent Offender* (U.S. Department of Health, Education, and Welfare, Office of Juvenile Delinquency and Youth Development, 1968), p. 35; and in Bernard L. Diamond, "The Psychiatric Prediction of Dangerousness," *University of Pennsylvania Law Review*, vol. 123 (December 1974), pp. 439–52.

17. Hawkins, "Parole Selection," p. 300.

The substantial correlations among the three variables above [institutional progress, discipline, and estimate of likely parole outcome] suggest that parole board members heavily weigh institutional behavior in forming their estimates of parole risks. If so, this logic is open to question . . . [A] random sample of 144 Youth Corrections Act original parole releasees from fiscal year 1969 was taken in order to examine the relationships between record of prison punishment and parole outcome. The results indicated that 55 percent of the 84 cases with no known prison punishment had favorable outcome (two-year follow-up) compared to 48 percent of the 60 cases with known prison punishment. *This difference is not statistically significant.*[18]

A study of male felons in California also showed mixed results. The subjects were persons admitted or readmitted to California prisons in 1964; the study relates parole outcome to their ratings on behavior, education, training, and participation in voluntary group programs during the first year after admission or readmission. The results were:

—New admissions (217 cases): (1) neither the ratings of specific areas of behavior nor the overall ratings were strongly related to parole outcome; (2) there was some association between participation in academic education and favorable parole outcome; (3) those receiving high ratings in work assignments or vocational training tended to perform less favorably on parole than those receiving poorer ratings; (4) a higher degree of participation in voluntary group programs was more strongly related to favorable parole outcome than was a lower degree.

—Readmissions (133 cases): (1) a high rating of performance in vocational training was predictive of not returning to prison; (2) parolees having one disciplinary writeup in the first year were more likely to return to prison than those having either none or more than one; (3) voluntary group participation among the readmissions was associated with a higher rate of return to prison than was nonparticipation.[19] Such findings give little guidance indeed to parole boards trying to judge future parole success from an inmate's behavior in prison.

It is interesting to note that since the study the California Adult Authority (parole board) "has abandoned participation and progress in rehabilitation programs as criteria for release from prison."[20]

18. Peter B. Hoffman, *Paroling Policy Feedback*, National Council on Crime and Delinquency, Research Center, Report no. 8 (Davis, Calif., February 1972), p. 21 (emphasis added).

19. Dorothy R. Jaman, *Behavior during the First Year in Prison. Report IV: As Related to Parole Outcome*, California Department of Corrections, Research Division, Synopsis of Report no. 44 (Sacramento, November 1971), p. 1.

20. "Follow-up," *Corrections Magazine*, vol. 1 (July–August 1975), p. 59.

There is, however, newer and clearer evidence that a combination of good behavior in a prison and participation in its programs tends to fore-shadow success on parole. Table 4-3 shows the results of a study of federal offenders two years after they were released to the community in 1970. The more disciplinary infractions in prison, the higher the percentage of fail-

Table 4-3. *Parole Success and Failure Rates of 1,367 Federal Adult Offenders Released in 1970, by Number of Prison Punishments*
Percent

Number of punishments[a]	Performance on parole		
	Success	Failure[b]	Unknown
None	69	23	8
One	57	33	10
Two	53	43	3
Three or more	52	40	9
Total	65	27	8

Source: U.S. Bureau of Prisons, "Success and Failure of Federal Offenders Released in 1970" (January 1974; processed), table 20, p. 34. Figures may not add to 100 because of rounding.
a. Punishments consist of any action on charges of prison rules violations resulting in with-holding of privilege, segregation, isolation, loss of good time, or any other deprivation.
b. Failure consists of parole revocation or any new sentence of 60 days or more during two years following release.

ures on parole. Participation in prison educational programs (when background characteristics of prisoners are controlled for), religious programs, "other" recreational programs, and "progress in counseling" all predict success.[21] These results offer encouragement but not yet firm support to parole board members who see prison behavior as an indicator of adjustment to the free community.

TIME SPENT IN PRISON. This is not a satisfactory factor for predicting success or failure on parole. For some types of crimes and offenders one can conclude from the research data that those long imprisoned are less likely to do well on parole than others. Nevertheless, "the complex of factors operating in any specific jurisdiction makes any hasty application of the generalizations drawn from the gross national data hazardous indeed."[22]

21. U.S. Bureau of Prisons, "Success and Failure of Federal Offenders Released in 1970" (January 1974; processed), pp. 50–52.
22. Don M. Gottfredson and others, *Four Thousand Lifetimes: A Study of Time Served and Parole Outcomes* (National Council on Crime and Delinquency, June 1973), p. 25. See also Steve E. Kolodney and others, *A Study of the Characteristics and Recidivism Experience of California Prisoners* (San Jose, Calif.: Public Systems, Inc., 1970), p. 22.

The Trouble with Prediction

Many other examples could be given of efforts to relate prisoners' characteristics to success on parole.[23] Those discussed so far are relatively primitive, oversimplifying a problem that has numerous hard-to-control variables. More sophisticated information can be obtained by constructing configuration tables that present several variables at once, such as age, prior incarceration, and longest period on a job in the free community.[24] But even if a board has such information, the extent to which its members should be guided by it is still in question.

The trouble with prediction is simply that it will not work—that is, it will not work for individuals, only for groups. A parole board may know that of a hundred offenders with a certain set of characteristics, eighty will probably succeed and twenty fail on parole. But the board members do not know whether the man who is before them belongs with the eighty or the twenty. Therefore they release some who succeed and some who fail and they keep in the damaging, often destructive, prison environment some who would have succeeded outside as well as some who would have failed. Those potential successes who are kept in prison are called, in research terminology, "false positives."[25]

Prediction tables are useful to parole boards in reminding members of factors they may have overlooked and in providing something for them to compare their own less scientific judgments with.[26] But there is a counterbalancing disadvantage: the prediction table could influence the board to deny parole to a prisoner who might be perfectly successful in the community. Parole boards need to give some hard thought to the relative disadvantages of their let-them-out mistakes and their keep-them-in mistakes, and to remember that they cannot be sure of any prediction.[27]

Given the difficulties with prediction, the critical question facing the

23. For an orderly, readable summary, see Vincent O'Leary and Daniel Glaser, "The Assessment of Risk in Parole Decision Making," in D. J. West, ed., The Future of Parole (Duckworth, 1972), pp. 135–98.

24. Daniel Glaser, Routinizing Evaluation: Getting Feedback on Effectiveness of Crime and Delinquency Programs (National Institute of Mental Health, 1973), chap. 9, esp. pp. 145–55.

25. For a discussion of the "false positive" problem in prediction and, consequently, of the logical flaws and social costs of confining those who may return to crime, see Andrew von Hirsch, "Prediction of Criminal Conduct and Preventive Confinement of Convicted Persons," Buffalo Law Review, vol. 21 (Spring 1972), pp. 717–58.

26. David Dressler, Theory and Practice of Probation and Parole (Columbia University Press, 1969), p. 150.

27. For a research approach to this problem, see Peter B. Hoffman, "Mandatory

THE DECISION TO RELEASE

parole board member "is not so much whether or not a parolee is classified as being in a poor risk group, it is: when is the best time to release this inmate? *No parole predictions device has been yet developed which will answer that question and there is no parole official who would claim that he has the gift of making omniscient decisions.*"[28] Maybe not, but we observed board members who believe that there is a single best time (a "peaking" period) for release, after which a prisoner's chances of making it outside go down, and that they can render sound judgments based on their experience as to when the prisoner starts down the other side of the peak.[29] These members tend to decide cases of prisoners who are past their peak in a negative sort of way: "More time in prison will do him no good." "What can we do with a guy who has used everything the prison has to offer?" "He may seem a bad risk, but we simply can't deny parole any more."

How Parole Boards Decide

The decision reached by the board during and after the hearing is the result of each member's evaluation of the factors in the prisoner's file, and in his demeanor, that seem relevant to his future. The "parole ballot" (p. 58) filled out by members of the Georgia board can help us to visualize the mental process the member follows. Each member, without knowing the judgments of the others, goes over the prisoner's file, looking for the information called for on the ballot. He signs opposite each reason listed that supports his decision for grant or denial. The board member also records his recommendations on types of assistance and degree of supervision required when the inmate is paroled. The whole process takes five to fifteen minutes per case, according to one board member. (He is quicker than others, however, because he has a staff member go through the inmate's file first and mark important factors for his attention.) Boards in other states may not use written ballots and factors considered may be phrased or emphasized differently, but the main considerations are the same.

Release: A Measure of Type II Error," *Criminology*, vol. 11 (February 1974), pp. 541–54.

28. Stanton, *Success Rates of Male Parolees*, p. 9 (emphasis added).

29. A similar view was expressed by a member of the Washington State Board of Prison Terms and Paroles in a public television documentary, "Parole," shown January 21, 1974. The New York State Board also holds to this view (Citizens' Inquiry, *Prison without Walls*, p. 167).

State Board of Pardons and Paroles

Atlanta, Georgia

PAROLE BALLOT

NAME _____ COUNTY _____ NUMBER _____

DATE SET_____ MAXIMUM EXPIRES _____

GRANT PAROLE, VOTE IS TENTATIVE UNTIL DATE OF ACTUAL RELEASE ON PAROLE	DENY PAROLE
	DATE RESET _____
BY _____ DATE_____	BY_____ DATE_____
CLEMENCY RECORDED _____	DENIAL NOTICE ISSUED _____

REASONS FOR GRANT		REASONS FOR DENIAL
	CIRCUMSTANCE	
	PAST PROBATION RECORD	
	PAST PAROLE RECORD	
	EMOTIONAL STATUS	
	PATTERN OF BEHAVIOR:	
	CRIMINAL RECORD	
	ALCOHOL PROBLEM	
	DRUG PROBLEM	
	EMPLOYABILITY	
	INSTITUTIONAL RECORD:	
	ATTITUDE	
	USE OF TIME	
	DISCIPLINARY REPORTS	
	ESCAPE	
	ATTEMPTED ESCAPE	
	RELEASE PLANNING:	
	EMPLOYMENT	
	RESIDENCE	
	COMMUNITY:	
	SUPPORT, REPUTATION, RECOMMENDATIONS	
	RESOURCES	
	PHYSICAL AND EMOTIONAL NEEDS	
	FAMILY NEEDS	
	POSITIVE EFFORTS ON BEHALF OF OTHERS	
	DETAINER	
	SENTENCE LENGTH	
	OPPORTUNITY	
	SUPERVISED ADJUSTMENT PERIOD	
	WORK RELEASE	
	OTHER	

1. POOR INSTITUTIONAL PROGRESS   2. AVERAGE, INSTITUTIONAL PROGRESS   3. GOOD INSTITUTIONAL PROGRESS

RECOMMENDATIONS FOR FUTURE REHABILITATION

_____ EDUCATIONAL TRAINING
_____ JOB TRAINING
_____ ALCOHOL TREATMENT
_____ DRUG TREATMENT
_____ COUNSELING
_____ BETTER USE OF SELF-IMPROVEMENT PROGRAMS
_____ CONSTRUCTIVE USE OF LEISURE TIME AND RECREATION
_____ ATTITUDE OF CO-OPERATION WITH STAFF AND INMATES

_____ INSTITUTIONAL ATTITUDE CHANGE TO HELPING YOURSELF BECOME A RESPONSIBLE PERSON
_____ COUNSELING FOR BETTER INSIGHT INTO YOUR PROBLEM WITH INCREASED ABILITY TO SOLVE AND HANDLE THESE PROBLEMS
_____ DEVELOPMENT OF PERSONAL GOALS WHICH WILL LEAD TO A MATURE LIFE STYLE
_____ OTHER _____

TYPE SUPERVISION REQUIRED: MAXIMUM _____ MEDIUM _____ MINIMUM _____
SPECIAL CONDITIONS: _____

FBI: NO PREVIOUS FBI RECORD ☐   IN FILE ☐   NONE ON FILE IN CORRECTIONS ☐   APD IN FILE ☐

REMARKS _____

What Research Studies Show

When researchers analyze how parole boards make decisions they look at the official guidelines, the members' perceptions of their own criteria, and the findings of prediction studies. The results reveal, not surprisingly, a complex process, with different boards placing emphasis on different factors.

Robert Dawson reviewed the parole decision processes of Kansas, Michigan, and Wisconsin as part of a comprehensive study of sentencing for the American Bar Foundation.[30] He found that these states' boards emphasize their predictive function: "The principal consideration in the decision to grant or deny parole is the probability that the inmate will violate the criminal law if released."[31] In judging this probability, they consider their perceptions of: psychological change in the inmate; his participation in institutional programs; his prison disciplinary record; his criminal record; his performance in prior periods of supervision in the community; the adequacy of the parole plan; and the circumstances of his offense.[32] The reader will remember that some of these factors involve highly subjective judgments and others are of dubious predictive value.

Other criteria are also listed and illustrated, some relevant to prediction, some to the maintenance of prison discipline, and some to the rehabilitation of the inmate.[33] One criterion that lies behind all the others is bluntly stated by Dawson, although it tends to be muted by most boards and commentators: to avoid criticism of the parole system.[34] Boards may keep an inmate in prison, even if the chances of parole success are favorable, because he is not welcome in the community or because repetition of his crime, however unlikely, would hurt the board's reputation.

A more limited but very revealing study by Joseph Scott in one midwestern state concentrates on criteria for deciding how much punishment the offender should receive.[35] Scott did a computer analysis of the relation-

30. Robert O. Dawson, *Sentencing: The Decision as to Type, Length, and Conditions of Sentence* (Little, Brown, 1969), particularly chap. 10, "Parole Information," and chap. 11, "The Decision to Grant or Deny Parole."
31. Ibid., p. 263.
32. Ibid., pp. 264–78.
33. Ibid., pp. 278–96.
34. Ibid., pp. 296–98.
35. Joseph E. Scott, "The Use of Discretion in Determining the Severity of Punishment for Incarcerated Offenders," *Journal of Criminal Law and Criminology*, vol. 65 (1974), pp. 214–24.

ship of various factors considered by the parole board to the number of months the offender was actually imprisoned. He found that the seriousness of the crime was the factor best related to severity of punishment.[36] Other less salient but clear findings were that severity of punishment is related to: the number of prison disciplinary reports received by an inmate; age (older offenders stay longer); intelligence (higher I.Q.s get out sooner); education (so do men with more education); marital status (so do married persons); and socioeconomic status (likewise those higher in this scale). Participation in institutional programs was not related to severity of punishment. Other findings are conflicting or inconclusive.[37] In contrast to the mixture of factors reported by Dawson, Scott emphasizes the retributive attitude of the parole board and its apparent lack of concern with rehabilitative or predictive considerations.[38] He concludes that "perhaps what should be seriously questioned at this point is the present usefulness of either indefinite sentences and/or parole boards."[39]

A very mixed bag of criteria is revealed in research on New York State parole by Keith Hawkins of Cambridge University.[40] His analysis of the board's decision making shows an unpatterned array of predictive factors, punitive considerations, prison-related matters, and personal impressions from the hearing. What the board members say they generally use as criteria, moreover, have no correlation with the criteria asociated by them with specific decisions. Table 4-4 shows the criteria New York board members said influenced their decisions to defer parole. This wide variety of factors is highly reminiscent of the conversation of parole board members in hearings we attended in Colorado, Wisconsin, California, and the District of Columbia. In those jurisdictions, as in New York, the nature of the crime, the prisoner's past, his demeanor, the suitability of the parole plan, and other considerations are used with varying emphasis in different decisions.

Federal Research and the Decision-Making Process

A somewhat narrower and much more orderly approach to decision making is now used by the U.S. Board of Parole after a tryout of nearly a year and a half in the Northeast. It was based on the results of more

36. Ibid., p. 217.
37. Ibid., pp. 219–21.
38. Ibid., p. 222.
39. Ibid.
40. Hawkins, "Parole Selection."

THE DECISION TO RELEASE

Table 4-4. *Criteria for Parole Deferral, by Their Actual Use and Stated Influence, New York State, 1968*[a]

Criterion present	Percent of cases deferred	Actual rank order	Rank order of stated influence
Poor behavior at hearing	100.0	1	8
Poor effect of release on prison morale	100.0	1	7
Poor attitude to authority	91.2	3	15
Poor readiness to assume responsibilities	90.0	4	16
Grave offense of selling narcotics	89.5	5	1
Too short a time served compared to maximum	88.5	6	18
Poor job opportunity	85.6	7	19
Grave offense against property	84.4	8	3
Grave offense to support drug habit	83.3	9	2
Poor parole plan	83.2	10	26
Poor proposed residence	82.8	11	22
Rule breaker in prison	82.6	12	29
Poor stability, maturity	81.7	13	23
Little attempt at completion of treatment	80.8	14	24
Great need for treatment or training	80.4	15	20
Light sentence compared with similar offenders	79.8	16	21
Poor I.Q. and skills	77.9	17	27
Grave offense of using narcotics	77.8	18	5
Poor past behavior under supervision	77.3	19	13
Poor employment record	76.8	20	16
Serious offense of selling narcotics	76.7	21	28
Extensive prior use of narcotics	74.8	22	9
Poor family attitude	74.5	23	25
Poor prior juvenile, criminal record	74.0	24	12
Average behavior at hearing	73.6	25	...
Serious offense of using narcotics	73.3	26	...
Serious offense to support drug habit	72.7	27	...
Average family attitude	70.1	28	...
Grave offense against person	67.7	29	...
Adverse attitude of other officials	67.6	30	14

Source: Keith Owen Hawkins, "Parole Selection: The American Experience" (Ph.D. dissertation, University of Cambridge, 1971), p. 326.

a. This table is based on a "decision schedule" designed by Hawkins on which board members were asked to "check factors they had considered, and to rate the extent to which these factors affected the decision" (ibid., p. 260). It is important to know that the board declined to respond to two predictive items, "probability of violating parole" and an estimate of the "prisoner's probability of successful completion of parole" (ibid., pp. 261–62).

than two years of intensive research on decision making conducted for the board by the National Council on Crime and Delinquency.[41] Part of the research, comparable to Hawkins's in New York, required the Cali-

41. For a brief, authoritative description, see Don M. Gottfredson and others, "Making Paroling Policy Explicit," *Crime and Delinquency*, vol. 21 (January 1975), pp. 34–44. For scholarly detail, see the series of numbered reports under the general

fornia Youth Authority (a parole board) members to complete an evaluation sheet after reviewing each case and before reaching a decision. Analysis then showed that "parole board decisions could be predicted fairly accurately by knowledge of their severity and prognosis ratings. Similarly, at review considerations, parole board decisions were strongly related to ratings of institutional discipline. . . . From this knowledge, the development of an explicit indicant of parole selection policy was possible. . . ."[42]

After further testing and development, the "indicant" was put into effect. The board's hearing examiners, working in two-member panels, review the prisoner's file, conduct the hearing with him, and write up an evaluation of his case that, by the use of the indicant, results in a decision as to the total number of months he should serve (see "Salient Factors" and "Adult Guidelines" sheets, pp. 64 and 65). Each examiner completes the worksheet, giving a value to each "salient factor"—those factors found by the NCCD research to be the most valid predictors of parole success. The total salient factor score—a measure of parole prognosis— is then applied to the list of offense characteristics—a measure of severity of the crime—to obtain the months of incarceration that are appropriate, the definition of appropriate being based on NCCD research into actual past parole decisions.

How the process works can be illustrated by filling out a salient factors worksheet for an imaginary post office burglar:

Item	Points
A. One prior conviction	1
B. One prior incarceration	1
C. Twenty years old when first committed to prison	1
D. No auto theft involved in the crime	0
E. Parole was once revoked for a new offense	1
F. No history of drug dependence	0
G. Did not complete high school	1
H. Did have a job for eight months	1
I. Will live with wife	1
Total score	7 ("good" prognosis)

Offense severity: high
Jail time served, 3 months; prison time, eight months—total 11
Guidelines used: adult

title *Parole Decision-making*, published in 1972–73 by the Research Center of the National Council on Crime and Delinquency, Davis, California, one of which is cited in n. 18 above.

42. Peter B. Hoffman and Don M. Gottfredson, *Paroling Policy Guidelines: A Matter of Equity*, National Council on Crime and Delinquency, Research Center, Supplemental Report no. 9 (Davis, Calif., June 1973), p. 5.

The guidelines point to twenty to twenty-six months for a high severity and good prognosis. Our burglar has served eleven months of jail and prison time, so the examiner could recommend anywhere from nine to fifteen months more in prison. He could recommend fewer if he believes there are mitigating circumstances or more if there are aggravating circumstances. If he makes a recommendation outside the guidelines it must be concurred in by a regional administrative hearing examiner. The prisoner may appeal a decision to his regional director (a member of the U.S. Parole Board), who may order a new hearing at the institution or a regional appellate hearing, or may affirm, reverse, or modify the examiner's decision. If he reverses, his judgment must be concurred in by at least one other regional director. Further appeal is possible to board members in Washington.[43]

Examiners have strongly tended to follow the guidelines: they did so in 86 percent of the cases decided in August through November 1974,[44] and in about 84 percent in mid-1975.[45] Examples of reasons given for decisions on longer imprisonment than the guidelines call for include "disciplinary reports," "narcotic problems," "worse clinic risks," "multi offense," and "disciplinary." Reasons for decisions on shorter imprisonment include "state time credit," "excellent progress," and "mental retardation." Inmates are notified in writing of how they were rated and, if parole is denied, what specific reasons are applicable.

These new techniques will certainly result in more consistent judgments and in better understanding by inmates of how parole decisions are arrived at, both highly desirable effects. Nevertheless, there are grounds for criticism, as there are for any system of parole decision making. Because the salient factor scores are based on prediction the system has the shortcomings already discussed. If the burglar in our example has no high school diploma and no wife to live with he loses two points, which may cost him months of freedom, yet he may in fact be a greater success on parole than another burglar with more points. That is, he is punished *as*

43. For complete official provisions, see 40 Fed. Reg. 10973–84 (1975): Rules and Regulations, chap. 1, Department of Justice, U.S. Board of Parole; pt. 2, Parole, Release, Supervisions and Recommitment of Prisoners, Youth Offenders, and Juvenile Delinquents. For a popularized explanation, see Robert Wool, "The New Parole and the Case of Mr. Simms," *New York Times Magazine*, July 29, 1973, pp. 14–16, 18–20, 24–25, 30.

44. Computed from data supplied by the U.S. Board of Parole concerning initial parole hearings. The percentages vary by region from 83.8 to 89.5 percent.

45. Data supplied by telephone by USPB staff.

R-2 part 2
(Rev. 4/74)

NOTICE OF ACTION - PART II - SALIENT FACTORS

Case Name _____ Register Number _____

Item A ---   ☐

    No prior convictions (adult or juvenile) = 2
    One or two prior convictions = 1
    Three or more prior convictions = 0

Item B ---   ☐

    No prior incarcerations (adult or juvenile) = 2
    One or two prior incarcerations = 1
    Three or more prior incarcerations = 0

Item C ---   ☐

    Age at first commitment (adult or juvenile) 18 years or
    older = 1
    Otherwise = 0

Item D ---   ☐

    Commitment offense did not involve auto theft = 1
    Otherwise = 0

Item E ---   ☐

    Never had parole revoked or been committed for a new
    offense while on parole = 1
    Otherwise = 0

Item F ---   ☐

    No history of heroin, cocaine, or barbiturate dependence = 1
    Otherwise = 0

Item G ---   ☐

    Has completed 12th grade or received GED = 1
    Otherwise = 0

Item H ---   ☐

    Verified employment (or full-time school attendance) for a
    total of at least 6 months during the last 2 years in the
    community = 1
    Otherwise = 0

Item I ---   ☐

    Release plan to live with spouse and/or children = 1
    Otherwise = 0

Total Score ---   ☐

Offense Severity: Rate the severity of the present offense by placing a check in the appropriate category. If there is
a disagreement, each examiner will initial the category he chooses.

Low ....   High ....
Low Moderate ....   Very High ....
Moderate ....   Greatest ....
                                       (e.g. willful homicide, kidnapping)

Jail Time (Months) .... + Prison Time (Months) .... =Total Time Served To Date .... Months.
Guidelines Used: .... Youth .... Adult .... NARA
Tentative Decision ....

Form R-3
(Rev. 1/75)

OFFENSE CHARACTERISTICS: Severity of Offense Behavior (Examples)	OFFENDER CHARACTERISTICS: Parole Prognosis (Salient Factor Score)			
	Very Good (11-9)	Good (8-6)	Fair (5-4)	Poor (3-0)
LOW Immigration Law Violations Minor Theft (Includes Larceny and simple possession of stolen property less than $1,000) Walkaway	6-10 months	8-12 months	10-14 months	12-16 months
LOW MODERATE Alcohol Law Violations Counterfeit Currency (Passing/Possession less than $1,000) Drugs: Marijuana, Simple Possession (less than $500) Firearms Act, Possession/Purchase/Sale (single weapon-not altered or machine gun) Forgery/Fraud (less than $1,000) Income Tax Evasion (less than $10,000) Selective Service Act Violations Theft From Mail (less than $1,000)	8-12 months	12-16 months	16-20 months	20-25 months
MODERATE Bribery of Public Officials Counterfeit Currency (Passing/Possession $1,000 - $19,999) Drugs: "Hard Drugs", Possession by Drug User (less than $500) Marijuana, Possession with Intent to Distribute/Sale (less than $5,000) "Soft Drugs", Possession with Intent to Distribute/Sale (less than $500) Embezzlement (less than $20,000) Explosives, Possession/Transportation Firearms Act, Possession/Purchase/Sale (altered weapon(s), machine gun(s), or multiple weapons) Income Tax Evasion ($10,000 - $50,000) Interstate Transportation of Stolen/Forged Securities (less than $20,000) Mailing Threatening Communications Misprision of Felony Receiving Stolen Property with Intent to Resell (less than $20,000) Smuggler of Aliens Theft/Forgery/Fraud ($1,000 - $19,999) Theft of Motor Vehicle (Not multiple Theft or for Resale)	12-16 months	16-20 months	20-24 months	24-30 months
HIGH Burglary or Larceny (other than Embezzlement) from Bank or Post Office Counterfeit Currency (Passing/Possession $20,000 or more) Counterfeiting (Manufacturing) Drugs: "Hard Drugs" (Possession with Intent to Distribute/Sale by Drug User to Support Own Habit Only Marijuana, Possession with Intent to Distribute/Sale ($5,000 or more) "Soft Drugs", Possession with Intent to Distribute/Sale ($500 - $5,000) Embezzlement ($20,000 - $100,000) Interstate Transportation of Stolen/Forged Securities ($20,000 - $100,000) Mann Act (No Force - Commercial Purposes) Organized Vehicle Theft Receiving Stolen Property ($20,000 - $100,000) Theft/Forgery/Fraud ($20,000 - $100,000)	16-20 months	20-26 months	26-32 months	32-38 months
VERY HIGH Robbery (Weapon or Threat) Drugs: "Hard Drugs" (Possession with Intent to Distribute/Sale for Profit (No Prior Conviction for Sale of "Hard Drugs") "Soft Drugs" (Possession with Intent to Distribute/Sale (over $5,000) Extortion Mann Act (Force) Sexual Act (Force)	26-36 months	36-45 months	45-55 months	55-65 months
GREATEST Aggravated Felony (e.g. Robbery, Sexual Act, Aggravated Assault) - Weapon Fired or Personal Injury Aircraft Hijacking Drugs: "Hard Drugs" (Possession with Intent to Distribute/Sale) for Profit (Prior Conviction(s) for Sale of "Hard Drugs") Espionage Explosives (Detonation) Kidnapping Willful Homicide	(Greater than above - however, specific ranges are not given due to the limited number of cases and the extreme variations in severity possible within the category)			

Notes: 1) These guidelines are predicated upon good institutional conduct and program performance.
2) If an offense behavior is not listed above, the proper category may be obtained by comparing the severity of the offense behavior with those of similar offense behaviors listed.
3) If an offense behavior can be classified under more than one category, the most serious applicable category is to be used.
4) If an offense behavior involved multiple separate offenses, the severity level may be increased.
5) If a continuance is to be given, allow 30 days (1 month) for release program provision.
6) "Hard Drugs" include heroin, cocaine, morphine or opiate derivatives, and synthetic opiate substitutes.

an individual for possessing the recidivistic characteristics of a group. The system also does not address the serious problem of whether twenty-six to thirty months in prison for post office burglary is a "wise" or "correct" decision considering the various rationales for incarceration; it only assures more even-handed application of past judgments on the severity of the crime. This is a step forward *if* it is concluded that parole boards should share in the sentencing process, an issue that is discussed further below.[46]

Contract Parole

Another new and exceptional development in parole decision making also reduces the haphazardness of the process. This is the idea of a parole "contract" or "mutual agreement programming" (MAP). The concept of an agreement with the parolee is not new; indeed, all paroling authorities put the conditions of parole in an agreement which the inmate signs.[47] What is new is a contract between the prisoner, the institution, and the parole board under which the inmate will achieve certain agreed-upon goals (in terms of behavior, therapy, or training) in order to be paroled on a predetermined date. A Parole Corrections Project within the American Correctional Association has been planning, promoting, and helping install mutual agreement programming in two of the states studied here, Wisconsin and California, as well as in Arizona.[48]

In each state the plan was put into operation on a limited, experimental basis after a difficult installation period in which resistance had to be overcome from all parties—from parole boards concerned over losing authority to make decisions, from prison staff fearful of departing from established methods of inmate control and treatment, from attorneys raising legal questions, and from inmates suspicious of any deal offered them by their

46. For an extensive critique of the USPB methods, see William J. Genego, Peter D. Goldberger, and Vicki C. Jackson, "Parole Release Decision Making and the Sentencing Process," *Yale Law Journal*, vol. 84 (March 1975), pp. 810–902.

47. Parole conditions are discussed below, pages 82–84.

48. For a description of the program, see American Correctional Association, Parole Corrections Project, *Mutual Agreement Programming: An Overview* (College Park, Md.: ACA, June 1974); and idem, *The Mutual Agreement Program: A Planned Change in Correctional Service Delivery*, Resource Document no. 3 (College Park: ACA, November 1973). A similar program in Michigan, though not part of the ACA project, is described in Henry B. Risley, "Michigan's Contract Service Program: The First Year's Experience" (Michigan Department of Corrections, March 23, 1974; processed); see also Steve Gettinger, "Parole Contracts: A New Way Out," *Corrections Magazine*, vol. 2 (September–October 1975), pp. 3–7.

custodians. The Wisconsin plan, centered mostly at the Wisconsin Correctional Institution at Fox Lake, includes therapy, disciplinary improvement, education, and vocational training as goals and has been linked to an intensive job-finding program. The California project transferred a group of thirty men from a prison to a Los Angeles halfway house and gave them vouchers with which to purchase education and training. After the experimental period ended, the program was continued and made statewide in Wisconsin. Arizona and California did not renew it.[49]

Evaluative research in all three states was conducted as part of the project. The California experiment was a washout for various policy and operational reasons, although it did prove that a voucher system was feasible.[50] In Wisconsin and Arizona the evaluations showed that the bargain was kept by all parties: the prison staffs provided the services called for by the agreements; a large majority of the inmates did fulfill their commitments; and the boards did release them as promised.[51] But the results were disappointing in two important respects when the participating offenders were compared with nonparticipants: there were no significant differences between the two groups in employment success and recidivism.[52] The program was, however, regarded as helpful by both offenders and staff in Wisconsin and by offenders in Arizona (where staff attitudes were not surveyed).[53]

The story of MAP thus far is a mixture of good news and bad news. The bad news is that (1) the program is based on the widely doubted and nearly discredited rehabilitation theory; (2) the contract is implicitly coercive—the offender participates in institutional activities (whether or not he thinks they will do him any good) in order to be certain of release;

49. Ellen Russell Dunbar, "Politics and Policy Change: Processes Which Aid or Impede Change When a Research Demonstration Project Is Used to Stimulate Change in Correctional Policy" (Ph.D. dissertation, University of Southern California, 1975). This provides an analytical account of MAP in all three states. An appendix discusses a promising start in Maryland and unsuccessful efforts to "sell" the program in New Jersey, Virginia, and the District of Columbia.

50. Anne H. Rosenfeld, An Evaluative Summary of Research: MAP Program Outcomes in the Initial Demonstration States, American Correctional Association, Resource Document no. 7 (College Park, July 1975), pp. 62–63; James O. Robison, MAP Markers: Research and Evaluation of the Mutual Agreement Program, American Correctional Association, Resource Document no. 5 (College Park, August 1975), p. 256.

51. Rosenfeld, An Evaluative Summary, pp. 23–25; Robison, MAP Markers, pp. 260–62.

52. Rosenfeld, An Evaluative Summary, pp. 25–32; Robison, MAP Markers, pp. 140–50, 156–208.

53. Rosenfeld, An Evaluative Summary, pp. 33–37.

and (3) thus far the experiment does not result in the offenders becoming better employees or less recidivistic. The good news is that issues are clarified and understandings increased and that the program can be seen as a base worth building from in reassessing institutional policies and in enlisting the aid of more community services that could help parolees.[54]

The Political Factor

Another influence on parole decision making is what can be called the political factor—the pressure on any government agency working in a democracy. Parole boards need to survive and function in a public, and hence political, environment of fear of crime and punitiveness toward criminals, and in a criminal justice system that is sensitive to that environment. This fact pressures boards to be conservative—to take a "when in doubt keep him in" stance—in the face of human and professional inclinations to be more lenient.

The boards observed in this study kept an eye on newspaper editorial pages and on the pronouncements of political leaders. More systematic information on public opinion is available to boards through polls, as when the Gallup poll reports that "crime and lawlessness (including drug abuse) are the public's greatest concern on the domestic front, second only to the economic situation" and that the leading reason for high crime rates (given by 25 percent of interviewees) is "Laws are too lenient (penalties not stiff enough)."[55] Yet the public may sometimes favor leniency: in a survey of San Francisco and Portland, Oregon, citizens, over half "asserted that offenders should serve three years or less in prison."[56] The same study showed differences between the two cities in views on incarceration:[57]

	Percent	
Opinion	San Francisco	Portland
Not enough offenders get prison terms	25	51
About right number get prison	23	28
Too many are put in prison	48	17
No response	4	4

54. Robison, MAP Markers, pp. 260–63.
55. Gallup Opinion Index, Rept. no. 82 (April 1972), p. 11.
56. Don C. Gibbons, Joseph F. Jones, and Peter G. Garabedian, "Gauging Public Opinion about the Crime Problem," Crime and Delinquency, vol. 18 (April 1972), p. 143.
57. Ibid.

Aside from public opinion, the board members are naturally influenced more directly by executive and legislative leaders in their governments. Two examples from the jurisdictions visited in the present study demonstrate this. In fiscal year 1971, 92 percent of the parolees released by the District of Columbia Parole Board were assigned to community centers (halfway houses for work-releasees); the next year the figure dropped to 42 percent, and remained stable in fiscal 1972.[58] The reason, according to a staff member of the board, was that the chief of police had publicly stated that many crimes were being committed by persons on work-release, on bail, or on parole. The D.C. Department of Corrections became reluctant to accept recommendations from the parole board to assign inmates to community centers as a preparole step, and the board modified its decisions accordingly.

The other example is in California. At the time of our field research the California prison population was rising but commitments from the courts were not, so the increase was due to more denials and revocations of parole.[59] Adult Authority members acknowledged that this was a deliberate policy, adopted because of increases in violent crimes in the state. The policy was also consistent with a law-and-order campaign featuring strong public statements by the state attorney general and by a prominent member of the state legislature.

Parole boards, of course, have no monopoly on such sensitivity to political or public moods. The same thing happens in the determination of eligibility for welfare: "The strongest reaction to this decision-making [on public assistance grants and eligibility] again seems to be the anticipatory reaction to public opinion or sentiment, either at the state or the local level."[60] There is nothing new or unnatural about public officials trimming their decisions to the winds of public opinion. What hurts is the injustice this causes for individuals. In the District of Columbia, for example, scores of men lost their chance to go on work-release. Some, to be sure, would have failed, but some would not. In California scores of men were kept in prison or put back in prison for reasons that would not have sufficed in a different political climate. Changes in public policy usually hurt somebody, but these are particularly painful examples.

58. Board of Parole of the District of Columbia, *Annual Report, Fiscal Year 1971*, table II; *Fiscal Year 1972*, table II.
59. Notes on staff meeting, California Department of Corrections, March 26, 1973.
60. Alan Keith-Lucas, *Decisions About People in Need: A Study of Administrative Responsiveness in Public Assistance* (University of North Carolina Press, 1957), p. 227.

There is a formal procedural manifestation of this concern with the political factor. When parole boards work through hearing examiners or panels they may provide for the full board to consider certain classes of cases: decisions involving notorious criminals, heinous crimes, or famous persons, or cases where there is sharp diagreement among the examiners or the panel. The U.S. Board of Parole, for example, used to hold *en banc* (full board) hearings on cases involving national security, organized crime, persons or crimes receiving "national or unusual attention," and long-term sentences. Under the board's new rules, such cases are "original jurisdiction" cases. The regional director concerned forwards the case with his vote to the national directors in Washington, and three concurring votes are required for decision.[61] Wisconsin and California also have difficult cases decided by the full board. The actual decisions in full-board cases may or may not be different from the decisions as normally made; the point is to spread the blame in case there are strong public reactions.

Legal Fairness and Due Process[62]

The problem of legal fairness permeates the parole decision-making process. A central question in parole selection as well as revocation (treated in chapter 6) is how much freedom of choice parole boards have under the Constitution as well as by statute, and how they use this freedom. Robert Dawson wrote in 1966 of parole boards' great discretion to grant or deny parole. Such discretion, he said,

is as a practical matter free of legal controls. It is virtually impossible in an individual case to challenge a parole board decision successfully by legal processes. Not only are the provisions lacking for effective judicial review, but there are few legal standards to which the decisions must conform. When discretion has been granted, its exercise is often regarded as a matter not of

61. 40 Fed. Reg. p. 10975.

62. This section is a brief introduction to the due process issues in parole decision making. For more detail, see files of the American Bar Association's *Prison Law Reporter* and the *Criminal Justice Newsletter*, published by the National Council on Crime and Delinquency. For other helpful discussions, see Donald J. Newman, "Court Intervention in the Parole Process," *Albany Law Review*, vol. 36 (1972), pp. 257–304; "Comments. Due Process: The Right to Counsel in Parole Release Hearings," *Iowa Law Review*, vol. 54 (1968), pp. 497–509; and John P. Quinn, "The Parole Board's Duty of Self-Regulation," *University of Michigan Journal of Law Reform*, vol. 6 (Fall 1972), pp. 131–53; Sol Rubin, "Developments in Correctional Law," *Crime and Delinquency*, vol. 19 (April 1973), pp. 244–47; Rubin, "The Impact of Court Decisions on the Correctional Process," ibid., vol. 20 (April 1974), pp. 129–34; and David Gilman, "Developments in Correctional Law," ibid., pp. 169–81.

concern to the law and lawyers—the law sets the boundaries of discretion; it does not interfere with decisions within those boundaries.[63]

These statements now are becoming less true, as litigious inmates file suits challenging parole board processes.

Considerable impetus was given to the move to regularize the parole process by the publication of Kenneth Culp Davis's *Discretionary Justice*.[64] Davis had the U.S. Board of Parole in his sights, as well as several other government administrative bodies, when he urged openness and fairness in proceedings. More specifically, he said that the board should:

(a) develop open standards, as specific as possible, to guide its decisions,
(b) state findings and reasons when parole is denied, and when it is granted on the basis of a policy determination that may have value as a precedent,
(c) open proceedings and records to the public except to the extent that confidentiality is essential,
(d) develop a system of open precedents, and
(e) move toward group decisions made by members who deliberate together. In addition
(f) courts should review parole denials for errors of law, unfair procedure, or abuse of discretion.[65]

More support for adoption of the openness principle came in a report by Phillip Johnson to the Administrative Conference of the United States, which urged that parole boards give reasons for denials promptly, state reasons for granting parole in important cases, and make decisions and opinions public.[66] He also recommended that prisoners be allowed to see their own files ("except where compelling considerations require confidentiality in specific instances") so that they can dispute inaccurate or immaterial statements.[67] The conference substantially accepted these recommendations and added, with respect to the disclosure of the file, that "the prisoner should be given an oral summary or indication of the nature of any relevant adverse information which is not directly disclosed to him." The conference said further that the prisoner should be permitted counsel to help him both in examining his file and in his hearing.[68]

The federal board's new procedures announce the criteria for parole, tell the prisoner how he was rated, and give him reasons if parole is denied

63. Robert O. Dawson, *Sentencing*, p. 244.
64. Kenneth Culp Davis, *Discretionary Justice* (University of Illinois Press, 1971).
65. Ibid., p. 130.
66. Phillip E. Johnson, "Federal Parole Procedures: Report in Support of Recommendation 72-3," in *Recommendations and Reports of the Administrative Conference of the United States* (July 1, 1970–December 31, 1972), pp. 730–32.
67. Ibid., pp. 733–35.
68. "Recommendation 72-3: Procedures of the U.S. Board of Parole," in ibid., pp. 60–61.

(see the "Notice of Action Worksheet" on p. 73).)[69] He is also allowed to be represented by counsel and can appeal decisions within the board. In these respects the U.S. board is ahead of most others in applying the principles advocated by Davis and Johnson. Most states, as noted in chapter 3, do not give reasons for denials, and many take their time in letting the inmate know what the decision is.

Giving Reasons for Denial

This resistance to telling the prisoner why parole has been denied may seem surprising. One would think that the rationale behind a personal meeting with the inmate would also require telling him why he will not be paroled.

Knowing why he is not being paroled does not make the decision more acceptable to the inmate, only a little more understandable. A federal prisoner can discover from the notice-of-action sheet what severity and prediction factors apply to him; he may learn that his disciplinary record or need for institutional treatment is keeping him in longer.

Parole boards, however, have objected to giving reasons on the theory that parole is a privilege or an act of grace; that being on parole is an alternative to incarceration; that correctional authorities, including parole boards, must be in control of the situation; and that giving reasons for adverse decisions exposes this control to unnecessary challenge and has a weakening effect. This position has been under attack in the courts, and there has been a growing number of decisions requiring boards to give reasons.[70] Pressures in the same direction have been exerted by the National Advisory Commission on Criminal Justice Standards and Goals[71] and the board of directors of the NCCD.[72]

69. This is the form filled out by the hearing examiner when he decides the case. The relevant data and paragraphs are then typed on a notice of action form, which is sent to the prisoner within fifteen days.

70. For example, *Childs* v. *U.S. Board of Parole,* 371 F. Supp. 1246 (D.D.C. 1973) aff'd, no. 74-1052 (D.C. Cir., Dec. 19, 1974); *Burton* v. *Ciccione,* 484 F.2d 1322 (8th Cir. 1973); *U.S.* ex rel. *Johnson* v. *Chairman,* 363 F. Supp. 416 (E.D.N.Y. 1973), 500 F.2d 925 (2d Cir. 1974), *vacated as moot,* Sup. Ct., Nov. 18, 1974; In re *Sturm,* 11 Cal. 3d 258, 521 P.2d 97 (1974); *King* v. *United States,* 492 F.2d 1337 (7th Cir. 1974); *Bradford* v. *Weinstein,* no. 73-1751 (4th Cir., Nov. 22, 1974); and *Cook* v. *Whiteside,* 505 F.2d 32 (5th Cir. 1974).

71. National Advisory Commission on Criminal Justice Standards and Goals, *Corrections* (GPO, 1973), p. 422.

72. Board of Directors, National Council on Crime and Delinquency, "Parole Decisions: A Policy Statement," *Crime and Delinquency,* vol. 19 (April 1973), p. 137.

Form R-2
(Rev June 1974)

NOTICE OF ACTION WORKSHEET

CASE NAME_____ REGISTER NUMBER _____

REASONS: (CIRCLE AND COMPLETE EACH APPLICABLE REASON)

1. YOUR OFFENSE BEHAVIOR HAS BEEN RATED AS _____ SEVERITY.
   YOU HAVE A SALIENT FACTOR SCORE OF _____. YOU HAVE BEEN IN CUSTODY
   A TOTAL OF _____ MONTHS.

2. GUIDELINES ESTABLISHED BY THE BOARD FOR (ADULT) (YOUTH) (NARA)
   CASES WHICH CONSIDER THE ABOVE FACTORS INDICATE A RANGE OF
   _____ MONTHS TO BE SERVED BEFORE RELEASE FOR CASES WITH
   GOOD INSTITUTIONAL PROGRAM PERFORMANCE AND ADJUSTMENT. AFTER CAREFUL
   CONSIDERATION OF ALL RELEVANT FACTORS AND INFORMATION PRESENTED, IT
   IS FOUND THAT A DECISION OUTSIDE THE GUIDELINES AT THIS CONSIDERATION
   (DOES NOT APPEAR WARRANTED.) (APPEARS WARRANTED BECAUSE _____
   _____
   _____
   _____
   _____.)

3. YOU HAVE (A SERIOUS) (REPEATED) INSTITUTIONAL DISCIPLINARY INFRACTION(S).

4. YOU NEED ADDITIONAL INSTITUTIONAL TREATMENT, SPECIFICALLY _____
   _____, TO ENHANCE
   YOUR CAPACITY TO LEAD A LAW ABIDING LIFE.

5. OTHER: _____
   _____
   _____.

6. BOARD POLICY LIMITS A CONTINUANCE TO NOT MORE THAN THIRTY-SIX MONTHS
   WITHOUT REVIEW. YOUR CONTINUANCE HAS BEEN LIMITED BY THIS POLICY.

7. YOU HAVE NOT BEEN CERTIFIED AS ELIGIBLE FOR RELEASE PURSUANT TO SECTION
   4254 OF PUBLIC LAW 89-793 BECAUSE OF INSUFFICIENT PROGRESS IN THE NARA PROGRAM

NOTE: FOR GREATEST SEVERITY OFFENSE BEHAVIORS ONLY, YOU MAY USE THE FOLLOWING:

8A. YOUR RELEASE AT THIS TIME WOULD DEPRECIATE THE SERIOUSNESS OF THE OFFENSE
    COMMITTED AND THUS IS INCOMPATIBLE WITH THE WELFARE OF SOCIETY.

8B. THERE IS NOT A REASONABLE PROBABILITY THAT YOU WOULD LIVE AND REMAIN AT
    LIBERTY WITHOUT VIOLATING THE LAW BECAUSE _____
    _____
    _____.

The Georgia Board of Pardons and Paroles began giving written reasons for denial in 1973, using generalized language to meet various types of cases. Here are two samples:

Your record of emotional instability indicates that you have not consistently used good judgment when faced with problems.

The attitude you have shown indicates that you do not realize the seriousness of your past behavior or the need for self-improvement. The Board feels that you have not put a sincere effort towards changing your attitude to one that is mature and responsible.

Such messages are about as useful to the inmate as they are acceptable.[73] There is more realism and human validity to the practice in Colorado and Wisconsin of giving no written reasons but of the board or panel talking to the inmate about why they believe he should stay in prison. There may be less validity in their urging him to attend therapeutic or training activities as an implied condition of release, but there is little else they can do if they wish to be constructive. As long as indeterminate sentences are used, parole authorities will have to say to the inmate, in effect, "You're not good enough to get out now."

Disclosure of Information in Files

Even more difficult is the issue of whether to disclose to the inmate what is in his file—that is, what factors are working against his release. Due process considerations argue for letting him see what is in his record. As the head of the National Prison Project of the American Civil Liberties Union Foundation points out,

The parole board's current closed system not only generates the appearance of unfairness but also is filled with the real danger of factual error. Past records of criminal convictions which are erroneous, hearsay misinformation by investigating or prosecutorial officials, filing errors . . . and informal observations about a prisoner's institutional behavior . . . are to be found in a large percentage of the individual files of prisoners considered by parole boards. Prisoners have no opportunity to correct or rebut the information in these files. Openness alone could have a great effect upon the board's quality of performance. In playing God, the board is almost completely immune to criticism by anyone, and it should not be. Openness would serve as a protection

73. A more constructive approach was adopted later. The board now interviews the prisoner the second time he comes up for parole consideration. This affords an opportunity for more specific discussion of reasons for denial.

against administrative arbitrariness, too, in the same way that the constitutional guarantee of a public trial is designed as a protection against judicial arbitrariness.[74]

Yet correctional officials and parole boards resist. The U.S. Board of Parole, for example, is still taking a hard line on this issue despite its provision of greater legal fairness in other respects. Disclosure is opposed by the correctional establishment and boards on the grounds that the material revealed would impair the prisoner's rehabilitation (for example, by letting him see upsetting psychiatric evaluations); aggravate inmate enmities (by disclosing informants in cases of disciplinary infractions); cause prison staff to prepare bland, uninformative reports; and encourage unproductive controversy and litigiousness over small details of behavior. Yet these objections, to the extent that they are valid, can be mitigated by screening the files to remove some material temporarily or by oral summarization, as the Administrative Conference recommended. In the same spirit the Standard and Goals Commission recommended that "parole procedures should permit disclosure of information on which the hearing examiner bases his decisions. Sensitive information may be withheld, but in such cases nondisclosure should be noted in the record so that subsequent reviewers will know what information was not available to the offender."[75]

There remains a great gap between such policy recommendations and the necessities perceived by prison officials and parole boards. It can be bridged by executive policy decisions, new legislation, and court decisions. And parole boards, of course, do not have to wait for courts, legislatures, or governors to force them to state their criteria, open their files, give reasons for decisions promptly and specifically, allow counsel to represent inmates, and provide for appeals. Yet as conscientious and heavily burdened officials they are understandably reluctant to incur additional workload and criticism. Nevertheless, such reluctance adds to public suspicions of arbitrary and capricious decision making and tends to undermine confidence in the parole process. Whether the current trend toward more emphasis on due process continues strong, weakens, or stops depends in large measure on political currents and on public opinion on criminal justice issues.

74. Alvin J. Bronstein, "Rules for Playing God," *Civil Liberties Review*, vol. 1 (Summer 1974), p. 120.

75. National Advisory Commission, *Corrections*, p. 422. New federal legislation (P.L. 94-233, March 15, 1976) requires the U.S. Parole Commission (the board's new name) to give the prisoner a summary of the information relied upon.

Evaluation and Alternatives

To appraise parole decision making as a whole requires a look at sentencing practices, since parole boards decide how much of the original sentence will actually be served. They do so by applying, explicitly or implicitly, a mixture of the underlying concepts of incarceration: retribution, incapacitation, deterrence, and rehabilitation. Which function of imprisonment is emphasized varies from board to board and even from case to case, but parole boards generally depend heavily upon prediction of future criminality, especially dangerousness. This leads to preventive imprisonment—a questionable concept, given our basic traditions of fairness. Its validity is particularly dubious because predicting dangerous behavior is so difficult. Nevertheless, it is widely supported by judges, political leaders, and the general public. While practicing preventive detention, parole boards also emphasize and preach rehabilitation, though the evidence is that prisons are ineffective in accomplishing it.

Parole boards are, in effect, second-guessing the sentencing judge.[76] It may be argued that the boards are in a position to correct the much-deplored disparities in sentencing. But they do not approach this in a systematic fashion, except for the U.S. Board of Parole, whose guidelines are not used by the judges. Furthermore, no parole board can do anything about the major sentencing disparity, whether or not the offender is put on probation.[77] Parole boards make their decisions, moreover, without giving the offender nearly as much procedural fairness, or due process, protection as a person on trial recives in court.

Observations like these raise three interlocked questions: Should parole boards participate at all in determining length of sentence? Can they do (or do more effectively) anything that the sentencing judge cannot do? Should indeterminate sentences continue to be used? Negative answers to all three questions are suggested not only by the discussion thus far but also by the findings of several other studies.

Alternatives Proposed by Other Studies

The recent Yale Law School study looks at these matters and concludes that when the U.S. Board of Parole evaluates offense severity and likeli-

76. Genego and others, "Parole Release Decision Making," p. 893.
77. Ibid., pp. 896–97.

hood of risk it is making decisions that could and should be made only by judges. "[It] is difficult to see any purpose in having two independent decisions with respect to the same individual, based on the same data, aimed at achieving the same purpose, unless one is explicitly and intelligently assigned as a review or check on the other."[78] The authors argue that deficiencies in the sentencing process should be corrected by the judicial branch.[79] Although they would do away with the board's release function, they would not end indeterminate sentences. It is suggested that the judge might set "a presumptive date of conditional release" at sentencing; then the actual date of release would be determined by prison officials' administration of "good time" rules. As an alternative model, "Congress might find that certain circumstances warrant limited postponement of the presumptive release date [and] . . . might authorize a parole board to postpone the presumptive release date upon a finding that the inmate needed a certain amount of time to complete specific institutional programs or that there was substantial probability, based on specific evidence, particular to the individual inmate, that the inmate would engage in further criminal activity."[80] This proposal is undesirable because it falls into the prediction and rehabilitation traps discussed at length already.

The Committee for the Study of Incarceration would abandon the indeterminate sentence and all bases for incarceration except what we have been calling retribution and is called the "commensurate deserts principle" by the committee: "Our theory undercuts the need for indeterminancy. The commensurate-deserts principle looks to the past—to the seriousness of the defendant's crimes. Seriousness—the extent of the harm done or risked and the degree of the actor's culpability—can just as well be ascertained at the time of conviction as at an indefinite later date; for this purpose as Marvin Frankel states, 'whatever complexities and imponderables there are—and there are plenty—there is none that is not knowable on the day of sentencing.' "[81] Under the committee's plan, sentences would be much more definite, with the judge's discretion limited:

• Graded levels of seriousness would be established, and the guidelines would specify which offense categories belong on which seriousness levels.

• For each level of seriousness, a specific penalty—the presumptive sentence

78. Ibid., p. 898.
79. Ibid., p. 899.
80. Ibid., p. 898.
81. Andrew von Hirsch, *Doing Justice: The Choice of Punishments*, Report of the Committee for the Study of Incarceration (Hill and Wang, 1976), p. 102.

—would be prescribed. An offender convicted of a crime of that gradation of seriousness would ordinarily receive this sentence.

• For those offenders who had been convicted before, there would be a prescribed increase in the presumptive sentence, depending on the number and seriousness of the prior crimes.

• The judge would have authority to raise the penalty above or reduce it below the presumptive sentence, in cases where he finds there were special circumstances affecting the gravity of the violation and where he specifies what these circumstances of aggravation or mitigation were. But such variations could not depart from the presumptive sentence by more than a prescribed amount. The limits on the permitted variations should be designed to preserve the basic ranking of penalties—and restrict overlaps in the severity of punishments for offenses of characteristically distinct seriousness. Intentional homicides, even under mitigated circumstances, would preserve their rank above, say, burglaries.[82]

The plan also calls for reduced sentences because "Many judges now impose long sentences in the expectation (not always fulfilled) that a parole board will permit earlier release. Under our approach, the initially imposed sentence would be the one actually served."[83]

This recommendation is consistent with the conclusions of an earlier study made for the American Friends Service Committee. This report urges, "Whatever sanction or short sentence is imposed is to be fixed by law. There is to be no discretion in setting sentences, no indeterminate sentences, and unsupervised street release is to replace parole."[84] The elimination of parole supervision is a touchy point. Parole boards sometimes feel uneasy about decisions to release inmates but claim that the community will be protected and the offender benefited by supervision. This is doubtful, as shown in chapter 6.

Similar reforms have more recently been proposed by the governor of Illinois. He asks that a legislative commission be set up to study his recommendations that fixed, not indeterminate, sentences be used; parole be ended; and evaluation of rehabilitation not be a factor in prison releases. Sentences would be shortened by "good time"—a day's reduction for each day of good behavior.[85] These recommendations have been supported by strong criticisms of present sentencing and parole practices similar to those made here.

82. Ibid., pp. 99–100.
83. Ibid., p. 102.
84. *Struggle for Justice: A Report on Crime and Punishment in America Prepared for the American Friends Service Committee* (Hill and Wang, 1971), p. 144.
85. "News from the Office of the Governor" (press release, Feb. 18, 1975; processed), p. 1.

In New York State, parole decision making was extensively criticized in the report of the Citizens' Inquiry on Parole and Criminal Justice. The "long-term recommendations" say in part: "The goals of rehabilitation ...are unrealistic and should not shape sentencing and release decisions.... Sentences should be shorter and have a narrower range of indeterminacy. The criteria used to determine the length of terms and the justifications for indeterminacy must await further research."[86]

A study by the University of Connecticut for that state's Commission on Parole Techniques and Rehabilitation recommends in part that *"the present structure of indefinite sentences should be replaced with one of definite sentences....."* and that "parole should be abolished both as a means of release prior to serving a full term in custody and as a status after release"[87]

The attorney general of the United States more recently expressed his sympathetic understanding of the need to impose sentencing guidelines and possibly to eliminate parole.[88]

Conclusions

The conclusions of this study and those just cited point clearly to the need for reform of the process for determining whether and for how long an offender shall be incarcerated. The inconsistencies and irrationalities of the present combination of sentencing and parole are insupportable. There is a temptingly simple solution that should be considered: eliminate the indeterminate sentence, greatly reduce judges' sentencing discretion, and abolish the decision-making powers of parole boards. Under such a plan the community would be protected from the more threatening criminals by the longer sentences given to repeat offenders.

But, as with all alternatives, there are problems. Any legislative body inclined toward such a plan would encounter strong resistance from judges who are unwilling to relinquish their wide sentencing discretion. Legislators, having gotten the message from public opinion that punitiveness is good politics, would also be reluctant to reduce statutory prison terms. If

86. Citizens' Inquiry, *Prison without Walls*, p. 178.
87. "Staff Report, Prepared for Commission on Parole Evaluation Techniques and Rehabilitation" (State of Connecticut, Sept. 1, 1975; processed), pp. 21, 22 (emphasis in original).
88. Press release, U.S. Department of Justice, "Address by Hon. Edward H. Levi before the [Wisconsin] Governor's Conference on Employment and the Prevention of Crime" (Feb. 2, 1976; processed).

parole were abolished and terms not reduced, most prisoners would have to serve longer terms than they do now for the same offenses. Even if legislatures did pass definite sentencing laws that provided for appropriately short sentences, their intent could be frustrated by prosecutors and judges. For instance, an offender could be charged on multiple counts and then sentenced nonconcurrently.

Thus, if one looks to the judiciary itself to lead the way in a more consistent criminal justice philosophy and equitable sentencing, the problem of judicial independence is encountered. Judges under the American system are difficult to coordinate and direct; their very independence is a protection against abuses elsewhere in the criminal justice system. The best that can be expected, therefore, is legislative action based on clear facts and sound research. Changes will be incremental and controversial. At present, however, sentencing imperfections are partly and irregularly mitigated by release on parole, however irrational that process may be.

CHAPTER FIVE

The Parolee under Supervision

So the prisoner is released; he is now a parolee. He comes out of prison into a program intended both to protect society from him and to help him. These two purposes are intermingled—the parole officer is responsible for both—but they are discussed separately here. This chapter and the following one cover parole surveillance, first introducing the parole officer and his routine supervision of the offender, then exploring in chapter 6 what happens when the parolee goes wrong. Chapter 7 deals with the help available to the parolee in the community, partly from the parole officer, mostly from others. These processes require further exercises in decision making. There are difficult judgments to be made about the methods and frequency of surveillance; about possible returns to prison; about discharge from parole; and about the means of assistance to be used.

While the offender is on parole he is legally in the custody of the government. In reality he is still being punished; otherwise, crime-free periods spent by absconders could be counted toward the completion of parole. The parolees are fully aware that parole is part of their punishment and that they are "paying their debt" by submitting to surveillance.[1]

Most people would react poorly to being under surveillance, and a typical parolee faces his abrupt transition from prison to life in the community with painfully mixed emotions. He experiences "a period of confusion, filled with anxiety, missed cues, embarrassment, over-intense impulses, and excitement followed by depression."[2]

In his own language:

They were talking and doing different things, I felt like a fool.

1. Letter to the author from Professor Elliot Studt, University of California at Los Angeles, Jan. 2, 1975, based on her study of parole processes in California.
2. Elliot Studt, "Reintegration from the Parolee's Perspective," in *Reintegration of the Offender into the Community*, U.S. Law Enforcement Assistance Administration, Criminal Justice Monographs (GPO, June 1973), p. 43.

The clerk asked me what I wanted and for a minute I couldn't understand her. It was like I didn't understand her.

I mean, I was shook, baby. Things were moving too fast everybody rushing somewhere. And they all seemed so cold, they had this uptight look.[3]

Such feelings of disorientation and anxiety are natural accompaniments to the massive change from the total institution to the relative freedom of parole. Parolees are apprehensive, too, because their expectations of the parole experience may have been influenced by parole violators who have been reimprisoned and present an unfavorable picture of the situation.[4] Furthermore, they understand that they face demeaning and damaging legal handicaps: inability to vote, to sue in the courts, and to be licensed to engage in certain occupations.[5]

The Parole Agreement

⤳ Before he is released, the prisoner must sign an agreement containing the conditions of his parole. In greater or lesser length, detail, and stringency, they prescribe how he shall conduct himself. His liberty depends on how well he complies with them. A condition may be as vague as "I agree to conduct myself as a good citizen at all times; I understand that my attitude and behavior must justify the opportunity granted to me by this parole";[6] or as specific as "You shall make a complete and truthful written report (on a form provided for that purpose) to your probation [parole] officer between the first and third day of each month. . . ."[7]

One state imposes as many as twenty conditions; others, as few as four. The median is thirteen.[8] Like the examples above, they can be grouped into two main types: "reform" conditions that urge him toward a non-

3. Quotations from interviews in John Irwin, *The Felon* (Prentice-Hall, 1970), pp. 114–15.

4. Jerome H. Skolnick, "Toward a Developmental Theory of Parole," *American Sociological Review*, vol. 25 (August 1960), pp. 544, 549.

5. For an extensive review of convicts' legal disabilities, see Walter Matthews Grant and others, "Special Project: The Collateral Consequences of a Criminal Conviction," *Vanderbilt Law Review*, vol. 23 (1970), pp. 929ff.

6. State of California, Adult Authority, *Agreement of Parole* (Sacramento, June 1, 1973), Condition 12 (in part).

7. U.S. Board of Parole, *Certificate of Parole* (rev. January 1972), Condition 5 (in part).

8. Resource Center on Correctional Law and Legal Services, *Survey of Parole Conditions in the United States* (Washington, D.C.: American Bar Association, Commission on Correctional Facilities and Services, December 1973), pp. 15–16.

criminal way of life and "control" conditions that make it possible for the parole staff to keep track of him. Reform conditions might include the following: comply with laws; maintain employment and support dependents; refrain from use of drugs; refrain from excessive use or (in some governments) any use of liquor; refrain from (or get permission for) use of firearms. Common examples of control conditions are: get permission for (or notify parole officer of) change of job or residence, or marriage or divorce; get permission for out-of-state or (less frequently) out-of-locality travel; report to parole office upon release and periodically afterward; cooperate with parole officer; get permission to own or use a motor vehicle. In the least-used parole conditions, parolees are urged, though not required, to attend church (in three states) and must refrain from gambling (in two).[9]

A 1973 survey by the American Bar Association (ABA) showed that some states had cut down on the number of conditions but that no nationwide trend was discernible. Those most frequently abandoned were ones whose realism is questionable, including: "avoid undesirable associations [the parolee's brother or father may have a prison record]; refrain from use of alcohol; get permission to own or use a motor vehicle [how else will he get to work?]; and get permission for marriage or divorce."[10] In contrast, at the time field research for this study was going on the California Adult Authority was making its parole conditions more numerous and specific in order (members said) to facilitate decisions on contested parole revocations. The Wisconsin Board of Parole was considering a similar step.

The conditions described so far are general conditions, applicable to all parolees of the government imposing them. In forty-six of the jurisdictions, special conditions have been added to fit individual parolees' cases, such as: "You will not visit or telephone your former wife." "You will not be in contact with Julius B—— or John M—— [parolee's crime partners]." "You will participate fully in the South Springfield Drug Clinic program."

Parole conditions in most jurisdictions are so numerous and either so specific or so vague that "most free citizens would find it difficult to avoid violations of parole regulations if all were rigorously enforced."[11] Technically a parolee may be returned to prison for any one breach—failing to

9. Ibid., pp. 10, 12–13.
10. Ibid., p. 2.
11. William Parker, *Parole: Origins, Development, Current Practices and Statutes*, American Correctional Association, Parole Corrections Project Resource Document no. 1 (College Park, Md.: 1975), p. 36.

make a report, staggering drunkenly out of a tavern—but this is rarely done. Nevertheless, the parolee lives with the knowledge that the parole authorities can use this power if they wish.

Some conditions are called "constitutionally suspect" in the ABA study: requiring permission to travel out of state, prohibition of associating with undesirables, and (in eighteen states) requiring the parolee to permit visits to his home or job.[12] With the increase in offenders' rights litigation, court decisions in these matters can probably be expected. Meanwhile the parolee must treat the conditions as if they were laws.

Assignment to a Parole Officer

When the parolee leaves prison, he is instructed in writing to report on or before a certain day to a parole office in the community where he will live. He must do this almost immediately, so that contact with him is not lost. The parole office will already have received a file of information about him from the prison. In most instances the office will also have commented on his parole plan and hence will be familiar with his case.

He will also have already been assigned to a particular parole officer[13] who will be his overseer, counselor, and, possibly, friend. Usually the assignment is routinely made to the parole officer who works in the part of town where the parolee will live or, if there is a choice, to the officer working there who has fewer cases to supervise.

The assignment is a more complex matter in governments where parole officers specialize by type of case. In California, Georgia, the District of Columbia, and some federal parole offices, parolees are classified on the basis of their records as needing maximum, medium, or minimum supervision. Parole officers responsible for maximum supervision are required to see or call the parolee more frequently and therefore are assigned fewer cases than are those handling medium or minimum supervision. Some parole officers may also have a reduced case load because they specialize in narcotics offenders, who are supervised more closely.

California's classification and assignment program, called the Work

12. ABA Resource Center, *Survey*, pp. 9–11.

13. The term "parole officer" is used in this book although such an official may have another title—"parole agent" in California and Colorado, for example. Where the official is responsible for both probation and parole supervision (see pp. 87–88 below) the title may reflect this: "probation and parole agent" (Wisconsin); "probation-parole supervisor" (Georgia); and federal "probation officers" who handle both probation and parole.

Unit Parole Program,[14] is a complex system of allotting staff time on the basis of parolees' estimated needs. For the first five years after its initiation in 1965 it was hailed as one factor in reducing the proportion of parolees who were caught in new crimes or who failed to make it for other reasons.[15] At the time of our field research in 1973, however, the rising recidivism statistics cast doubt on such claims. By then work unit had become a synonym for difficult or risky types of parole cases that the board felt required maximum supervision.

Whether parolees are assigned randomly or on the basis of assumed risk, almost nowhere are they assigned on the basis of personal compatibility. Obviously some parolees would respond better to authoritarian treatment, others to a more permissive attitude, but it is apparently assumed that all parole officers treat their clients the same. So there are inevitably cases like that of one parolee we interviewed who told of his despair when, soon after he came out of prison, his wife left him and he was unable to get anything but temporary, rock-bottom jobs. Needing someone to listen, sympathize, and help, he went to his parole officer, who genially clapped him on the shoulder and told him to be a man. Another example was that of one of the few women we interviewed, a young parolee assigned to a "stern, elderly person." He told her that all he expected of her was to go to church regularly and not cause any trouble. Said she, "I need white trash advice like that like I need a private jet."

None of the jurisdictions studied here made any effort to match parole officer and parolee, although an official in one state did say, "Well, we wouldn't assign an older man to a long-haired boy just out of college." It is understandable that the diagnostic and administrative problems of ensuring significant compatibility between parolee and parole officer would seem too great to overcome in a busy parole field office. An already-busy office supervisor would have to do careful analytical work on the characteristics of the parole staff and of incoming parolees. And even then the "right" officer for a parolee might be already overburdened.

14. So called because supervisory time requirements were translated into work units for assignment purposes. Each parole agent was allotted 120 units in total, but parolees were classified as follows:

Special (maximum) supervision	4.8 units, or	25 parolees per officer
Regular (medium) supervision	3 units, or	40 parolees per officer
Conditional (minimum) supervision	1 unit, or	120 parolees per officer

California Department of Corrections, Parole and Community Services Division, *A Report to the Legislature on the Work Unit Parole Program* (December 1971), p. 6.

15. Ibid., pp. 10–12.

Still, more effort toward matching personalities may pay off in improved performance, according to research in the Community Treatment Program of the California Youth Authority.[16] Offenders closely matched with their community workers had a significantly lower failure rate than those not closely matched.[17] The researcher adds that there is a negative advantage, too, in that matching "systematically obviat[es] unproductive relationships or serious personality clashes that might otherwise result from worker-client combinations, competent supervision notwithstanding."[18]

Another matching experiment in California, however, provided "no evidence . . . that parole agent and client characteristics impacted parole outcome."[19]

Parole officers themselves object to being classified into categories for purposes of assignment, according to an analysis by three leading criminal justice scholars.

Attempts to classify officers and move from the GP [general practitioner] model have been limited by resistance on the part of the officers themselves to be categorized as external-internal; punitive-protective-welfare-opportunist; welfare-paternal-passive-punitive or, for that matter, according to any other scheme. The resistance of "professional" staff to such, or similar, categorization is understandable, but unfortunate. Variations among officers in terms of capabilities and skills are somehow seen by officers as personal deficiencies when in fact they may be assets.[20]

In general, then, assignments on the basis of personal compatibility would seem to be desirable but are of unproven value, pose administrative difficulties, and are hard to sell to the parole staff.

Before treating the parole officer–parolee work relationship in detail, more needs to be said about parole officers—how they are organized, their characteristics, and their careers.

Organization of Parole Staffs

Parole officers and their supervisors used to work for parole boards in a majority of jurisdictions, but the pattern has now changed. The em-

16. The present study did not include this agency.

17. Ted B. Palmer, "Matching Worker and Client in Corrections," *Social Work*, vol. 18 (March 1973), p. 101.

18. Ibid.

19. M. G. Neithercutt and Don M. Gottfredson, "Case Load Size Variation and Difference in Probation/Parole Performance" (Administrative Office of the U.S. Courts Probation Division, 1973; processed), p. 6.

20. Robert M. Carter, Daniel Glaser, and E. Kim Nelson, "Probation and Parole

phasis on comprehensive departments of corrections (or large departments that include corrections) has left only eighteen state boards that
supervise field staffs.[21] It has been argued that the boards as policymakers
should oversee the administration of their policies and decisions. The
counterarguments, which have generally prevailed, say that the growing
use of prerelease programs and community-based facilities requires "a
close meshing of institution and field activities and a heavy expenditure
of field staff energy for many months before an inmate's release on
parole."[22] This means that a consistent approach to the whole system of
punishment—institutional programs, work-release, and parole supervision
—is necessary, and it is reasonable to assume that a corrections department
can better provide this than a parole board. Furthermore, there is no reason why boards cannot communicate both formally and informally with
parole staffs without being in charge of them. The boards already have
enough administrative detail to be concerned with in their decision-
making function.

Four of the parole staffs studied for this book were under the corrections department: the District of Columbia, California, Georgia, and
Wisconsin.[23] Georgia had recently transferred supervision of the parole
staffs from the parole board to regional offices of the Department of Offender Rehabilitation. Colorado parole staffs are under a department of institutions along with the corrections division. The federal parole officers
are also probation officers and work for the court system, which brings us
to the next point.

Combined Probation and Parole Staffs

Along with the federal government, Georgia and Wisconsin use the
same officers for probation and parole work. This has been a common but
not universal arrangement. Thirty-five states have officers who do both
kinds of work, although six of them also have some officers who are

---

Supervision: The Dilemma of Caseload Size" (Administrative Office of the U.S. Courts
Probation Division, February 1973; processed), pp. 12–13.

21. Vincent O'Leary and Joan Nuffield, *The Organization of Parole Systems in the
United States* (Hackensack, N.J.: National Council on Crime and Delinquency, 1972),
p. xvi. See also *Human Resource Agencies: Adult Corrections in State Organizational
Structure* (Washington, D.C.: Council of State Governments, 1975).

22. O'Leary and Nuffield, *Organization of Parole Systems*, p. xvi.

23. More precisely, parole in Wisconsin is under the corrections division, which is
part of the Department of Health and Social Services.

assigned only to parole. Probation-parole officers outnumber parole-only officers by about five to two.[24]

There are several reasons in favor of the combined arrangement: (1) the same goals are sought and the same knowledge and skills are required; (2) the same approach should be applied to all offenders in the same jurisdiction; (3) only one supervisory hierarchy, one set of offices, and one set of directives are required instead of two of each; and (4) since some probationers "grow up" to be parolees, it is efficient to have the same organization in charge of them.

On the other side are these arguments: (1) probation is a staff service for judges, so it must be promptly and flexibly available to them—under their control and separate from the correctional bureaucracies; (2) since probation officers deal with unhardened criminals whom society wishes to keep out of prison, while parole staffs must deal with an older, tougher, prison-damaged group, different organizations and different officers should be responsible for the different clienteles; and (3) judicial-branch patronage and executive-branch patronage or the civil service are more comfortably kept separate.

In the three governments studied, probation-parole officers were questioned about the combination. Their only significant response was that judges' work had to be treated by them as more urgent, so that parole duties had to be delayed on some occasions.

Supervisors

Between the individual parole officer and the director of corrections (or parole board) are two or three intermediate layers of parole administrators. The officer's immediate supervisor may be a straw boss, handling a case load himself as well as directing a few officers, or he may supervise so many officers (perhaps eight or more) that he is a full-time administrator. This first-line supervisor trains the new parole officer, assigns cases to him, reviews his reports and desk records to see that he is making the required contacts with parolees, and suggests solutions to problems of surveillance or assistance. He probably is involved in any case where the parolee has disappeared or where revocation is being considered. This first-line supervisor works for a higher administrator who is in charge of

24. *Probation and Parole Directory: U.S. and Canada* (National Council on Crime and Delinquency, 1976 ed., forthcoming).

parole staff for a region of the state or for a large city. The federal probation organization is different. Each of the ninety-four district courts has
its own probation staff located in one, two, or more cities, the average
being two.

Thus parole staffs, except in the smallest states, are substantial bureaucracies with scores or even hundreds of officers organized hierarchically.
The administrators in charge impose controls, reports, and rules intended
to produce a reasonably uniform and effective level of performance. The
individual parole officer must conform as best he can while he tries to
supervise and help his extremely difficult and diverse group of parolees.

The Parole Officer and His Job

A typical parole officer, at least in New York State, is "a forty-three
year-old man; five feet ten inches tall, weighing one-hundred eighty-one
pounds. His experience in the Division of Parole would amount to more
than ten years. Chances are 13 out of 14 that he is a college graduate; 1.78
out of 2 that he has taken post-graduate courses; and 1 out of 2 that he
holds a Master's or Law Degree. He is active in at least two community
service projects unrelated to his work, enjoys the usual varied hobbies, and
is married, with at least two children."[25] There is also a 30 percent chance
that he is black.[26] The typical parole officer interviewed in our field research is like this except that he is a little younger, has two or three years
less experience, and is less likely to have a graduate degree.[27]

There is generally more than one level of parole officer job, but this
discussion refers to what some states call Parole Officer I—the basic position to which the employee is appointed and in which he actually supervises parolees on his own. There are other levels: some governments have
trainee jobs and there are also higher levels, based on the extent of responsibility. Table 5-1 shows examples of the parole officer and supervisor jobs
in the governments we studied with their salaries and qualifications.

25. New York State Division of Parole pamphlet, quoted in Citizens' Inquiry on
Parole and Criminal Justice, *Prison without Walls: Report on New York Parole*
(Praeger, 1975), pp. 14–15.
26. Steven R. Weisman, *New York Times*, Jan. 1, 1973.
27. For a comparable description of California parole agents, See David Joseph
Bentel, "Parole Officer: An Examination of the Occupational Career of California
Parole Agents" (D.Crim. dissertation, University of California, Berkeley, 1970), pp.
94–96.

Table 5-1. *Qualifications and Monthly Salaries for Parole Officers, 1975*[a]

Government	Trainee or pre-Journeyman	Journeyman (basic job)	More qualified, nonsupervisory	Supervisor	Higher supervisor	Highest supervisor
Federal (U.S. Courts)	Probation Officer Trainee: $920; bachelor's or master's degree Assistant Probation Officer: bachelor's degree and two years' experience, or other options	Associate Probation Officer: $1,355; qualifications for assistant level plus one year experience in "personnel work for welfare of others"	Probation Officer: $1,616; qualification for assistant level plus two years of similar experience	Supervising Probation Officer: $1,909; three years of similar experience with at least one as probation officer	Chief Probation Officer: $2,238; four years of similar experience with at least one as chief or supervising probation officer	Chief Probation Officer (larger district): $2,609; four years of similar experience with at least one as chief or supervising probation officer
California	Correctional Case Work Trainee: $849; bachelor's degree and general knowledge of counseling, casework Parole Service Associate: $791; one year experience at next lower level and one year college, or three years' experience plus two years' college	Parole Agent I: $1,218; one year experience at lower level (two years as Correctional Officer plus bachelor's degree or equivalent experience)	Parole Agent II (specialist or supervisor of small unit): $1,344; one year as Parole Agent I	Parole Agent III (staff specialist or unit supervisor): $1,483; one year as Parole Agent II	Parole Administrator I (district supervisor or assistant to regional administrator or staff specialist): $1,595	Parole Administrator II (regional administrator or staff specialist): $1,846
Colorado	Parole Agent: $822; bachelor's degree or correctional experience	Parole Agent B: $952; completion of training program	Parole Agent C: $1,103; two years as Parole Agent B or three years in probation or parole work	Parole Supervisor I (supervises a specialized parole unit): $1,277; one year as Parole Agent C or 4 years in probation or parole work	Parole Supervisor II (supervises a major geographical unit): $1,408; five years of parole experience with at least two at Parole Agent C level	Parole Supervisor III (directs one of largest units): $1,478; six years of parole experience with at least two at Parole Supervisor I level

Georgia		Probation/Parole Supervisor I: $650; bachelor's degree, social sciences	Probation/Parole Supervisor II: $746; one year as Probation/Parole Supervisor I or master's degree in behavioral science	Probation/Parole Supervisor III (directs small group): $815; two years in probation/parole work	Probation/Parole Unit Coordinator (directs large group): $891; two years in probation/parole or related fields including supervisory experience	Social Services Administrator I (directs a parole region): $1,544; similar background; ability to represent the program to outside groups
Wisconsin	Social Worker I: $881; bachelor's degree and prerequisites for admission to a school of social work	Social Worker II: $1,036; two years graduate training in school of social work, or two years social work experience, or combination	Social Worker III (more independent work): $1,117; same requirements as for Social Worker II	Social Services Supervisor I (directs a parole unit): $1,193; background in administration and casework, knowledge of laws, rules, procedures	Social Services Supervisor III (directs a parole district): $1,418; similar background	
District of Columbia	Parole Officer, GS-7: $920; bachelor's degree with 24 credits in social sciences, plus one year experience. Parole Officer, GS-9: $1,124; one additional year experience	Parole Officer, GS-11: $1,355; one year experience at GS-9 level	Parole Officer, GS-12 (supervises seven youth and adult parole officers): $1,616; promotion by competition from GS-11	Parole Officer, Branch Chief, GS-13 (supervises three areas): $1,909; one year at GS-12; promotion by competition from GS-12	Chief Parole Officer, GS-14 (supervises entire parole program): $2,238; one year at GS-13; promotion by competition from GS-13	

Source: Personnel documents supplied by the governments studied. Data are simplified for presentation here.

a. Salaries shown are the lowest rate of each pay range as of 1975.

Note the different meanings of "supervisor"—supervising parolees in Georgia, supervising parole staff in Colorado and Wisconsin.

Qualifications and Pay

The basic parole officer job calls for college graduation with a major in one of the social or behavioral sciences. Some governments require also either a year or more of graduate study in the same fields or an equivalent amount of work experience in some field involving supervision, counseling, or teaching.

The starting pay for state jobs, according to the salary survey of the U.S. Civil Service Commission, ranges from $600 a month up to $1,320. The median is $777, and over three-quarters of the starting rates are clustered between $650 and $900.[28] By the time a state parole officer is an experienced journeyman his pay is roughly $150 a month above these salaries.

Comparing the probation and parole job in this survey with other jobs in the same states, one finds that the salaries approximate those for social service worker, vocational rehabilitation counselor, and public health nurse. Hence the parole job is considered professional and is equated with other healing, problem-solving professions, but on what might be called the second tier: parole officers are more like nurses than physicians, more like counselors than attorneys.

The parole officer job in the Civil Service survey calls for college graduation, as do those in the governments studied here, though substitution of experience for education is sometimes permitted. Of the twenty-five parole officers we interviewed, twenty had bachelor's degrees, of whom three also had master's degrees and one had a law degree; three were not college graduates; and no educational information was obtained about one. Only four officers began parole work right after college; others had been teachers, caseworkers, employees of other government agencies, or policemen. Some had been correctional officers in prisons; the California personnel system especially encourages movement from prison to parole work. It may seem logical to interchange personnel in these two parts of the criminal justice system: both jobs require an understanding of the offender's needs and the ability to deal with him firmly and constructively. However, several state officials told us, "No, it takes a different kind of guy"—meaning that the correctional officer who can endure and advance

28. U.S. Civil Service Commission, Bureau of Intergovernmental Personnel Programs, "State Salary Survey, 1975" (C.S.C., Aug. 1, 1975; processed). These data are from forty-nine states (excluding North Carolina) and the District of Columbia for the entry-level job of "probation and parole officer."

in a custody-comes-first environment is not the best guide for a parolee in the community.

Nevertheless, correctional experience and social work experience are equally emphasized in the personnel standards recommended by the American Correctional Association[29] and the Federal Probation Officers Association.[30] This equal treatment is borne out in part by the results of a research study of New York State parole officers: it was found that differences in officers' employment backgrounds had no significant relationship to their attitudes toward reintegrating the parolee into the free community.[31]

Training

How does the professional parole officer learn his complex and difficult duties? The older officers interviewed for this study said they "swam because they were pushed off the dock." If they were lucky they accompanied experienced officers for a week or two as observers before they started work on their own case load. It is now recognized that more systematic training is beneficial. Several states (see table 5-1 for examples) appoint trainee parole officers who receive a mixture of group instruction and on-the-job training. Colorado, California, and the U.S. Probation Division all have formal training programs. After-hours university training at government expense is also widely available, thanks to financing by the Law Enforcement Assistance Administration. Wisconsin puts parole officers on reduced work load while they study for their master's degree in social work. Parole officers are also guided by detailed manuals or directives and by reviews of their work papers and case discussions with their supervisors.

Help from Aides

A small part of parole officers' work load has been assumed by nonprofessional assistants, or aides, in several governments, including all of the

29. American Correctional Association, *Manual of Correctional Standards* (Washington, D.C., 1969), p. 121.

30. Federal Probation Officers Association, "Professional Standards Endorsed by the Federal Probation Officers Association" (brochure, 1965), p. 6.

31. Richard Dembo, "Orientation and Activities of the Parole Officer," *Criminology*, vol. 10 (August 1972), p. 204.

six studied here.[32] These jobs are usually filled by persons from the ethnic and socioeconomic groups from which many offenders come. Some of the aides are exoffenders themselves. They are paid at rates below the lowest paid to professional parole officers. The jobs have been set up for three main reasons.

First, the aides do some of the interviewing, counseling, checking, or job developing that the parole officers would otherwise do, thus enabling the officers to serve more parolees, or give more service to the same number. However, the aides' work is not clear gain because they need considerable training and supervision by the parole officers.

Second, aides communicate better with parolees than officers do. An Ohio study says that parolees found them "easier to talk to, more trustworthy, more concerned, more helpful in finding jobs . . . more understanding, and easier to find when needed . . . than were parole officers."[33] Without going that far, a research evaluation of an aide program in the Chicago federal probation office found "a positive working relationship. . . . Their ability to empathize and simply listen proved an obvious benefit to the clients. . . . The level of mutual rapport and client identification appeared to be unusually high. . . ."[34]

Third, there is both social and economic value in creating constructive work for members of underemployed groups, particularly when they are exoffenders. It is better yet when it is possible for aides to advance, when qualified, to professional positions, as in the federal program.

Aides are typically used in a counseling and helping capacity, notably in finding jobs and housing. On the policing side of the parole job they may be effective in persuading a slipping parolee to get in touch with the parole office instead of missing appointments, absconding, or violating parole in some other way. One federal official remarked that the aides, paradoxically, tend to be tougher on parolees than the parole officers. Being less experienced, they become frustrated and think of no alternatives to cracking down.

They are also used for less difficult and more menial tasks like reminding parolees of appointments and providing transportation for them. But unless this kind of overprotective service is kept at very modest levels it is

32. No field research was done on this subject in the present study.

33. Joseph E. Scott and Pamela A. Bennett, *Ex-Offenders as Parole Officers: An Evaluation of the Parole Officer Aide Program in Ohio* (Ohio State University, Program for the Study of Crime and Delinquency, 1974), p. iii.

34. Donald W. Beless, William S. Pilcher, and Ellen Jo Ryan, "Use of Indigenous Nonprofessionals in Probation and Parole," *Federal Probation*, vol. 36 (March 1972), p. 14.

bad both for parolees and aides. The parolee must learn to live indepen-
dently in the community, and the aide must learn to take a professional
approach to his work.[35]

The Routine of Surveillance

According to parole law and doctrine, society is protected from relapses
into criminality by the parolee because the parole officer is keeping an eye
on him. Yet detailed supervision is actually not feasible, partly because
of parole officers' work loads and partly because of wide acceptance of the
rehabilitative purposes of parole. "The days are gone," a veteran parole
officer said, "when we hung around bars in bad parts of town hoping to
catch one of our parolees there." Present-day precautions consist of a
system of required contacts, varied in some jurisdictions according to how
the parolee is classified.

The first contact, as already mentioned, comes soon after release from
prison. A few parolees never show up but make a run for it. In such cases
the parole officer makes a few efforts to find him through relatives or employers mentioned in the records. If not found he is listed as an absconder
or a parolee-at-large, and the police are notified. If and when the man is
found steps will normally be started to revoke his parole.

In most cases, however, the parolee reports as scheduled. The parole
officer uses this initial meeting to get acquainted and to talk over the conditions of parole. He may already have met the parolee in a visit to the
prison, but this is not universal practice. The parole officer finds out what
the parolee's job is, if he has one, where it is located, what his housing
arrangements are, how he will travel to and from work, whether he has
any family problems, and what his financial situation is. If the parolee
needs help on any of these matters the parole officer is supposed to help
him or to steer him to an appropriate community agency (see chapter 7).
In going over the parole agreement with the parolee, the officer usually
emphasizes certain conditions of parole that he thinks this particular
parolee needs to be warned about on the basis of his previous history,
such as promptly reporting job changes, attending a narcotics clinic, avoiding excessive drinking, never having a firearm. Then he tells the parolee

35. For a detailed guidance program for aides, based on a long-term Chicago
project, see Raymond D. Clements, "Para-Professionals in Probation and Parole: A
Manual for Their Selection, Training, Induction, and Supervision in Day-to-Day
Tasks" (University of Chicago Law School, Center for Studies in Criminal Justice,
1972; processed).

exactly what contacts he is required to make with the parole office, urges him to come in or telephone any time he has a problem that threatens the success of his parole, and gives him a business card with the address and phone number of the parole office.

Frequency of Contacts

What the parolee is told to do and how often he is seen depends on how he is classified, if the parole organization uses such a system. Maximum supervision in the District of Columbia requires four contacts a month; medium supervision, two. Two of the states studied require heavier supervision at first, then may reduce it later. California starts with four contacts a month with the parolee plus one "collateral contact" (parent, employer, girl friend) a month for the first six months. After six months, if all is well, the parolee is put on "regular" supervision: two parolee contacts a month plus one collateral contact. New York does about the same thing, reducing parolees from "intensive" to "active" supervision after three months.

The nature of the contacts is usually ordained for the parole officer in rules, a procedural manual, or instructions from his supervisor. The New York requirements are laid out in detail:[36]

Type of contact	Intensive supervision	Active supervision	Reduced supervision
Reporting to parole office	Weekly or semi-monthly	Monthly or up to but not exceeding every two months	Quarterly, or less frequently up to and including annually
Employment check	Monthly	Every two months	Same as reporting
Employment visit	Every three months	Every three months	At least as frequently as reporting
Home visit	Every three months	Monthly	Not mentioned
Other and collateral visits	More frequently than active or reduced	Not mentioned	Not mentioned

Office Visits

Visits at the parole office are becoming the principal means of parolee control, according to field observations and interviews in the present study.

36. Citizens' Inquiry, *Prison without Walls*, pp. 105–06. There are also three additional types of more intensive supervision.

The parolee comes into the office, say once or twice monthly, bringing a simple form he has filled out with some such statement as "Still working for Acme Construction," and reporting any change in his address. Parole officers hold office hours some evenings to accommodate employed parolees. The contact is typically amiable, superficial, and brief, something like this:

"How have you been doing?"
"Oh, fine."
"Still living with Betty?"
"Yes."
"Working at Acme still?"
"Yes, but I might move—I'd rather work for a smaller firm."
"O.K. Let me know if you make a change."

The interview is much longer and more significant if the parolee has real problems and feels like sharing them with the parole officer. This may lead to counseling on employment, housing, financial, or family problems; referral to community agencies; or direct aid by the parole officer in finding a job or house or quick loan. Some parolees (though these do not predominate) just like somebody to talk to.

The parole officer may feel the need for evidence of the parolee's progress. So he may ask to see the driver's license the parolee intended to get, the receipt for auto insurance, or a pay stub showing that he is really employed. This may strike us as repugnant policing, but most parole officers have learned the hard way not to believe everything their clients say. After all, a parolee who is not performing well has little to lose by trying to con his parole officer, and prison life is good training for doing so.

Other forms of policing may be combined with the office visit. One parole officer we observed kept and administered an alcoholic parolee's every-few-days dose of antabuse (a drug which if taken regularly causes a person to be very sick if he drinks alcohol). The parolee did not trust himself or anyone else to handle this. In another jurisdiction parolees with drug problems were required to contribute a urine sample for analysis. This required the parole officer to exercise enough surveillance to make sure he had the correct person's sample. Distasteful and time-consuming as this was, there was an even worse problem: the laboratory was taking two months to send back reports on the samples, and then not on all the samples, thus making this aspect of the surveillance meaningless.

Another problem with office visits is that when the parolee comes in his parole officer may not be there even though he is supposed to be. He may be participating in a revocation hearing or working on an emergency problem of another parolee. In such instances the parolee simply drops off the required form, or asks the office clerk to note that he was there, or is seen by another parole officer who is not familiar with his case. Thus the visit still has some utility as a means of policing. The staff know that the parolee is in the locality and cooperating, at least to this extent, though they would probably miss danger signals that his own parole officer might detect (or would when there is good understanding between parole officer and parolee).

In several of the parole offices we visited the parolees were checking in by telephone. Obviously this is a much less reliable means of surveillance. The parolee could be anywhere, doing anything, and telling the parole officer anything he pleases. All the latter knows is that the parolee is co-operative (or careful) enough to make the call.

Job Visits

The parole officers we interviewed showed a strong consensus on avoiding visits to parolees on their jobs. Employers do not like their workers to be interrupted, even if the interruption is practicable. Often it is not; the parolee may be a machinist on a production line, a bricklayer's helper on a high building, or a truck driver. The parolee resists the visits, too, either because he does not want to be interrupted or because it is distasteful to be checked on the job—especially if he has not told the employer of his criminal record. Even if the parolee can be contacted on the job it is difficult to have a satisfactory conversation under such circumstances. A few parole officers told of visiting the place of employment and asking a foreman or timekeeper if the parolee worked there. A less intrusive method, as mentioned earlier, is asking the parolee to bring a pay stub to the parole office.

Home Visits

Seeing the parolee at home is a time-honored method of checking up and maintaining contact. About one-fourth of the parole officers interviewed believed in dropping in at a parolee's home without prior notice. The others preferred to tell the parolee when they were coming, either specifically or perhaps "some evening next week" or "some Tuesday evening soon." The unexpected visit can be considered good surveillance because the parole officer may catch the parolee at home when he is supposed to be working or going to school. The parole officer may even, in some states, search the premises for weapons, drugs, or other evidence of criminal activity. One of the parole officers we interviewed collects urine samples during surprise home visits. New York State directs its parole officers to make late-night surprise visits if they have reason to believe that there may be a violation of parole.[37]

If the parolee is not at home his mother, father, wife, or girl friend may give the parole officer some useful information. Parole officers gave us numerous examples of relatives who reported incidents showing that the parolee was getting into trouble. Some relatives will do this in an effort to keep the offender from new crimes; others will lie or cover up for him. The more positive home visits are those when the parole officer and parolee have a chance to discuss progress and problems. And if family members are present the parole officer gets some understanding of relationships in the home that may be good or bad for the parolee.

A night of unscheduled visits can be almost devoid of personal contacts, as a *Washington Post* reporter found in accompanying a parole officer checking on "a few of his 102 parolees."

[John Thomas] Pell, a D.C. corrections parole officer, made eight unannounced house calls that night, seeking parolees. He found only one: Robert Wooten. At the homes of the other seven men, Pell left messages with: a grandmother, mother, girlfriend, sister, halfway house director, and the landlord of a rooming house.

In the jargon of the District's department of corrections, the messages left for the men to contact Pell by phone the next day counted as "indirect contacts." The one man Pell did find at home, Wooten, who lives at 1205 4th St., N.W., counted as a direct "eyeball to eyeball" contact although it lasted less than 30 seconds.

"How ya doin?" Pell asked Wooten as he stepped into the darkened hallway of the two-story attached house.

"Fine. Just fine," Wooten answered expressionlessly as Pell shook his hand.

"I just stopped by to see how you're making out and if there are any problems," Pell told Wooten.

"No, there are no problems and I'm doing just fine," Wooten said again as the two men stood staring at each other.[38]

This stiff, shallow encounter is typical, as noted earlier, of surveillance interviews. An evening like Parole Officer Pell's keeps some pressure on the parolees, but it is a burdensome job.

37. Ibid., p. 76.
38. Leon Dash, *Washington Post*, March 17, 1974.

There are times when the parolee is obviously lying to the parole officer about his activities, other times when he admits that he is "just hustlin' " (stealing), like another parole interviewed by the *Washington Post*. This parolee, "Pinocchio" Fredericks, said

he sees parole officer Pell about twice a month, usually after Pell has left a message at his mother's house on one of the parole officer's evening calls.

Asked if Pell is concerned about him jumping from job to job or not working at all, Fredericks said, "No, he doesn't press me at all. All you have to do is make a report" to the parole officer, Fredericks said, "and most of the contact is by phone."[39]

We encountered in our own interviewing cases of parolees admitting to their officers drug use, fighting, and violation of various conditions of parole. The parole officer often takes no action because he does not think the violations are serious enough to justify revocation.

Reactions other than Wooten's coolness and Fredericks's defiance may better typify the parolees' feelings of being under surveillance. Elliot Studt's account of a California "parole action study" speaks of "the embarrassment and intrusiveness of the surprise visit; and the tension that develops over what can be done with the evenings when the agent has telephoned to say 'I will probably be by this evening; if not tonight, then tomorrow night,' and then does not appear until the next week," and "the misunderstandings and uneasiness that sometimes appear in personal relationships after a person close to the parolee has talked with the agent; or the anxiety that spreads through the family when the agent leaves a message that the parolee should get in touch with him immediately."[40] It also tells how parolees are conscious "of being watched during each contact, knowing that whatever is observed registers in the agent's mind as information that can be used, whenever the agent feels it is needed, as either positive or negative evidence supporting an important decision about the parolee's life. . . . They wonder, 'What did he find out about me this time?' "[41]

Surveillance is even rougher when the parole officer appears at the home without warning and searches the premises, the parolee's wife's

39. Ibid., March 19, 1974.

40. Elliot Studt, *Surveillance and Service in Parole: A Report of the Parole Action Study* (University of California, Los Angeles, Institute of Government and Public Affairs, 1972), pp. 78–79.

41. Ibid., p. 79.

handbag, or even her person for incriminating objects. Thus far courts have upheld the constitutionality of such searches,[42] but the problem is now in litigation again.[43]

Our own interviewees (mostly parolees who are succeeding and co-operating) showed less objection to home visits. They expressed either general acceptance of parole supervision as a necessary evil or else a general resistance to it because they feel they were punished and watched enough while they were imprisoned.

Does Surveillance Work?

Any combination of visits and reports keeps pressure on the parolee to be law abiding and to stay in touch with the parole office. It is very hard to say whether such supervision really prevents relapses into crime. A parolee determined to make it does not need surveillance; a parolee determined to con his parole officer, evade him, or engage in illicit activities can find ways to do so.[44] A parolee who is not committed either way may be induced to accept guidance and help.

The Parole Relationship

The parole officer and parolee, like the army private and his squad leader or the prisoner and his caseworker, did not ask to be put together. The parolee is not (or feels he is not) in a position to ask for another parole officer if he would prefer one. The parole officer is not likely to get out of the relationship unless he is transferred or promoted. A supervising parole officer in one state was asked if changes could be made to increase compatibility. He said, "This would be highly desirable but it is simply not possible under the system. Even if an officer is doing a poor job it is considered his case, and a case is never taken away from an officer."

42. Citizens' Inquiry, *Prison without Walls*, pp. 109–11.

43. *Diaz et al.* v. *Ward et al.*, no. 75c 1194 (Southern District of New York).

44. Someone has invented the near-ultimate in policing, which might set limits on such parolees. The person being monitored would wear an electronic transmitter, and a receiver in the parole office would detect whether he was somewhere he should not be. This idea raises some immediate questions: Is this legal? Is it humane? Will funny accidents happen to the transmitters? Described in Ralph Schwitzgebel, "Electronically Monitored Parole," *Prison Journal*, vol. 48 (Autumn–Winter 1968), pp. 34–35.

If the parolee is changed to another level of supervision (say maximum to medium) he may change parole officers or may stay with the same one. For the most part the two are expected to stay together and to make the relationship work. If both are well motivated the expectation helps ensure good performance by both. On the other hand the forced association is unnatural from a human standpoint. As one author says, "The parolee–parole officer link is by nature the social anathema [he probably means antithesis, but the word is not inappropriate] of a voluntary relationship."[45]

A compulsory relationship is strained enough, but the tension is worse if one party is policing the other. The strain becomes even more complex and unreasonable if the supervisory party is required to be the other's primary source of advice and help. How do they handle this? Field observations of parolee–parole officer contacts, plus interviews with them, suggest that they make the relationship "work" through brief, shallow contacts. Real animosity is rarely shown, and truly friendly relationships, though less rare, are still exceptional. Parolees are accustomed to handle an unnatural personal relationship rather routinely; many of them have been supervised by reform school officers and probation officers, and all have dealt with prison caseworkers. Most of the parolees we interviewed did not comment on relationships with parole officers in general but talked about the specifics of their own cases, avoiding evaluative remarks. A few expressed a generalized distaste for being under supervision; a few others commented favorably on their parole officers.

These observations are consistent with the findings of the major, multiyear California study by Elliot Studt. The researchers talked to scores of parolees and parole officers ("agents") and observed many of their interchanges. The report says:

All the evidence from every source supports the Study's findings that parolees are, in general, not actively hostile toward the agents as persons, tending instead to blame "the system," that they often find agents more decent as persons than they expected . . . On the other hand, the Study's evidence suggests equally strongly that most agent-parolee relationships are superficially friendly; and that the ambiguous structure in which interaction occurs, together with the critical jeopardy inherent in it for the parolee, tends to press both agents and parolees toward (1) the maintenance of an interaction relationship that is bland and diffuse, and (2) the avoidance of confronting tough issues until a problem situation becomes openly critical.[46]

45. Robert E. Wolin, "After Release: The Parolee in Society," *St. John's Law Review*, vol. 48 (October 1973), p. 17.
46. Studt, *Surveillance and Service*, p. 109.

We also saw frequent instances of what Studt observed:

Some agents assumed a jocular, "us boys together," approach toward most parolees, as though to underline their essential good will and to ward off the recognition of possible conflicts between their interests.[47]

The relationship will be better than what these statements describe when the two parties like each other, and particularly when the parolee is succeeding. What happens when he is failing is the main topic of the next chapter.

47. Ibid., p. 106.

CHAPTER SIX

The Parolee in Trouble

THE PAROLEE who is trying, or allowing himself, to get back into illegal activities may be detected in such efforts. He may have no intention of leading a law-abiding life or he may be reacting to readjustment problems that are too hard for him to handle. In either event the parole officer may pick up signs of slippage. The parolee may miss occasional appointments or be late with his reports. An alcoholic parolee may appear bleary-eyed and shaky. The parole officer may see needle marks on an addict's arm. The parolee may be cited for misdemeanors such as disorderly conduct. The parole officer may get tips from a beaten-up wife, another parolee, or other sources that his client seems headed for trouble or is already there. The parolee himself may tell the parole officer he is in difficulty, as a cry for help and to forestall worse trouble. In an extreme case in this study a parolee confessed to a burglary to his parole officer, who did not report him.

It would be a mistake to assume, however, that normal surveillance is the major way in which parolees' misdeeds are brought to light. On the contrary, most violations are discovered when the parolee is caught by others. A study in California reports that "since the [parole] agent's contacts with the parolee total no more than two hours per month, the agency depends on other sources for information about parolee activities. A review of 1,023 emergency reports prepared by agents on parole incidents shows that 71.2 percent of the reports are based on information supplied by law enforcement agencies [police and routine narcotics testing]."[1] However he learns of problem situations, the parole officer must decide what to do about them.

1. Paul Takao Takagi, *Evaluation Systems and Adaptations in a Formal Organization: A Case Study of a Parole Agency* (Ph.D. dissertation, Stanford University, 1967; microfilm), p. 109.

The Road to Revocation

The parole officer's first response may be to look at lapses or even (rarely) crimes as temporary setbacks in a situation that he expects will improve. He decides that he must give his man more attention, to the extent that his work load permits. He increases efforts to reach the parolee by telephone, to leave messages, to see him at home. If he does succeed in seeing him, he will discuss the problems. He may have a constructive solution to suggest or may simply scold, warn, or threaten. This increased attention is seen by some parolees as sincere helpfulness, by others as "hassling" or "put-downs"; the reaction depends on how motivated they are to stay out of crime. Both parties know it is not hard to find a basis for starting revocation proceedings; parole conditions are so numerous and either so vague or so specific that, as pointed out earlier, almost any citizen could be found in violation.

Short-Term Jailings

"So then I throw him in the slammer for a few days," a parole officer told us. More accurately, he asks the local sheriff or police to jail the parolee for a day or two, a weekend, or even one or two weeks. These are not cases where the parole officer is at that time planning to recommend revocation, nor are they cases in which the parolee is jailed because he is an imminent threat to public safety. The intent is usually to impress a wayward parolee with the seriousness of his conduct or to dry out a drunk. One parole officer told us with pride of having jailed a parolee for two weeks to keep him away from friends who were trying to get him back on drugs.

Parole officers represent these jailings as positive therapeutic measures. If challenged, the parole officer will say that the man is being held for investigation of possible violation of parole, but there is not likely to be a legal challenge. Officers say such jailings are not illegal under state laws or federal court decisions governing due process for parole revocations. Furthermore they are easily and informally arranged within the close working relationships between parole officers and local law enforcement officials. Wisconsin, however, has formalized the process in its parole hierarchy. The parole officer can jail a man for five days or less, but he must get his supervisor's approval for six through ten days; his district chief's approval for eleven through fifteen days; and his division chief's (or deputy's) for over fifteen days. Not all jurisdictions condone this practice, however; it is not used, for example, by the federal government.

Short-term jailing has not been systematically evaluated, to my knowledge, and judgments about it are largely subjective. One can argue, as some parole officers do, that short-term jailing is an effective way of dealing with immature and recalcitrant parolees who are testing their parole officers; reimprisonment impresses on them the fact that limits have been set on their behavior and that parole is a serious business. Opponents of this view, some of them also parole officers, reply that incarceration does nobody any good and that it is unjust to imprison a parolee without action by a court or parole board. One legal scholar maintains that any detention of a parolee at the initiative of a parole officer without parole board action is illegal, except when the public safety is involved, and only then for the length of time needed to report the facts to the board.[2] The National Advisory Commission on Criminal Justice Standards and Goals also labels such "jail therapy" an abuse of parole powers.[3]

How Many Parole Failures?

According to data reported by various jurisdictions to the National Council on Crime and Delinquency, 73 percent of offenders paroled in 1970 were still under supervision, or parole had been terminated without violation, after two years. Eight percent went back to prison with new major convictions; 5 percent absconded; and 15 percent were returned to prison as technical violators.[4] The nature of these types of failures needs some explanation now.

Arrests for New Crimes

The surest road to revocation is for the parolee to be arrested for a new crime. The parole officer may learn about it in any of several ways.

2. Paul H. Robinson, "Comments. Parole Holds: Their Effect on the Rights of the Parolee and the Operation of the Parole System," *University of California at Los Angeles Law Review*, vol. 19 (June 1972), pp. 759–803.

3. National Advisory Commission on Criminal Justice Standards and Goals, *Corrections* (GPO, 1973), p. 407.

4. "Parole Nears 75% 'Success' Rate," *Criminal Justice Newsletter*, vol. 6 (Sept. 29, 1975), p. 5. Figures are from the Uniform Parole Reports project of the NCCD. Most paroling jurisdictions report complete data; the rest send in reports based on samples.

He may be called by the parolee, by a relative, by an attorney for the parolee, or by the police. The police may have been supplied with a list of parolees, or, more likely, they find the parole officer's card or other identifying papers on the parolee. The suspect himself may tell them that he is on parole. The parole office may also routinely make a daily check of arrest lists in the community.

However he finds out, the parole officer must give prompt attention to the problem, in case the parolee should be released and then disappear. The parole officer reads the arrest report, talks to the suspect, and may interview the arresting officer and witnesses. He then prepares a report to the parole board, routed through his superiors for approval, in which he may recommend that the board issue a warrant and proceed with revocation. He may recommend instead that the warrant not be served until the new case against the parolee has been decided. He may recommend no action at all if the parolee has had a good record so far and if the arrest is not for a serious crime.

In cases of felonies, the prosecutor may discuss with the parole officer or his superiors the relationship of the new offense to possible parole revocation. Rather than prepare a case to convict the parolee of, say, armed robbery, the prosecutor may prefer to ask the board to revoke parole for possession of a weapon, failure to report the arrest, associating with criminals, or whatever other parole condition has been violated. This is done when a milder penalty is desired. A parolee convicted of a felony for the second or third time faces years more in prison, but if his parole is revoked he may be eligible for reconsideration for parole in a year or less.

An illustration of revocation in lieu of prosecution came up in our field observations. A parolee charged with a new felony was active in a vengefully militant organization, and witnesses were unwilling to appear against him; for the authorities, parole revocation was the easier way out. One can argue, however, that trial for the major offense would be fairer to the suspect since, as discussed below, he gets less of a day in court in a revocation proceeding than he would in a trial. This also means, of course, that he can be incarcerated more easily through revocation when the case against him is weak.[5]

5. In another example of the use of revocation, in Washington state a parolee was acquitted of assault charges in a criminal prosecution, but the court upheld use of the same evidence to revoke his parole, holding that there was a difference in burden of proof. *Standlee* v. *Smith*, no. 42,729 (Wash. Sup. Ct., Jan. 31, 1974), *Prison Law Reporter*, vol. 3 (July 1974), pp. 216–18.

Automatic Revocation?

The question may arise, "Why bother with the revocation process when the parolee has committed a new crime? Has he not abdicated his status as a parolee by doing so?" The answer is that under a 1972 U.S. Supreme Court decision a formal revocation procedure is required. Even before the decision, however, a majority of parole boards did not provide for automatic revocation.[6] Thus the parole boards can consider the offender's entire record and the circumstances of his crime in deciding whether or not to revoke parole. Normally they do use their power to revoke parole when the offender commits a new felony.[7]

Absconding

Some parolees go into hiding locally or take off for distant places. The typical parole officer, overloaded with cases, will make several efforts over a few weeks to reach the parolee through his last known home address or employer. If he has more than the typical amount of time and enterprise, the parole officer will really look for the parolee, visiting his favorite bar or asking his friends. One parole officer who covers miles of sparsely settled territory in southern Colorado said that he takes gifts to old women in small communities who make everybody's business their business and asks them about missing parolees from that area.

When all efforts have failed and a specified time has elapsed—one month in some states, two in others—the parole staff reports the parolee as an absconder. An arrest warrant is obtained from the parole board, and all

6. The NCCD survey showed that thirty-three out of fifty-two jurisdictions did not revoke automatically for felonies and forty-nine out of fifty-two did not for misdemeanors. See Vincent O'Leary and Joan Nuffield, *The Organization of Parole Systems in the United States* (Hackensack, N.J.: National Council on Crime and Delinquency, 1972), pp. 1–167.

7. Though other complications may arise, like these observed in one of the states we studied. (a) A parolee for whom there is good evidence of guilt on a new felony charge may be discharged from parole (thus becoming a "success" in the statistics) to stand trial for the new offense. This is done sometimes out of "kindness," to prevent a consecutive sentence on the new offense, and sometimes out of "spite," to assure that the offender cannot avoid another conviction by merely being returned to finish his sentence as a parole violator. (b) A parolee may be revoked and required to serve his maximum sentence for some part of the new felony—for instance, possession of a firearm—and be "allowed" to stand trial on the major offense—armed robbery. A new sentence is then imposed by the court, to run either concurrently or consecutively with the old one.

police departments are notified. If the parolee is found, he may face revocation proceedings. An absconder is not usually found unless he has been rearrested for a new misdemeanor or felony; and again, the revocation becomes entangled with the new charge.

Technical Violations

A technical violation is a violation of any condition of parole other than commission of a new crime (though it may also include a new crime of a minor nature). It may or may not include absconding, depending on the practice of the jurisdiction. Bluntly stated, it is a justification for imprisoning a parolee for some act or failure for which other persons would not be punished. The threat of reimprisonment after revocation thus constitutes a means of controlling parolees.

Revocation in lieu of prosecution for new crimes has been discussed above; it is also used in cases where the parolee is suspected of crime but there is no basis for even arresting him. Two good examples of this came up in our field studies. In one state the police were certain that a parolee had caused several murders to be committed but could not pin them on him, so his parole was revoked for failure to make the required monthly reports. The parole official who handled this case admitted that it was unjust and said that he would recommend such action only rarely. He believed, however, that he was protecting society from a dangerous person.

In the other case a frightened witness came to the parole board and complained that a parolee had beaten him badly. He begged the board not to identify him, saying that the parolee would kill him. The board revoked the attacker's parole for failure to notify the parole officer of change of address and change of employment. The parolee had no opportunity to defend himself against the real reason for his reimprisonment. Here again the action was defended as a protection to the community. These cases were exceptional in our field research, but they show how the broad discretion to revoke parole is open to the possibility of abuse by both parole officers and boards.

Technical violations are more likely to result in revocation when there has been a series of failures by the parolee that the parole officer sees as adding up to a return to criminality. They also lead to a feeling of frustration and irritation on the part of the parole officer—he has "had it up to here" with the parolee. The board will sometimes go along with the parole officer, sometimes not. In one Wisconsin case a parolee was cited for two misdemeanors, but the parole officer took no action. The parolee was then caught making obscene phone calls. The parole officer and his supervisor decided that there was a pattern of deteriorating behavior and that they should recommend revocation. The case was heard by a hearing examiner who ruled that only the third infraction, not the two misdemeanors, could be considered and that this was not a sufficient basis to revoke parole. The parole staff were irate; how, they asked, could they stop a man from sliding back into crime if such rulings were made? (One possible answer is to punish him for the misdemeanors.)

A case with a contrasting outcome was observed in another state. A young parolee with a good job and a stable home life kept getting into trouble for reckless driving and driving without a permit. After three such incidents the parole officer recommended revocation, and the parole board after some hesitation agreed. In this case, as in the previous one, the parole staff thought they were protecting the community and even doing the parolee some good. But in both cases they showed how insensitive they had become to the inequity of putting a man in the penitentiary for a relatively minor transgression.

Short-Term Return as an Alternative

California has developed a "short-term return program" as a less drastic alternative to revocation for selected parolees (and for narcotics addicts under civil commitments) who have not committed new felonies and who are having trouble making it on parole. The parolees are placed in any of thirteen special housing units within state correctional institutions for a median stay of four and a half months instead of the fifteen to eighteen months they would have to serve if they were reimprisoned for parole violations in the usual manner.[8] The parolees assess the difficulties they have had in adjusting to community life and then set short-term goals for themselves (as in the experiment in mutual agreement programming discussed in chapter 4). Programs of education, counseling, group activity, and work assignments are available to them.[9] The participants' performance on parole was not better than that of parolees in general, but it must be remembered that the participants were selected because they were already in trouble on parole.[10]

8. California Department of Corrections and Adult Authority, *Short-Term Return Program* (Sacramento, 1971), p. 1.
   9. Ibid., p. 3.
   10. Ibid., pp. 9–10.

Whether such an alternative can be considered useful depends both upon future statistical evaluations and upon the resolution of the civil liberties issues involved. If short-term return is considered by the courts to be revocation, each case will be subject to the same rather burdensome formalities. Parole officers and their supervisors will then have to decide if they want to go through the necessary procedures for the sake of only two or three months of reincarceration.

Arrests and Weapons

When a parole violation is serious enough so that revocation must be considered and when the violator is not already in custody, the parole officer may have to arrest him. He needs a warrant to do so in twenty-one of the paroling jurisdictions surveyed by the NCCD, including the federal government, the District of Columbia, and Georgia. In the rest, including California, Colorado, and Wisconsin in the present study, the parole officer has temporary authority to detain.[11]

The arrest itself is normally no problem. The parolee knows that he has erred and that the parole officer has a warrant or the full power of the law behind him, so he generally submits quietly. On rare occasions, however, the parole officer may fear trouble—a belligerent drunk, a parolee with a history of violence, a bad part of town at a bad time of night. In such cases he is usually expected to have a policeman or deputy sheriff go along with him. Parole officers may also be called upon to escort parolees from one location to another; they may, for example, have to bring back a parole violator arrested in another state.[12]

There are elements of danger, of course, in arrest and escort duties, as well as in some visits to parolees' homes. This raises the question of whether parole officers should be armed. There is no standard rule on this point. Parole officers are forbidden to carry weapons by the federal government, the District of Columbia, California, and Wisconsin. Georgia allows parole officers to be armed when they are transporting offenders or conducting searches. With some exceptions, Colorado arms parole offi-

11. O'Leary and Nuffield, *Organization of Parole Systems*, pp. xl–xli, xlv–xlvi. Also Howard Abadinsky, "Should Parole Officers Make Arrests and Carry Firearms?" *New York State Division of Criminal Justice Services Newsletter*, vol. 3 (September 1975), pp. 4–6.

12. See discussion of the Interstate Compact for the Supervision of Parolees and Probationers, pp. 122–24 below.

cers in the countryside but not in the cities; this policy reflects not the relative danger to the officers but local customs within the state.

The arguments for arming parole officers are obvious. Any officer with surveillance and arrest powers should be able to defend himself in case of trouble and to make his authority effective by force if necessary. It is also argued that policemen who accompany parole officers into sticky situations prefer them to be armed. The no-guns policy is defended on several grounds. The most important is that a parole officer is more likely to be accepted as a counselor and helper if he does not have a pocketful of ordnance. The parolee is being trusted (to a degree), tried out, and aided to succeed in the free community; knowledge that his guide can use a gun on him must surely be destructive. Furthermore, the parole officer is actually safer without a gun than with one because the parolee knows that the officer is not going to resort to violence. If the parolee escapes during an attempted arrest, efforts can be made to have police capture him later.

Some parole officers in no-gun jurisdictions pack pistols anyway. One officer in a California city told us, "I'm not allowed to be armed, but I wouldn't go into the —— Park section without my briefcase" (winking and patting the briefcase). One can imagine him trying to get his pistol out in a hurry.

The Formal Revocation Process

After the parolee has been caught in a violation and placed (or kept) in custody and after the parole office has recommended revocation, the more formal processes begin. These are governed by a landmark decision of the U.S. Supreme Court, *Morrissey* v. *Brewer*,[13] which imposed minimum requirements of due process.

There must first be a preliminary hearing to find out if there is "reasonable ground to believe that the arrested parolee has violated a parole condition."[14] This hearing must be conducted by someone not directly involved in the case, usually a parole officer not responsible for the parolee. Two of the governments we studied, however, used others. Georgia assigned this task to parole review officers from the parole board staff, and Wisconsin used supervisory parole staff. The parolee must be notified of the hearing and be permitted to appear, to present evidence and witnesses

13. 408 U.S. 471 (1972).
14. Ibid.

on his own behalf, and to question adverse informants. The hearing officer prepares a summary of the case and determines whether there is probable cause to hold the parolee for a decision by the parole board on revocation.

The Full Revocation Hearing

The Supreme Court identified these minimum requirements of due process for revocation proceedings:

(a) written notice of the claimed violations of parole; (b) disclosure to the parolee of evidence against him; (c) opportunity to be heard in person and to present witnesses and documentary evidence; (d) the right to confront and cross-examine adverse witnesses (unless the hearing officer specifically finds good cause for not allowing confrontation); (e) a "neutral and detached" hearing body such as a traditional parole board, members of which need not be judicial officers or lawyers; and (f) a written statement by the factfinders as to the evidence relied on and reasons for revoking parole. We emphasize there is no thought to equate this second stage of parole revocation to a criminal prosecution in any sense. It is a narrow inquiry; the process should be flexible enough to consider evidence including letters, affidavits, and other material that would not be admissible in an adversary criminal trial.

We do not reach or decide the question whether the parolee is entitled to the assistance of retained counsel or to appointed counsel if he is indigent.[15]

These requirements, if faithfully observed, would obviously discourage arbitrary revocations based on minor infractions; but, as the examples cited earlier show, they are not complete deterrents. Nevertheless, revocations now require more care and more work on the part of both parole officers and parole boards than in the past. Statistics are not available to compare the number and content of revocation proceedings before and after *Morrissey*. However, board members and parole officers interviewed said that fewer revocations are now proposed on the basis of technical violations. Generalizing from their comments, one could say that revocations are increasingly rare except for new crimes, cases of absconding, and cases of prolonged and eventually intolerable uncooperativeness.

The states were actually in partial compliance with the *Morrissey* requirements even before that decision. Thirty-five states, for example, gave notice of specific charges, and thirty-two allowed the parolee to present witnesses.[16] Virtually full compliance in the future can be expected, both

15. Ibid., at 489.
16. O'Leary and Nuffield, *Organization of Parole Systems*, p. xlviii. See the analysis of pre-*Morrissey* due process provisions in ibid., pp. xl–lii. For an early analysis of post-*Morrissey* compliance, see American Bar Association, Resource Center on Correctional

as a matter of conscience and as a result of pressure from writ-writing offenders and prisoners' rights attorneys. It should not be assumed, however, that compliance will guarantee the parolee a fair shake in any realistic sense. In the revocation hearings we attended few parolees presented witnesses; and when they did, the witnesses were relatives. The parolees were incompetent in presenting their defense and questioning either their own witnesses or adverse witnesses. In those respects the due process requirements ring hollow indeed.

Right to Counsel

Such deficiencies point to the parolee's need for counsel, an issue that the Supreme Court specifically avoided in *Morrissey*. In a later decision it held that representation by counsel should be decided on a case-by-case basis by the body conducting the hearing but that counsel should be provided

where the indigent probationer or parolee may have difficulty in presenting his version of disputed facts without the examination or cross-examination of witnesses or the presentation of complicated documentary evidence. Presumptively, counsel should be provided where, after being informed of his right, the probationer or parolee requests counsel, based on a timely and colorable claim that he has not committed the alleged violation or, if the violation is a matter of public record or uncontested, there are substantial reasons in justification or mitigation that make revocation inappropriate.

3. In every case where a request for counsel is refused, the grounds for refusal should be succinctly stated in the record.[17]

This language describes what is in fact the normal parole revocation situation, and therefore generally obligates the government to provide counsel for the parolee.

Field studies for this book took place before the effect of this decision had been felt. As a matter of policy California and Colorado did not permit counsel, but the other four jurisdictions studied did—the District of Columbia, the U.S. Parole Board, Wisconsin, and Georgia.[18] The hearings we attended usually did not have parolees' attorneys present because the parolees could not afford them and the government had none available. They were obviously badly needed by parolees who were inarticulate,

---

Legal Services, *Survey of Parole Revocation Procedures: State Parole Board Compliance with* Morrissey v. Brewer (Washington, D.C.: ABA, 1973).

17. *Gagnon* v. *Scarpelli*, 411 U.S. 778 (1973).

18. Colorado now provides counsel also.

poorly educated, defensive, and facing a group of college graduates repre-senting the correctional establishment.[19]

Plight of the Parole Officer

The parole officer is also in difficulty in the revocation hearing: he be-comes in effect a prosecutor. "Mr. ——," board chairmen were heard to say, "you will present the case against the parolee." The parole officer has already been trying to be both helper to and policeman over the parolee; now he becomes his legal adversary. This generally ends any useful rela-tionship that may remain between them. Another cause of difficulty is that he is not trained to present a case. Should he state all the evidence at once or let it come out in questions and answers? How does he cope with the defenses and objections of the parolee's attorney if there is one? Will he be helped or overpowered by parole board members with legal training? The parole officer's job is difficult enough without his being required to act like a prosecuting attorney.

The Decision to Revoke

For the parole board, revocation decisions are much like release deci-sions. The same theoretical, political, and organizational considerations are before them. The main difference is the specific attention focused on the circumstances of the violation. Again, however, board members are in effect asking themselves: How much more punishment for this viola-tion (retribution)? Does society need to be protected from this person for more time (incapacitation)? Will return to prison convince him and other parolees that parole conditions must be complied with (deterrence)? What will more incarceration do for him—or to him (rehabilitation)? Again, they think of the political and public reaction to a decision to return the parolee to prison or to leave him at liberty.

Above all they listen to the parole officer. He presents and interprets the information against the parolee, telling the board why the parolee has not been a success in the community. The board, for obvious reasons, is more likely to believe the parole officer than the parolee if there is a differ-ence in their stories. Members have a natural inclination to back up the

19. An organization to defend parolees in revocation proceedings has been estab-lished by the New York City Legal Aid Society under a grant from the state govern-ment. See Patricia Conroy, "Parole Revocation Defense Unit" (New York: Institute of Judicial Administration, 1975; processed).

parole officer as their colleague in the correctional establishment; they also may want to err on the side of protecting society and therefore lean toward revocation. These are powerful influences, but they are not always compelling. Board members may feel that the parolee can make it if given another chance despite the parole officer's recommendation. They may also want to keep down the number of parole failures shown in the statistics. Nevertheless, research in California showed that "nearly 80 percent of the recommendations of parole agents against revocation and over 90 percent of their recommendations for revocation were accepted by the Adult Authority [parole board]."[20]

PAROLE OFFICER ORIENTATION. Differences in personality and attitudes of parole officers have been stressed earlier. These factors will obviously affect the way a revocation case is handled. In the six governments covered in this study it was possible to categorize parole officers by the emphasis they placed on different aspects of their work.[21] Twenty-two percent tended to be surveillance-minded—more interested in control, oversight, pursuit, capture. Thirty-three percent tended to be assistance-minded—more interested in counseling, providing services, solving problems. Forty-four percent could not be said to lean one way or the other. Other categorizations have been made by sociologists: for instance, classifying the parole officer as either a "punitive officer," a "protective agent," or a "welfare worker."[22] A New York researcher classified parole officers as demonstrating either "punishment orientation" or "reintegrative orientation."[23] His study proved that a "high reintegrative score is positively related to low rate of clients declared in technical parole violation."[24]

BUREAUCRATIC PRESSURE. Not only the parole officer's social orientation but also his organizational membership and status influence revocation

20. James Robison and Paul T. Takagi, "The Parole Violator as an Organizational Reject," in Robert M. Carter and Leslie T. Wilkins, eds., *Probation and Parole: Selected Readings* (John Wiley and Sons, 1970), p. 235.

21. Categories were determined by analysis of parole officers' answers to two questions: (1) "Please summarize what you do in working with a parolee, beginning with when you first learn that he is assigned to you." (2) "Please describe what you do and what generally happens when parole is revoked." (Interviewers were supplied with guides for more detailed probing under each of these questions.)

22. Lloyd E. Ohlin, Herman Piven, and Donnell M. Pappenfort, "Major Dilemmas of the Social Worker in Probation and Parole," *National Probation and Parole Association Journal*, vol. 2 (July 1956), p. 215. See also characterizations on p. 86 above.

23. Richard Dembo, "Orientation and Activities of the Parole Officer," *Criminology*, vol. 10 (August 1972), pp. 193–215.

24. Ibid., p. 205.

decisions. A California researcher has documented pressure exerted by the headquarters parole staff on field supervisors of parole officers to reduce technical violation rates.[25] And the rates did indeed fall. He and a colleague later reported: "While there is some indication that the [parole] agent's personal background (his educational specialty and prior types of job) has a bearing on these judgments [recommendations to revoke or to continue on parole], and that his current value orientation is involved *the most definite value correlate shown in the present study was the agent's assessment of his supervisor's orientation.*"[26] Another researcher shows that the same things happen in Iowa:

> The parole agent is clearly an agent of the system, and he takes his organizational cues from both his supervisor, and his fellow agents. . . .[27]

> The agents felt pressured (some less than others) to attain a 10 percent personal revocation rate and so were reluctant to revoke parolees. . . .[28]

> Several of the agents noted that a 10 percent revocation rate didn't mean that they were any more effective, or that their parolees were behaving any better, than when the parole system had a 35 percent revocation rate. A couple of agents suggested that if the director wanted a 1 percent revocation rate, then that probably could be achieved as well.[29]

This susceptibility to pressure produces a major flaw in criminological research and statistics because returns to prison for parole violation are used as a measure of failure on parole and sometimes of failure of the entire prison-parole process. If the measure responds to bureaucratic pressure, what is it really measuring? This state of affairs is even more shocking from the standpoint of civil liberties and simple humanity. Parolees are being returned to prison in part to help protect the cohesion and political security of the correctional establishment, their own behavior being a secondary factor.[30]

THE COMMITMENT OFFENSE FACTOR. Further evidence of uneven standards in revocation decisions appears in an NCCD study of thousands of cases, which relates parole violation rates and returns to prison to the

---

25. Takagi, "Evaluation Systems and Adaptations," pp. 182–85.

26. Robison and Takagi, "The Parole Violator," p. 253 (emphasis added).

27. Robert Charles Prus, *Revocation-Related Decision Making by the Parole Agent: A Labeling Approach* (Ph.D. dissertation, University of Iowa, 1973; microfilm), p. 177.

28. Ibid., p. 179.

29. Ibid., pp. 182–83.

30. For further development of this problem, see, in addition to the Takagi and Prus dissertations already cited, James Orval Robison, "Unraveling Delinquency: Caseworker Orientation and Client Characterization" (D.Crim. dissertation, University of California, Berkeley, 1971).

types of offenses for which the parolees were imprisoned by the courts. It found that during their first year on parole 27.1 percent of all the parolees were "moved against for violating parole conditions." Tabulated by type of commitment offense, the violation rate was 19.6 percent for parolees who had been imprisoned for offenses against persons, but 31.5 percent for those imprisoned for property offenses.[31]

Despite the much higher violation rate for property offenders, offenders against persons are more likely to be returned to prison for technical violations.[32] The researcher suggests that *"person offenders are being returned to prison on a different set of criteria than are property offenders,* a set of criteria which holds the former to a much more rigid (and arbitrary) standard of conduct."[33] And "if, as appears from our data, property offenders are allowed to remain in the community even when showing 'signs of deterioration in parole adjustment' much more frequently than are person offenders, it seems clear, too, that criminal justice functionaries and citizens could well ask themselves whether this is a practical arrangement."[34] Apparently a criterion of dangerousness is being used, but it is being applied unevenly and without being reflected in formal policies.

The revocation process is becoming a little more orderly and fair following the *Morrissey* decision, and it is being applied in a diminishing number of cases, according to our field interviews. It is nevertheless a process that invites inconsistency and arbitrariness in administration and decision making.

Reparole after Revocation

Back in prison, the former parolee can now add his unfortunate experiences to the sad tale told to other convicts on the subject of parole. Depending on his mood and his associates, he decides on (or, more likely, drifts into) a pattern of conduct, education, and work. As in the case of his original release, this institutional behavior is an important factor when reparole is considered. The board also reviews carefully his record on parole and the reasons for his revocation.

In every jurisdiction but one, Nebraska, reparole after revocation is

31. M. G. Neithercutt, "Parole Violation Patterns and Commitment Offenses," *Journal of Research in Crime and Delinquency,* vol. 9 (July 1972), p. 89.
32. Ibid., pp. 89, 93.
33. Ibid., p. 89 (emphasis in original).
34. Ibid., p. 93.

possible. The laws are complex, but generally provide for reconsideration on either an unscheduled or a scheduled basis:[35]

Reparole basis	Number of jurisdictions
Unscheduled; reconsidered by parole board on individual basis	24
Reconsidered every two years or "at least every two years"	3
Reconsidered annually or "at least annually"	21
Reconsidered every six months	1
Reconsidered on individual basis but at least every eight months	1
Inmate may apply after six months	1
Revoked parolee ineligible for reparole	1

Revoked parolees in some states are enormously concerned with one particular legal provision: whether their time spent on parole (called "street time") is credited toward the maximum sentence. The NCCD survey shows that twenty-nine governments do credit this time; twenty-two do not; and one (Pennsylvania) credits street time when the revocation is for a technical violation but not when it is for a new crime.[36] Five of the six jurisdictions included in this study did not give credit for parole time, Wisconsin being the exception.[37]

Laws that take away the parolee's street time are apparently based on the idea that the parolee has been a failure, so he should put in the time again. The parolee's viewpoint is different: he performed satisfactorily on parole until his violation—why punish him for what he did well as well as for what he did badly? Certainly the denial of credit for street time cannot aid the rehabilitation of the parolee. Moreover, it seems unfair to add this time to the punishment he is already getting for the violation.

Some governments emphasize punitiveness even more by taking away good time earned on parole if there is revocation. On this point the NCCD survey shows the following:[38]

Good time	Number of jurisdictions
Lost upon revocation	13
May be lost	8
Rarely lost	1
Not lost	20
Not specified	10

35. Tabulated from O'Leary and Nuffield, *Organization of Parole Systems*, pp. 1–167.

36. Ibid.

37. The new federal parole law (P.L. 94-233, March 15, 1976), however, provides for crediting street time.

38. O'Leary and Nuffield, *Organization of Parole Systems*, pp. 1–167. Includes the federal government.

This penalty seems fairer, since good time is a reward for good performance. It is taken away for bad behavior in prison, and one can argue that the same policy should prevail on parole. The counterargument has already been advanced: the parole violation is punished severely enough by reimprisonment, without making it worse.

Discharge from Parole

How long shall the parolee be under surveillance? The maximum in most cases is until he has served, in prison and parole combined, his maximum sentence.[39] Most parole laws recognize, however, that it is pointless, as well as irritating and tiresome to the parolee, to continue to supervise an offender who has made a successful adjustment. So in all but thirteen jurisdictions a parolee can be discharged sooner.[40] In three states the corrections department decides (in Wisconsin, it is the Department of Health and Social Services, which includes the corrections division); in the other governments, the parole board. Some require a minimum period of satisfactory parole; some do not. The various practices can be summarized in simplified fashion like this:[41]

Discharge possible	Number of jurisdictions
Not before end of maximum sentence	13
No minimum period required	13
One year minimum	12
Two year minimum	6
Other periods	4
Not specified	4

Unfortunately a parolee in about half of the jurisdictions is not home free even after discharge. He faces barriers to full citizenship and employability because the law does not give him back his civil rights. Again, a simplified summary:[42]

39. In a few states parole surveillance may continue until after the original maximum sentence has ended because laws require a minimum period of parole supervision before discharge.

40. O'Leary and Nuffield, *Organization of Parole Systems*, pp. 1–167.

41. Tabulated from O'Leary and Nuffield, *Organization of Parole Systems*, pp. 1–167. One state, Louisiana, forbids discharge before the expiration of the maximum sentence less good time. In all states, of course, pardons and commutations of sentence are possible. The new federal parole law (P.L. 94-223) encourages discharge from parole before the end of the maximum sentence.

42. Tabulated from O'Leary and Nuffield, *Organization of Parole Systems*, pp. 1–167.

Civil rights	Number of jurisdictions
Not lost upon conviction	6
Restored upon discharge	18
Not restored upon discharge	23
Not restored, but offender can apply for restoration	3
Not specified	2

A thorough, multiyear research study was made of the processes and outcomes of parole discharges in California, beginning in the autumn of 1965.[43] The major findings have valuable implications for policy both there and in other jurisdictions.

1. There were great variations in rates of recommendation for discharge and of actual discharge at different times, organization levels, and parole districts.

2. When parole officers recommended against discharge "a decision to this effect was almost invariably made by all subsequent reviewers."[44]

3. Recommendations for discharge met with increasing levels of conservatism (that is, opposition) at subsequent levels of review.[45]

4. The policy on discharges became demonstrably more conservative in 1972 following a publicized conflict in one prison and some crimes in the Los Angeles area attributable to offenders on passes or work furlough.[46]

5. Few of both the discharged parolees and those continued on parole were in serious trouble during the first year following consideration for discharge. Of 386 parolees discharged, 10 percent were convicted of offenses resulting in a fine, a short jail term, or probation, and 1 percent were returned to prison for a new felony or civil commitment. Of 1,069 parolees left under parole supervision, 5 percent were returned to prison for technical violations and 3 percent for new commitments.[47]

The researchers conclude from these and other data that far more parolees could safely have been discharged and that this was prevented by overcautious attitudes in the parole agency and board.

43. Margo N. Robison, "Case Decisions and Operating Policy in Early Discharge from Parole" (Berkeley, Calif.: Criminological Research Associates, January 1974; processed). See also Dorothy R. Jaman, Lawrence A. Bennett, and John E. Berecochea, *Early Discharge from Parole: Policy, Practice, and Outcome*, California Department of Corrections, Research Division, Research Report no. 51 (Sacramento, April 1974). See also an earlier study in the same series, James O. Robison and others, *By the Standard of His Rehabilitation*, Research Report no. 39 (January 1971).

44. M. Robison, "Case Decisions," pp. 13–14.

45. Ibid., p. 16.

46. Ibid., pp. 36–39.

47. Ibid., p. 29.

In a later article the head of research of the California Department of Corrections and an NCCD staff member reviewed the above data and compared them with nationwide figures. They conclude that "those completing their first year on parole with no or minimal difficulty tend to have a nine out of ten chance of satisfactorily completing the second and third years of parole obligation without serious difficulty."[48] This is encouraging information. It would be even more interesting and useful to know how well the same offenders would have performed if they had had no parole supervision at all.

Mandatory Releasees

There are some people "on parole" who have never been paroled. These are offenders who are released before their maximum sentences have expired (usually because of good time accumulated) and who are required by law to be supervised as if on parole. Such mandatory release laws are in effect in twelve of the governments surveyed by the NCCD, including Colorado, the District of Columbia, the federal government, and Wisconsin.[49] As two mandatory releasees pointed out in interviews, it seems unfair for them, who have done most of their time, to be treated the same as regular parolees, who may have served only a fraction of their sentences. They might also have asked why they have to be policed as a "reward" for satisfactory prison performance.

Parolees from Other States

The discussion so far has assumed that offenders are paroled in the same jurisdiction where they are sentenced. This is not always so. Every state has a substantial number of parolees from other states who make the parole supervision task more burdensome and complex than it would otherwise be. In fiscal 1972 there were over 7,000 such parolees, according

48. Lawrence A. Bennett and Max Ziegler, "Early Discharge: A Suggested Approach to Increased Efficiency in Parole," *Federal Probation*, vol. 39 (September 1975), p. 30.

49. From O'Leary and Nuffield, *Organization of Parole Systems*, pp. 1–167. The Colorado provision has been repealed since the NCCD survey.

to the Council of State Governments, with the out-of-state load ranging from over 900 in California down to 21 in Vermont and Wyoming.[50]

Many an offender wants to be paroled to a different state than the one where he was sentenced in order to be with relatives or friends, to find more suitable job opportunities, or simply to seek a totally fresh start. If this makes sense to his caseworker and the parole staff in his present location, the "sending state" dispatches a request for investigation, including the offender's case summary and criminal record, to the "receiving state." The receiving state must accept him and provide parole supervision if he "is in fact a resident of or has family residing within the receiving state and can obtain employment there."[51] If he is not a resident and has no family there, the receiving state can choose to accept him or not.

These and other provisions are part of the Interstate Compact for the Supervision of Parolees and Probationers, which has been adopted by all fifty states, plus Puerto Rico and the Virgin Islands. Each state designates a parole or correctional official as its compact administrator for purposes of communicating with other states. This is a big job in California, with its 900-plus out-of-staters under supervision, and is only a trifling matter in the low-population states.

The state parole staffs are fully occupied with supervision and assistance to their own parolees, and they are naturally reluctant to accept out-of-state parolees whose records suggest that they would be threatening to the public, hard to handle, or in need of many services. This is, of course, a predictive judgment, subject to all the uncertainties already discussed, but it may be decisive. The reluctance of the receiving state may be a matter of stated policy, such as declining to accept parolees who have been sex offenders or drug sellers. Or it may reflect the feelings of an individual parole officer who rejects a parole plan proposed for an offender from another state. One parole officer we interviewed said, "We take only the cream of the interstate cases."

However, reciprocity can balance reluctance, for a state that is unwilling to receive parolees may be less successful in sending away its own. Although some states send away far more parolees than they receive, others

<hr>

50. Council of State Governments, "The Interstate Movement of Parolees and Probationers under the Parole and Probation Compact. Annual Report: July 1, 1971–June 30, 1972: I. Out of State Parolees under Supervision" (New York: CSG, n.d.; processed). (Figures are from only thirty-six states; more complete and recent statistics have not been compiled.)

51. Council of State Governments, *Handbook on Interstate Crime Control* (Chicago: CSG, 1966), p. 2.

do the opposite, and the typical state comes out even. According to the Council of State Governments' 1972 figures, the ratio of other states' parolees under supervision to own parolees assigned out of state ranged from 1:2.5 for Colorado and Kansas to 1:0.4 for Idaho and Rhode Island. The median states at 1.0:1.0 were Arizona, North Dakota, Vermont, and Wyoming.[52] Parole officers interviewed in this study say the interstate system works well on the whole, even though they complain in individual cases of having poor risks dumped on them.

Once a parolee is accepted he must be supervised under the same standards used by the receiving state for its own parolees.[53] Thus he makes the same reports and receives the same surveillance as do parolees in his new state. If such a parolee commits a technical violation serious enough that revocation must be considered, the receiving state makes a report of the violation and recommends action to the sending state.[54] Since the *Morrissey* decision, the receiving state conducts the preliminary (probable cause) hearing and reports its finding to the sending state. If probable cause is found the latter then decides (usually) to bring him back for a regular revocation hearing. The sending state could decide to continue him under supervision or even to discharge him from parole—decisions that would be accepted but resented by officials of the receiving state.

Can the Parole Officer Do It?

The limits on the time and ability of the parole officer to police his parolees has already been questioned; his helping duties have not yet been discussed. To the parolee the parole officer is the central figure—as instructor, guide, overseer, and sometimes prosecutor. How does the officer manage to do all of this? It should be remembered that some parole staffs are also probation staffs. In the governments studied here this is true in the federal government, Georgia, and Wisconsin. In these jurisdictions the parole officers are under extra strain simply because they serve two masters—the regular parole hierarchy, with its ties to correctional officials, and the sentencing judges. Questions of priority inevitably come up

52. Computed from tables I and II in Council of State Governments, "The Interstate Movement."
53. Council of State Governments, *Handbook*, p. 2.
54. Ibid., p. 10.

and must be resolved. In all three governments parole officers told us that work for judges (usually probation investigations) came first.

Time Studies

How federal parole officers spend their working time was the subject of a time study made by the Federal Judicial Center in January and February 1973.[55] A sample of 16 percent of the officers kept detailed records of the hours devoted to various duties. The results showed (see table 6-1)

Table 6-1. *Distribution of Federal Probation Officers' Working Time, by Type of Activity*
Percent

Type of activity	Time spent
Supervision	28.7
Probation	20.1[a]
Parole	8.5[b]
Investigation and reports	33.3
Presentence	25.9
Prerelease	1.7
Violation	1.3
Other	4.4[c]
Noncase-related	38.0
Administration	31.8
General preparation	3.9
Community relations	2.4

Source: Adapted from Federal Judicial Center, "Probation Time Study" (Feb. 26, 1973; processed), table II. Figures may not add to subtotals because of rounding.
a. Includes 0.3 percent for supervision of offenders whose prosecution is deferred.
b. Includes 1.0 percent each for mandatory releasees and military parolees.
c. Includes 0.2 percent for preliminary, 0.4 percent for postsentence, 1.6 percent for collateral, 0.3 percent for special, and 2.0 percent for other.

that a third of their time was spent on investigation and reports, mostly presentence, and more than another third on office work not related to cases. This leaves 28.7 percent for supervision of offenders, which means, according to the researchers, that

each offender under supervision [probationer or parolee] could expect to receive *6.4 hours of supervision from his probation officer in the course of a year—or 32 minutes a month or 7 minutes a week . . .*

55. Federal Judicial Center, "Probation Time Study" (Feb. 26, 1973; processed).

Based on [additional positions] now authorized . . . there will be a slight improvement. Each offender can expect 7.7 hours of supervision per year—or 38 minutes a month or 9 minutes per week.

The study has also determined that with present staffing levels, only one-third of the time devoted to supervision can be spent in face-to-face meetings between the offender and the officer. Therefore, this most desirable form of supervision and support will be available at present staffing limitations at the rate of 3 *minutes per week*.[56]

Obviously, neither parolees nor probationers can get much supervision. The ratio of the number of probationers supervised to the number of parolees supervised is 3.1:1, while the ratio of probation supervision time to parole supervision time is 2.3:1.[57] So parolees are getting at least their fair share of the little supervisory time available.

Some very general and tentative data from a time study of Georgia parole officers (who also handle probation) are not very different from the federal study results. In an average day the percentage of working time spent by officers on various functions is:[58]

Activity	Time spent (percent)
Supervision	20
Court-related	20
Paperwork	13
Discussion with other staff	13
Presentence investigation	20
Travel	13

If this supervision figure (20 percent) is treated the same way as the federal figure (28.7), and assuming that the federal case load was 80.5 offenders per officer and the Georgia case load about 100, the Georgia parole officer spends 7.2 *hours per year, 36 minutes per month, and 8 minutes per week* in supervising each offender.[59]

In this amount of time the parole officer is expected to find out about the parolee's home life, employment, vices, and emotional condition *and*

56. Ibid., pp. 3–4 (emphasis added).

57. Computed from ibid., tables I and Ia.

58. Computed from data in a letter to the author from Dr. Thomas C. Neil, College of Education, University of Georgia, Nov. 12, 1973. Court-related time increases to 40 percent during weeks when courts are in session.

59. The figure of 100 was given to us in interviews in Georgia. A study completed by the Department of Offender Rehabilitation soon after our visit showed an average case load of 123 (Susi Megathalin, "Probation Parole Caseload Review" [Georgia Department of Offender Rehabilitation, November 1973; processed]). Using this figure, the Georgia parole officer spends 5.9 hours per year, 29 minutes per month, and 6.5 minutes per week on each offender.

see that he gets the various kinds of help he needs. Obviously something has to give. What gives is detailed surveillance of those parolees thought to be less likely to fail on parole. As indicated earlier, home visits twice a month tend to be replaced by office drop-ins or telephone calls once a month.

The imposibility of doing all that is expected of him leads the parole officer to stress form, quantity, and going through the motions, instead of the real content of his dealings with parolees. This is also the conclusion reached by a scholar who explored the California system in depth, first as a parole officer, later as a researcher.[60] Unable to meet his professional responsibilities, the parole officer "tries at least to maintain his administrative relations."[61] If a parole case blows up, the parole staff must show that they are not to blame, that they did the work expected of them. Thus

agents and supervisors engage in adaptive and maladaptive coping responses, such as reducing levels of supervision, making superficial contacts, in an effort to "satisfy" the minimum standards. There is an emphasis upon the administrative aspects of the task rather than the casework responsibilities; and since the way the requirements are satisfied does not entail the rehabilitation of the client, the situation provides for the possibility of sanctions [meaning that the agent is checked by his supervisors on his enforcement of parole conditions rather than on the rehabilitation of the parolee].[62]

These observations are confirmed and reinforced by those of the Standards and Goals Commission:

Although the rhetoric of the organization [the traditional parole agency] is couched in such phrases as "helping the offender" and "developing a positive relationship," organizational controls tend to be attached to activities designed largely to foster the surveillance work of the agency or protect it from outside criticism. Parole officer performance most often is judged by the number of contacts that have been made with parolees, often with little regard for the quality of events that transpired during these contacts. Complete and prompt reports showing compliance with agency policies, such as written travel permits for parolees, are valued highly and require a major investment of parole officer time.[63]

This tendency to go through certain motions for organizationally protective purposes (the bureaucratic factor) is also a component of revocation decisions, as noted earlier.

60. Takagi, "Evaluation Systems and Adaptations."
61. Ibid., p. 88.
62. Ibid., p. 155.
63. National Advisory Commission on Criminal Justice Standards and Goals, *Corrections*, p. 409.

The Effect of Case Load Variation

Will a parole officer do a better job of supervision if he has thirty-five parolees (as suggested by The President's Commission on Law Enforcement in 1967)[64] instead of a hundred? He can more frequently counsel them, help them find jobs or homes, threaten them, look for them, and spy on them. Common sense certainly suggests that this will help them stay out of prison, but common sense appears to be an inadequate guide: the evidence, found in scores of case load research studies, is inconclusive.

Two recent papers prepared by recognized experts in correctional research for the Federal Judicial Center summarize and evaluate the extensive work that has been done in this field.[65] The first, by Neithercutt and Gottfredson of the NCCD, reviews studies with results like these: Early experimental evidence shows that clients of parole officers with smaller case loads do better than others, followed by later studies that show no significant difference. Fifteen-man case loads do no better than thirty-man case loads. Narcotics users in thirty-man case loads do no better than those in seventy-five-man case loads. More parolee–parole officer contacts seem to increase the chance of detecting violations. California's "work unit" (smaller case load) parolees show no difference in parole outcomes from parolees on conventional supervision. "Intensive" supervision of probationers *and* parolees produces no different results from "regular" supervision, except the former had far more technical violations. Small case loads result in more technical violations and no reduction in recidivism. Probationers showed no significant increase in success when part of small case loads.[66]

The second paper, by Carter, Glaser, and Nelson of the University of Southern California, is less explicit in quoting other research but agrees as to the inconclusiveness of the findings. Both papers emphasize that con-

64. *Task Force Report: Corrections* (The President's Commission on Law Enforcement and the Administration of Justice, 1967), p. 70.

65. M. G. Neithercutt and D. M. Gottfredson, "Case Load Size Variation and Difference in Probation/Parole Performance" (Administrative Office of the U.S. Courts, Probation Division, 1973; processed); and Robert M. Carter, Daniel Glaser, and E. Kim Nelson, "Probation and Parole Supervision: The Dilemma of Caseload Size" (Administrative Office of the U.S. Courts, Probation Division, February 1973; processed). For an earlier and less critical review of this subject, see Stuart Adams, "Correctional and Caseload Research," in Norman Johnston, Leonard Savitz, and Marvin E. Wolfgang, eds., *The Sociology of Punishment and Correction* (Wiley, 1970), pp. 721–32.

66. Neithercutt and Gottfredson, "Caseload Size Variation," pp. 2–15.

centration solely on case load size as the solution is an unproductive venture: "All of the data available indicate that there is no such thing as an ideal caseload size and that a continued search for the magic number is inappropriate and most likely futile."[67]

After a similar review, Martinson concludes that the burden of research evidence is that reductions in case load size alone have no "treatment effect."[68] That is, there is little support for the notion that recidivism would be reduced if the parole officer would put more effort into trying to rehabilitate the parolee.

All sorts of other variables may affect the outcome of efforts by both parole officer and parolee: the number of times they see each other; the duration and content of each transaction; their own characteristics and how they interact; the attitudes and methods of the parole officer's superiors; the size and characteristics of the community in which the parolee is supervised. Many more could be added to this list.

In short, research does not yet provide clear guidance on the optimum case load size. The standard social science remedy for such a problem is to recommend more research, to design studies in which case load size is related to other factors and in which rigorous attempts are made to control other variables (the word to emphasize here is *attempts*). But it would be even more useful to take a bolder approach to experimentation, as suggested below, by dispensing with parole supervision entirely in selected localities and monitoring the results. It would not be possible to control all the variables, but the characteristics of the community, of the parole bureaucracy, and of the parolees could be identified in enough detail to yield more information about how effective parole supervision really is.

The Parole Officer's Performance and Attitudes

How well does the parole officer work on the case load he has? It is hard to say, except in the case of those who are obviously lazy, uncooperative, or abrasive. A parole officer may be carefully selected, systematically trained, and well supervised, but it is nearly impossible to tell how good he is in his work. What constitutes good performance? He cannot be judged on the extent to which his charges stay out of trouble; after all, he works with parolees who have long been conditioned to be in trouble. He cannot be

67. Carter, Glaser, and Nelson, "Probation and Parole Supervision," p. 21.
68. Letter to the author from Robert Martinson, Dec. 17, 1974.

judged by what his parolees say about him, or by what judges, policemen, or even parole board members say about him. He can be and is judged by his superiors on the quality and timeliness of his paperwork, his faithfulness in keeping appointments, his compliance with the parole officers' manual, and the agreeableness and incisiveness of his working personality. He should be seen as busy, cooperative, on the ball. All this *may* increase the chances that a parole violator will be caught or a wavering parolee helped past a crisis, but it is no guarantee. Some parolees will fail no matter how "good" the officer is; some will succeed no matter how "bad" he is.

Yet the officer's basic orientation does have something to do with whether his clients succeed or fail. Robison, Takagi, and Prus have emphasized the bureaucratic factor in parole revocation.[69] Dembo has shown that there is a definite relationship between high reintegrative scores (that is, officers who strongly want the parolee to succeed in the community) and low rates of technical parole violations.[70]

Profession versus Practice

Whatever his orientation, the parole officer is frustrated much of the time by the unattainability of his goals and by the conflicts between his policing and helping functions. As noted previously, Studt found that the parole officer seems driven toward shallow, meaningless exchanges with the parolee[71] and Takagi discovered that the officer moves toward increasingly bureaucratized performance.[72] The conscientious, professionally minded parole officer, particularly if educated as a social worker, is painfully aware of the conflicts between his professional values and the goals and practices of the parole organization.[73]

The dilemmas he faces are presented by three perceptive scholars in this way:

The social worker [parole officer] desires a warm, neutral, and nonjudgmental relationship with his client. He recognizes, however, that the client regards him as a participant in the punitive and condemning system of apprehension, judgment, and correction. He knows that the offender is compelled to come to him as a condition of probation or parole and often

69. See nn. 25–30 above.
70. Dembo, "Orientation and Activities," pp. 205, 211–12.
71. See p. 102.
72. See p. 117.
73. For a discussion of such conflicts in the professions generally, see David T. Stanley, "New Pressures on Professionals: Unions, Politics, Bureaucracy," *The Chemist*, vol. 151 (September 1974), pp. 18–23.

approaches him with hostility and an interest in concealing facts and feelings. For example, both he and his client know that the actual decision on revocation usually is the worker's, even though the formal authority is lodged elsewhere. His profession tells him that this is "an initial obstacle to be worked through," but it does not teach or tell him what to do. This is a major though not insuperable barrier for the recruit who has no specific training to apply.[74] The last sentence is, alas, too hopeful; the barrier clearly is insuperable in many cases. The relationship is never really developed, communication is on the surface only, and the parolee avoids the parole officer as much as possible. The authors recognize this in part of their conclusions: "[The parole officer's] responses to the unexpected and painful dilemmas include withdrawal to another setting, experimental-evasive-manipulative tactics, and alienation from his professional identification."[75]

Getting Ahead and Hanging On

In this uncomfortable situation the parole officer knows that the way his performance is seen by his superiors determines his ability to advance. Promotions mean relatively little more pay (see the rather compressed salary levels in table 5-1), but they do give a sense of achievement and progress. Some officers are gratified by promotion to supervisory jobs, others do not want them, and others can't get them because there are not enough to go around.

Despite the limited promotional opportunities, parole staff, at least in the governments we studied, had low turnover. No quantified study was undertaken, but parole directors reported losing staff mainly to the retirement rolls and occasionally to higher paying jurisdictions (especially the expanding federal probation service),[76] or to other jobs in the same state government.

The parole officers interviewed were clearly interested in their cases. They were understandably depressed by failures (a vicious crime by a trusted parolee, an attempted suicide by a parolee returned to prison) and stimulated by successes (an office visit by a satisfied exparolee, a college degree for a young offender). A few experienced officers displayed a weary doubt about the worth of the effort. This coincides with Dembo's finding

74. Ohlin, Piven, and Pappenfort, "Major Dilemmas of the Social Worker in Probation and Parole," p. 216.

75. Ibid., pp. 223–24.

76. Three hundred and forty new probation officer jobs were authorized for fiscal year 1974, 320 for FY 1975.

in New York that more experienced parole officers are more likely to express "conservative attitudes and job dissatisfactions due to difficult cases, political aspects, constant crises [sic] situations or long hours."[77] Dembo, a former parole officer himself, suggests that the long-term parole officer tends to shift his dissatisfactions from problems of client care to those of the system in which he works.[78] An officer who has reached this point finds it difficult to make a job change, so he hangs on until eligible to retire.

Evaluation and Alternatives

Clearly, parole-as-surveillance is hard to disentangle from parole-as-release and parole-as-assistance; all three influence the parolee's ability to stay out of crime, the ultimate test of success. Chapter 8 brings together these three strands. Meanwhile, some concluding remarks can be made about the surveillance and revocation processes discussed in this chapter.

Parole: Unsatisfactory in Practice

Parolees dislike supervision but naturally find it preferable to prison. They find the use of rules by the parole officers to advise, reprimand, and correct them "petty, harassing, and mechanical, an added burden unrelated to the real business of making a life for oneself in the community. For almost all parolees the use of rule violations as the basis for sending a man back to prison, as though such acts were equivalent to criminal behavior is 'dirty pool,' an indication of the 'system's' essential injustice."[79]

Parole officers are strained by their work loads and by their role conflicts as counselor, helper, policeman, and prosecutor. Despite their efforts, they cannot possibly give their parolees the degree of surveillance needed to be sure they are not getting into trouble. Board members, too, often find themselves ambivalent about revocations. Though well aware of the bureaucratic pressures in revocations they hesitate to overrule the parole staff. In many cases they are uncomfortable about returning the offender

77. Dembo, "Orientation and Activities," p. 207.
78. Ibid., p. 208.
79. Studt, Surveillance and Service, p. 149. For an even more severe analysis, see John Irwin, "Adaptation to Being Corrected: Corrections from the Convict's Perspective," in Daniel Glaser, ed., Handbook of Criminology (Rand McNally, 1974), pp. 983–85.

to prison and equally uneasy about leaving him in the community, and they lack adequate criteria for a valid decision.

No Supervision?

Parole supervision is an awkward status: custody which is not custody, surveillance which is not surveillance. The question naturally arises, Why do it?

The case for the affirmative depends partly on believing in the effectiveness of the "treatment" the parole officer gives the parolee, a matter discussed in chapter 7. It depends partly on the deterrent effect of parole policing—that the parolee will stay clean because he fears detection and revocation if he violates a condition of parole. Defenders of the parole system can say that "even the most optimistic reading of current evidence indicates that a sizeable percentage of those under parole supervision would wind up in prison if parole were to be abolished."[80]

Yet the evidence suggests otherwise. The case load studies discussed above point generally to the lack of effectiveness of parole officers' "treatment." The early discharge research in California concluded that far more parolees could safely have been removed from supervision.[81] Further, nationwide parole statistics show that three-quarters of parolees do not "fail" during the first two years on parole despite (or perhaps because of) the lack of attention they receive.[82] The "sizeable percentage," then, has to come from the 5 percent who abscond and the 15 percent who are revoked as technical violators.

Other research casts doubt on the extent of failures to be expected from the latter group:

A sample consisting of all violators in Los Angeles County for two months was studied in terms of their subsequent parole behavior . . . There were 99 parolees who had violated the conditions of parole but were continued on parole anyway. Their performance for the following 12 months was then analyzed. The results . . . surprised everyone. The parole violators who remained in the community got into only about as much trouble as we expect for new men coming out of the institutions. They were no more likely to be arrested (45.4% compared to 46.6%) during the next 12 months and not much more likely to be returned to prison (13.1% compared to 9.7%). Even at this the comparison was probably the wrong one to make. In California most minor

80. Vincent O'Leary, "Parole Theory and Outcomes Reexamined," *Criminal Law Bulletin*, vol. 11 (May–June 1975), p. 315.
81. Pp. 121–22 above.
82. P. 106 above.

violations are handled informally by the parole agent. Thus the study group included only those who had demonstrated difficulty in adjusting, unlike new releases. A fairer comparison of outcome would probably have been with parolees returned to short term institutional programs. This would be the board's second option for these cases. Comparable figures for releases from these programs show that 37% of the addicts, 22% of the non-addicts returned to prison within 12 months. In either case, however, the results are strong enough to speak for themselves.

Needless to say this data seriously challenges the traditional idea that parolees having problems are doomed to eventual failure or that small problems necessarily predict major difficulties to come and, therefore, it's best to get the parolee off the street. In addition, our statewide data on parolees involved in new felonies would seem to further question the credibility of that idea. At the same time the number of technical violators being returned to prison was being reduced the percentage of parolees committing new felonies and being returned to prison was going down. Those men released in 1967 (thus exposed to parole in 1967–68) had a one year new felony return rate of 7.1%. In 1968 the rate dropped to 5.9% and the following year to 5.1%. Releasees in 1970 (doing parole in 1970–71) improved on that with only 4.9% being returned with new felony convictions. Comparable figures for these same years for technical violators returned to prison were 11.8%, 9.7%, 7.0%, and finally 4.8% for the 1970 releases.[83]

The elimination of parole supervision, at least on an experimental basis, must be seriously considered. The parolee would not be monitored at all, and if he were caught committing any misdemeanor or felony he would be dealt with like any other exconvict committing such an offense. This idea will be given more attention in the concluding chapter.

83. Norman Holt, "Rational Risk-Taking: Some Alternatives to Traditional Correctional Programs," in *Proceedings: Second National Workshop on Corrections and Parole Administration*, American Correctional Association, Resource Document no. 4 (College Park, Md., March 1974), pp. 38–39.

CHAPTER SEVEN

Helping the Parolee
in the Community

PAROLE still involves problems in decision making as the parolee reenters the community. Most of the decisions must be made by the parolee himself, some by the overburdened and ambivalent parole officer, and some by helping agencies, both public and private. It is just as difficult to make constructive and just decisions at this stage of the parole process as it was earlier; resources are still not adequate, and the parties involved are still under stress.

The parolee's need for understanding assistance begins even before he leaves the penitentiary. The prospect as well as the experience of being paroled is stressful, even traumatic, for the typical prisoner. Although some offenders face the outside world with apparent cool confidence (whether or not they mean to stay on the right side of the law), many display anxiety to the point of feeling physically ill ("short-timer's pains"). They may suffer from hyperventilation, headaches, and other symptoms, even including increased acne.[1]

The affected inmate fears he will not be accepted on the outside by family, loved ones, or prospective employers. Some have adjusted too well to prison life and routine and fear returning to a more difficult way of life on the streets.[2]

Note. A few specific community service projects for prison releases are referred to in the latter part of this chapter. In some instances the program's effect on recidivism is assessed by the authors describing it, but the reader should be warned that such evaluative comment, though based on analysis, may not be supported by a rigorous methodology. It is difficult to control adequately for race, social class, age, and other variables in measuring the effect of such programs. Such projects are presented here as constructive efforts that have received some favorable notice; their value in reducing crime is not necessarily proven, either for the original programs or for duplications of them elsewhere.

1. Bertrand Agus, M.D., and Thomas E. Allen, M.D., "The Effect of Parole Notification on Somatic Symptoms in Federal Prisoners," *Corrective Psychiatry and Journal of Social Therapy*, vol. 14 (1968), pp. 66–67.
2. Ibid., p. 61.

. . . Parole for some represents a loss of security, job, or friends of his own age or sexual inclination.

. . . once an inmate has "caught a date" [is scheduled for parole] he is subject to a great deal of pressure from other inmates, some of whom may be jealous and others who may demand that certain debts be repaid (e.g., gambling or sex).[3]

Prerelease Indoctrination

Some prison systems try to ease transitional difficulties by providing prerelease preparation. This may range from a little counseling or a lecture or two to a several-week program in a separate institution, such as the pre-parole release center formerly operated by the State of Colorado in Canon City. There preparolees spent the last five weeks of their incarceration in an attractive setting attending classes and meeting with representatives of state agencies. They were instructed not only on the details of their own parole but also on other aspects of community adjustment: driver education, employment opportunities, family relations, planned parenthood, credit, social security, and many others. The instruction was given by community leaders and educators.[4]

Such programs obviously provide useful information and can help prevent some painful errors. However, they are not likely to succeed unless the inmates truly want to take part and think the topics are relevant to their own needs. Some apparently well-planned programs in California and Minnesota were found by evaluation studies to have little effect,[5] while other projects in Massachusetts and Maryland were found to have reduced recidivism.[6] It is doubtful that any indoctrination program can by itself keep an exoffender away from crime.

3. Ibid., p. 66.

4. Colorado Division of Corrections, "Colorado Pre-Parole Release Center" (March 1973), pp. 4–5. The center has been abolished as a separate program and absorbed by the medium-security prison. The building is now used for minimum-security incarceration.

5. Harmon Holt and Rudy Renteria, "Prerelease Program Evaluation: Some Implications of Negative Findings," Federal Probation, vol. 33 (June 1969), pp. 42–44; William F. McRae and others, "A Study of Community Parole Orientation" (St. Paul: Minnesota Department of Corrections, 1969; processed), p. 24.

6. Marie Buckley, "Enter: The Ex-Con," Federal Probation, vol. 36 (December 1972), pp. 24–30; Harris Chaiklin, "Final Report: The Community Integration Project" (Maryland Division of Corrections, 1973; processed); "Pre-Release Centers May Cut Recidivism," Criminal Justice Newsletter, vol. 6 (Sept. 15, 1975), p. 4.

Community Reentry

Despite such training efforts and despite prison rehabilitation programs, the parolee's return to the community is an enormous change that
involves all kinds of emotional and practical problems. As Elliot Studt
explains:

> While the parolee was an inmate in prison, he was a nonperson in every
> sense, so far as membership in the community of free citizens is concerned.
> However, in prison he was only one nonperson among many; and among his
> fellows he could establish a certain kind of recognized personhood. And in
> prison, the free part of the world had obligations to provide housing, food,
> clothing, work, and recreation for him while he lived through his punishment.
>
> As a parolee in the community, however, he bears his nonpersonhood
> among associates who are free persons in law and in action and with whom he
> must compete in order to survive. To remain in the community the parolee
> must exercise full responsibility for himself; and he can only do this by finding
> some mode of entry into the normal system of reciprocal relationships within
> which ordinary free men sustain themselves. Yet at no point is anyone obli-
> gated to provide such opportunities to him, while many doors are barred and
> others he enters at the cost of living under suspicion. Thus, the parolee often
> finds himself solely responsible for "reintegration"; he must prove himself in
> the community by "making bricks without straw."
>
> It is too *seldom recognized that "reintegration" is a two-way relationship
> requiring open doors and support from the community as well as responsible
> performance by the parolee.* No one can reintegrate *in vacuo.*[7]

She adds: "In the actuality of his experience, the parolee tends to find
that being on parole in itself sets up certain barriers against reentry into
normal systems; and that it often adds tasks and harassments to an already
difficult undertaking."[8]

The Parole Officer

The parole officer is a source of both tasks and harassments, as the
previous chapters have shown. He is also expected to be a source of help
and advice and a guide to other sources of help. This is a fantastic expectation, considering that he can spare each parolee only a few minutes at a

7. Elliot Studt, *Surveillance and Service in Parole: A Report of the Parole Action
Study* (University of California at Los Angeles, Institute of Government and Public
Affairs, 1972), p. 40 (emphasis added). (The final sentence appears as a footnote in
the original.)
8. Ibid., p. 41.

time, that he is avoided or resisted by many of his clients, and that the economic and psychological problems of reentry are so formidable.

The typical parolees under his supervision were neither wise nor competent to begin with: they chose crime; they were caught. They are neither well educated nor of high intelligence. Now they have been trained by prison experience to be dependent, and, to make things worse, they are upset. Such persons find it difficult to make choices, to decide on courses of action. It is hard for them to fill out a job application, get a driver's license, or deal with utility companies and landlords. There are others, of course, who display more ability and confidence, some in a straightforward manner, some manipulatively. In general, however, small problems become large and large ones overwhelming for the average parolee.[9]

In dealing with such difficult clients the parole officer must mix surveillance with assistance, and he has little time for the latter. The parole officer may feel that the parolee is in the wrong job, the wrong school, or the wrong home. Yet he may make no suggestions, partly out of reluctance to tell the parolee how to live, partly out of the sheer difficulty of helping the parolee find the "right" job, school, or home. He may feel that it is enough that the parolee is not actively criminal.

One parole and probation unit that functions entirely on the constructive side is the diagnostic and evaluation center in Macon, Georgia. This is a specially funded pilot project that concentrates on parolees with emotional, alcoholic, or drug problems. They receive diagnostic testing, special counseling (staff members have reduced case loads), and referral to appropriate therapy. The probationers and parolees do not receive routine supervision; that is, they come to the center not to fulfill a reporting-in requirement but to get counseling, treatment, or training. No job or home visits are made by the parole officers.

Parolees' Needs

When parolees are asked what they need most their replies are what one would expect: jobs, money, acceptance, companionship. They put material needs (a comfortable place to live, cash in their pockets, a car) a little ahead of social and psychological requirements; but, as for everyone else, these requirements are overlapping and interrelated. In a recent

9. For a vivid elaboration of the difficulties of parolees as "rehabilitation clients," see Richard C. Ericson and David O. Moberg, *The Rehabilitation of Parolees* (Minneapolis Rehabilitation Center, 1967), pp. 27–29.

sociological study, sixty California parolees were asked to rank their needs in priority order, with the following results:[10]

1. Education
2. Money
3. Job
4. Job training
5. Circle of friends
6. Home/shelter
7. Medical care
8. Recreational activities
9. Legal assistance
10. Sexual life
11. Dental care
12. Marriage/home life

Community agencies can do a great deal to meet these needs, but community attitudes and practices often stand in the way. Some of the agencies and some of the barriers relate only to exoffenders; some of each relate to any people who need help. In short, this is a complex situation, involving much more than the problems of parolees, and it must be given simplified treatment here in order to emphasize the elements that are most relevant to parole.

Community Services for Offenders Not Yet on Parole

Helping parolees is only one aspect of a broad range of services that are alternatives to incarceration—often called community-based corrections. Increasingly used in recent years, this approach has been emphasized both by The President's Commission on Law Enforcement and the Administration of Justice (1967)[11] and by the National Advisory Commission on Criminal Justice Standards and Goals (1973).[12] Greater and more effective use of both probation and parole is also part of this philosophy.[13]

10. Rosemary J. Erickson and others, *Paroled but Not Free: Ex-Offenders Look at What They Need to Make It Outside* (Behavioral Publications, 1973), p. 68. For another impressive list of "high frequency problems" of parolees, including both material and emotional needs, see Ericson and Moberg, *The Rehabilitation of Parolees*, pp. 31–32.

11. The President's Commission on Law Enforcement and the Administration of Justice, *The Challenge of Crime in a Free Society* (GPO, 1967), pp. 165–71; and *Task Force Report: Corrections* (GPO, 1967), pp. 38–44.

12. National Advisory Commission on Criminal Justice Standards and Goals, *A National Strategy to Reduce Crime* (GPO, 1973), pp. 121–23; and *Corrections* (GPO, 1973), pp. 221–45.

13. For a brief general review, see Bertram S. Griggs and Gary R. McCune, "Community-Based Correctional Programs: A Survey and Analysis," *Federal Probation*, vol. 36 (June 1972), pp. 7–13.

Some features of this effort emphasize community activities as an alternative to prison. They include:

—Diversion from the criminal justice system: suspending the criminal process and dealing with delinquents through noncriminal agencies and methods.[14]

—Pretrial release programs, in which offenders are counseled, employed, educated, and treated in the community in lieu of prosecution.[15]

—Increased use of probation in lieu of prison, coupled with counseling, educational, therapeutic, and employment assistance.[16]

Two other types of programs shorten or relieve the period of imprisonment and can be thought of as bridges to parole: work-release and furloughs. Both involve the exercise of options by the offender and by the correctional system.

Work-Release

Work-release programs are used in forty-one states.[17] They permit a prisoner to leave his institution to work for pay in the community but require him to return for his leisure and sleeping hours. His working situation is almost surely better paid and provides better training than his work in prison, and he is given an opportunity to show how he can use a limited amount of freedom.[18] Normally work-release is granted near the end of a

14. Commission on Standards and Goals, *Corrections*, pp. 73–96; Robert M. Carter, "The Diversion of Offenders," *Federal Probation*, vol. 36 (December 1972), pp. 31–36; Joe Hudson and others, "Diversion Programming in Criminal Justice: The Case of Minnesota," *Federal Probation*, vol. 39 (March 1975), pp. 11–19.

15. See, for example, Charles E. Ares, Anne Rankin, and Herbert Sturz, "The Manhattan Bail Project: An Interim Report on the Use of Pre-Trial Parole," *New York University Law Review*, vol. 38 (January 1963), pp. 67–95; Daniel J. Freed and Patricia M. Wald, *Bail in the United States: 1964* (New York City: Vera Foundation; U.S. Department of Justice, 1964), esp. pp. 56–66; and National Council on Crime and Delinquency, *The Des Moines Community Corrections Project: An Alternative to Jailing* (Hackensack, N.J., 1973).

16. Michigan Council of the National Council on Crime and Delinquency, *Saving People and Money: A Pioneer Michigan Experiment in Probation* (East Lansing, 1963); *Instead of Prison: A Report on the Community Treatment Project for Repeat Offenders, Oakland County, Michigan* (Hackensack, N.J.: National Council on Crime and Delinquency, n.d.); Joan Sturmthal, "California's Probation Subsidy Program," *State Government*, vol. 47 (Winter 1974), pp. 27–31.

17. Elmer H. Johnson and Kenneth E. Kotch, "Two Factors in Development of Work Release: Size and Location of Prisons," *Journal of Criminal Justice*, vol. 1 (March 1973), pp. 43–50.

18. For an article by an economist comparing prison work programs most unfavorably to work release, see Neil M. Singer, "Incentives and the Use of Prison Labor,"

prisoner's term so that it becomes both preparation and testing for parole. The District of Columbia parole board recommends to the Department of Corrections that certain potential parolees (the "good risks") be granted work-release for these purposes, and its recommendations are usually followed.

Some work-release programs continue to house their participants in state prisons; others arrange for them to live in county jails; but there is an increasing tendency to use "halfway houses" in the community. The reasoning behind this is obvious. If work-releasees return to prison at night they become really another class of prisoners, with damaging consequences for prison morale. The men themselves find it depressing to return to institutional life after a day in the community, particularly if they are required to pay for room and board. Furthermore, they are under pressure from other inmates to smuggle messages out and contraband in, according to informants in this study.[19]

If, on the other hand, they are housed in special community facilities —whether owned by the government or by private organizations under contract to the government—there are clear advantages. Since many traditional prisons are located in the country, work-releasees can be more accessible to the available employers and to educational facilities. Besides, living in the community with others can be part of the rehabilitative effort.[20] But while living in a work release center

may in fact operate to reduce the compression that a prisoner is reported to experience in the institution . . . it introduces him to stresses of its own. It places him under temptation to violate curfew hours, thus opening him to charges of absconding. It keeps him under daily surveillance by the center administrators when he had been anticipating freedom from the correctional

Crime and Delinquency, vol. 19 (April 1973), pp. 200–11. For descriptive and guidance material, see Community Work: An Alternative to Imprisonment (Principles and Guidelines) (Washington, D.C.: Correctional Research Associates, 1967); Elmer H. Johnson, "Report on an Innovation: State Work-Release Programs," Crime and Delinquency, vol. 16 (October 1970), pp. 417–26; Richard M. Swanson, "Work Release: Toward an Understanding of the Law, Policy and Operation of Community-Based State Corrections (Summary Report)" (Southern Illinois University, Center for the Study of Crime, Delinquency and Corrections, July 1973; processed); and, for a voluminous how-to book, Walter H. Busher, Ordering Time to Serve Prisoners: A Manual for the Planning and Administering of Work Release (U.S. Department of Justice, Law Enforcement Assistance Administration, June 1973).

19. See Lawrence S. Root, "State Work Release Programs: An Analysis of Operational Policies," Federal Probation, vol. 37 (December 1973), p. 55.

20. Ibid., pp. 55–57.

regime. And by reducing some of the "pains of imprisonment," the work release center may modify his calculus for the commission of new crimes.[21]

Are prisoners who have been on work-release more successful on parole than other prisoners? Statistically, they should be, if predictive data are used to help select work-releasees, as they sometimes are for parolees (though such selection has the familiar disadvantages of all predictive efforts). Political sensitivity as well as prediction, however, is reflected in this summary of the criteria used by forty states to exclude offenders from work-release:[22]

Reason for exclusion	Number of states
Violence	20
Sexual crimes	18
Narcotics sale	16
Narcotics use	12
Notoriety	12
Organized crime	10

Whether the reason is good selection or something else, work-releasees do adjust well to life in the community, according to several research studies. A Wisconsin study of the parole success (defined as remaining on parole for two years or being discharged from parole) of former work-releasees showed these results: 61 percent succeeded on work-release and succeeded on parole; 30 percent succeeded on work-release but failed on parole; 6 percent failed on work-release but succeeded on parole; and 3 percent failed on both.[23]

Research covering over 3,700 felons in California who had participated in work-release or training-release programs revealed that "on the basis of a 24-month parole follow-up, furloughees [work-releasees] had an 18.8% return-to-prison rate as contrasted with 26.6% return rate for the total parole population."[24]

A study of releasees from a California minimum security institution showed that inmates who had been on work-release, compared to other

21. Stuart Adams, "Evaluation of Work Release," in Emilio Viano, ed., Criminal Justice Research (D. C. Heath, 1975), p. 271. For a critical view of "halfway houses" financed by federal grants, see U.S. Comptroller General, Federal Guidance Needed If Halfway Houses Are to Be a Viable Alternative to Prison, Report B-171019 (GPO, May 28, 1975).

22. Root, "State Work Release Programs," p. 53.

23. Wisconsin Division of Corrections, "Work Release Study Release Program: 1970 and First Five-Year Trends," Statistical Bulletin C-63 (Madison, April 1972), p. 9.

24. California Department of Corrections, "A Report to the Legislature on the Work and Training Furlough Program" (Sacramento, December 1971), p. 1.

inmates, showed more favorable results on a variety of recidivism measures, including fewer arrests, less severe offenses, and fewer reconvictions. The researchers acknowledge: "it could very well be that the favorable showing of the work furlough [release] group was due to careful selection."[25]

In Alabama, early data from an evaluation project show that "work releasees have worked more, earned more, and, at three months postrelease, have been involved in fewer undesirable law encounters [than offenders in comparison groups]."[26] A North Carolina study is less conclusive: "At the most general level, the two groups did not differ significantly in parole outcome. For whites 29 percent of the work-releasees and 31 percent of the orthodox parolees were returned to prison. For Negroes, 40 percent of the work releasees and 30 percent of the orthodox parolees were returned to prison."[27]

After reviewing various research studies, Stuart Adams concludes that it is difficult to justify work-release in terms of improving offenders' attitudes or reducing crime rates, but that the program does promise reduced demand for new prison construction and occasionally generates new concepts and procedures in corrections.[28]

The economic benefits are plain, if the costs of recidivism are not considered:[29] work-releasees earn money, so they help support their families (who might otherwise be on welfare) and pay taxes, thus aiding the economy. This advantage, plus the merit of what Norval Morris calls "increments of increased freedom,"[30] makes work-release a useful preliminary to parole. Its potential is "as an alternative for those who need closer

25. Alvin Rudoff and T. C. Esseltyn, "Evaluating Work Furlough: A Follow-Up," *Federal Probation*, vol. 37 (June 1973), p. 52. See also earlier article by Rudoff, Esseltyn, and George L. Kirkham, "Evaluating Work Furlough," ibid., vol. 35 (March 1971), pp. 34–38.

26. Rehabilitation Research Foundation, Experimental Manpower Laboratory for Corrections, *Final Interim Report on Phase IV* (Montgomery, Ala., 1974), p. 60.

27. Elmer H. Johnson, "Highlights. Work Release: Factors in Selection and Results" (Southern Illinois University, Center for the Study of Crime, Delinquency and Corrections, December 1968), p. 5 (summary of more complete report).

28. Adams, "Evaluation of Work Release," p. 22. For another analytical commentary, see Elmer H. Johnson, "Work Release: Conflicting Goals within a Promising Innovation," *Canadian Journal of Corrections*, vol. 12 (January 1970), pp. 67–77.

29. Adams, "Evaluation of Work Release," p. 16. See also Virginia McArthur, Barbara Cantor, and Sara Glendinning, "Cost Analysis of the District of Columbia Work Release Program," D.C. Department of Corrections, Research Report no. 24 (June 1970; processed).

30. Norval Morris, *The Future of Imprisonment* (University of Chicago Press, 1974), pp. 41–42.

supervision and support than possible under probation, but are not considered grave threats to the community."[31] For that potential to be realized will require public education, for many a citizen is apprehensive about exoffenders in his workplace and in halfway houses in his community.

Study-Release Programs

These are operating in forty states, the District of Columbia, and the U.S. Bureau of Prisons, according to a recent survey. They are a recent development, thirty-nine of the forty-two having been started between 1966 and 1971. Over 3,000 offenders were participating in 1971—45 percent in vocational school, 25 percent in college, and most of the rest divided about evenly between high school and night school.[32] Very little has been written on this subject, but the need for the service is evident.

Furloughs

Brief furloughs[33] are another kind of bridge from the prison to the community. They give the prospective parolee a chance to get a job, find living quarters, or spend a few days with his family. When the time is used constructively, it reduces the number of problems confronting the offender when he starts on parole. Such thinking lay behind the recent enactment of a federal law permitting furloughs.[34] Another purpose is to permit an inmate to become reacquainted with his wife under less demeaning and artificial conditions than those permitted by conjugal visit privileges.[35]

Like paroles and work-releases, furloughs can be abused, and the state of Virginia had to cancel and later restrict furloughs in 1974 after some abuses.[36] The District of Columbia has had similar problems. On a more favorable note, a Minnesota study showed that in one year 727 furlough applications were received, 365 were approved, and only 15 of the offend-

31. Root, "State Work Release Programs," p. 58.
32. Robert R. Smith, John M. McKee, and Michael A. Milan, "Study-Release Policies of American Correctional Agencies: A Survey," *Journal of Criminal Justice,* vol. 2 (Winter 1974), pp. 357–63.
33. The term "work furlough" is used in California to mean work release. Here "furlough" means an approved leave for an inmate for other purposes.
34. P.L. 93-209, Dec. 28, 1973.
35. Michael Braswell and Paul DeFrancis, "Conjugal Visitation: A Feasibility Study," *Georgia Journal of Corrections,* vol. 1 (October 1972), pp. 171–80.
36. "Virginia Inmate Furloughs Are Canceled," *Washington Post,* Jan. 7, 1974; and Paul G. Edwards, "Godwin Tightens Rules on Prisoner Furloughs," *Washington Post,* Feb. 2, 1974.

ers (4 percent) violated their furloughs.[37] More recent figures published by the National Council on Crime and Delinquency show four large states with furlough success rates above 96 percent.[38]

The Money Problem

Money was near the top of parolees' lists of needs, but the need varies from one to another: "Well, when I got out, they gave me $42.50 and they said, 'Okay, here you are, and there's the front gate.' Now, if I hadn't had the friends I have, I would have been in real trouble. I might have been back by now."[39] "Nick gave me a place to stay, because I was out of money within four days . . . I gave him $25. . . ."[40] When I did get out this time I didn't have any trouble because I brought $240 out with me. . . ."[41] Most state governments give each releasee clothing, his transportation, and "gate money," ranging from $10 to $200—the median is $28. Fifteen states do not provide transportation; six do not provide clothing; three give neither; and two give no money.[42] The free clothing supplied is usually a work shirt and trousers; most releasees do not want to wear them. They may also have a few dollars or, in fortunate cases, a few hundred saved from prison earnings.

The policy for federal prisoners is to pay an amount which, when added to an inmate's personal funds, will "frugally provide for his needs for one week. BOP [the Bureau of Prisons] recently defined this as a minimum of $100."[43] Nonetheless, the average federal releasee in 1974 received only $45,[44] plus clothing and transportation.

Broke

The typical parolee is broke very soon, according to our interviews, and has real trouble making ends meet until his first payday. Even if he starts

37. "Temporary Parole Experience, October 16, 1971–October 15, 1972" (St. Paul: Minnesota Department of Corrections, February 1973; processed), p. 19.

38. "Illinois Furlough Program Succeeds," *Criminal Justice Newsletter*, vol. 5 (Sept. 23, 1974), p. 5.

39. Erickson and others, *Paroled but Not Free*, p. 42.

40. Ibid., p. 18.

41. Ibid., p. 3.

42. Computed from Kenneth J. Lenihan, *The Financial Resources of Released Prisoners* (Washington, D.C.: Bureau of Social Science Research, 1974), pp. 4–6.

43. U.S. General Accounting Office, *Use of Statutory Authority for Providing Inmate Release Funds* (GPO, Aug. 16, 1974), p. 3.

44. Ibid., p. 6. Figure is for the first half of fiscal year 1974.

on a job right away he will not be paid for a week, maybe two. Meanwhile, he buys some clothes, pays a fee for a driver's license, makes an advance payment on rent, buys food supplies or restaurant meals, and spends something on a celebration of his release. So he is in difficulty and may borrow from family, friends, community agencies, or from state funds. Field interviews showed few community agencies prepared to lend to re-leasees, and government loans are also rare. Only eighteen states have loan funds, and they are seldom used. Most of these states report lending money to only 3 or 4 men a year, although Michigan has loaned to 320 men a year and Wisconsin to 400.[45] The federal government makes loans only to those on work-furlough programs, and then for a maximum of sixty days; generally loans are not made to other releasees.[46] There were 287 loans to furloughees, averaging $60 each, in 1973.[47]

It is hard to get parolees to repay loans, and parole officers, according to interviews in California, are reluctant to press them. One regional parole administrator estimated that about 20 percent of the loans are repaid. I attended a meeting of the California Adult Authority (parole board) at which it was reported that $30,000 had been repaid out of $225,000 loaned. Consideration was given to making parolees repay as a condition of being discharged from parole. The board did not go that far but voted that such a debt should be reported to the board, which would consider it "a reason for not expediting the discharge of the parolee concerned."

Parolees who have been on work-release are better off because they have been working for, say, two to five months at prevailing community wages. No figures are available to show how many parolees nationwide have been on work-release, but the percentage would be small—possibly 10 percent of the total.[48]

Cash and Parole Success

Two West Coast states have experimentally given parolees money over a period of time. The results are inconclusive in one case and only faintly encouraging in the second.

45. Lenihan, *Financial Resources*, pp. 16–17.
46. U.S. General Accounting Office, *Inmate Release Funds*, p. 11.
47. Ibid., p. 14.
48. There were 5,584 offenders on work release in 1971 in the forty-eight states reported in the Lenihan study (*Financial Resources*, p. 15), from which we can extrapolate a nationwide total of 6,000. Even if all of them were paroled each year, they would constitute only 10 percent of the more than 60,000 persons paroled annually. Although most of these work releasees will be on parole for one or more future years, others will be discharged from parole or returned to prison.

In 1971 Washington began providing two kinds of support for parolees and other releasees. One is a "weekly stipend option" for those who need extended support while job hunting: it pays up to $55 a week for up to twenty-six weeks. The second is a "gate money" option, which gives releasees "$40, clothing, transportation costs up to $100 and, if needed, an additional $60 expense money." This plan is for persons who have definite job offers and seem to need only short-term support.[49] Neither option resulted in lower recidivism rates for those who received money than for offenders who were released before the programs were started.[50]

California tried an experiment of "direct financial assistance" (DFA) to parolees in one region.[51] An experimental group of 135 parolees was randomly selected, of which 23 were found by their parole officers not to need assistance. The others, at the discretion of their parole officer, were given up to $80 a week for twelve weeks. The average amount each one received was $735, or $61 a week. When the parole performance of this experimental group was compared with that of a control group, it was found that "nearly 80 percent of the financially-aided group of parolees remained successfully on parole as compared to only 71 percent of [the controls]. An analysis of background variables and social characteristics of the two groups showed no differences capable of creating such a difference in parole success rates. In fact . . . the control group should have exceeded the experimentals as more controls fell into sub-groups which have traditionally had lower recidivism."[52] The California authors warn that the principal finding (80 percent versus 71 percent success rate) is not statistically significant overall because of the small sample, but they claim that it "does show promise."[53]

Another California study looks at the offenders' performance on parole in relation to the number of visitors they had while in prison and to the amount of release money they had (see table 7-1). It concludes: "Among those men receiving two or more visitors the amount of release money is not associated with parole outcome. Among those men with only one or no visitors, the percentage experiencing no parole difficulties increases

49. Cameron R. Dightman and Donald R. Johns, "The Adult Correction Release Stipend Program in Washington," *State Government*, vol. 47 (Winter 1974), p. 32.

50. Ibid., pp. 34–36. Recidivism was measured by the percentage of released offenders returned to correctional institutions.

51. Scientific Analysis Corporation, "Direct Financial Assistance to Parolees Project: Research Evaluation" (San Francisco, July 1973; processed).

52. Ibid., p. 4.

53. Ibid., p. 51.

Table 7-1. *Difficulties Experienced during First Year of Parole,*
by Number of Visitors Received While in Prison and Amount
of Release Money[a]

Percent

	Seriousness of difficulties		
Item	None	Minor	Serious
Visitors: 0 or 1			
Release money: less than $20	42	42	16
$20–$79	51	43	6
$80 or more	57	35	8
Visitors: 2 or more			
Release money: less than $20	63	35	2
$20–$79	61	31	8
$80 or more	66	29	5

Source: Norman Holt and Donald Miller, *Explorations in Inmate-Family Relationships,*
California Department of Corrections, Research Division, Report no. 46 (Sacramento, January
1972), p. 44.
a. Amounts are inmate's account balance at the time of his parole board hearing.

from 42 percent for those released with less than twenty dollars to 57 percent for men with release funds of eighty dollars or more. It should be
noted, however, that in every financial category men with more visitors
are more successful than those with fewer visitors."[54]

In another experiment, the Bureau of Social Science Research in a
study called LIFE (Living Insurance for Ex-Prisoners) has been testing
whether economic support and employment assistance would reduce the
rearrest rate among 432 prison releasees in Maryland. Those helped financially received $60 a week for thirteen weeks. Preliminary results show that
those who received financial aid were less likely to be rearrested for crimes
of theft than those who were not, but this was not so for other types of
crimes.[55]

To say that unemployed parolees need money is a truism. The deci-
sional problem for correctional authorities is how much to distribute out
of their already-pinched budgets. More disciplined research is needed to

54. Norman Holt and Donald Miller, *Explorations in Inmate-Family Relationships,*
California Department of Corrections, Research Division, Report no. 46 (Sacramento,
January 1972), pp. 43–44.
55. Kenneth J. Lenihan, "Some Preliminary Results of the LIFE Project" (paper
prepared for the National Manpower Policy Task Force meeting, January 1975;
processed), p. 10.

find out the amounts and conditions that will do the most good in helping to keep parolees from returning to crime.[56]

Employment

Much of what has been discussed so far—work-release, furloughs, financial needs—leads straight to the heart of the parolee's problems: employment. Finding jobs is the central concern of efforts to help parolees in the community.

The typical parolee interviewed in the present study was employed and had had two jobs in the time he had been on parole. He said he had found his present job himself and that it was unrelated to any training he had received or work he had done in prison. He was not satisfied with his present employment but had neither optimism about nor a clear plan for making a change. (And at that, his situation was probably better than that of the average parolee because it was the successful, cooperative parolees who were available for interviews.)[57]

The manpower literature presents a bleak picture of the employment status and prospects of released prisoners. They tend to come disproportionately from vocationally disadvantaged groups—uneducated, untrained, victimized by discrimination. Their prison training is unlikely to give them marketable skills.[58] Furthermore employers generally are reluctant to hire persons with criminal records.[59] As a result, according to one federally

56. A radical alternative is the suggestion that released prisoners should be given "reparations" money *because* they have been incarcerated and that the amount should be proportional to the time served—say $100 per month of confinement. See Criminological Research Associates, *Rehabilitating Parole: An Alternative Model* (Berkeley, Calif., 1974), pp. 31–32.

57. Parolees were not sampled for this study but were interviewed incidentally in the course of visits to parole departments. The thirty-six interviewed were those who were reporting in at the time of our visit to a parole office or who were willing to come in at the invitation of their parole officers. Of the thirty-six, two were unemployed; sixteen had had one job; eight had two; nine, three; and one, four.

58. See p. 17. See also Michael J. Miller, "Future Employment Prospects and Vocational Training in Prisons," *Georgia Journal of Corrections*, vol. 1 (1972), pp. 103–11; and Philip J. Cook, "The Correctional Carrot: Better Jobs for Parolees," *Policy Analysis*, vol. 1 (Winter 1975), pp. 47–48.

59. See Robert Taggart, "Manpower Programs for Criminal Offenders," *Monthly Labor Review*, vol. 95 (August 1972), pp. 17–24; Taggart, *The Prison of Unemployment: Manpower Programs for Offenders* (Johns Hopkins University Press, 1972), pp. 1–5, 17–21; Roberta Rovner-Pieczenik, A *Review of Manpower R & D Projects in the Correctional Field (1963–1973)*, U.S. Department of Labor, Manpower Administra-

sponsored study, released prisoners have a high rate of unemployment. Statistics on employment of exoffenders are old and rare, but table 7-2 shows that they are more than three times as likely to be unemployed as are workers in general.

Table 7-2. *Employment Status of Male Federal Parolees and Mandatory Releasees and the National Male Civilian Labor Force, June 1964*
Percent

Employment status	Federal Exoffenders (N = 892)	National civilian labor force (N = 50,000,000)
All employed	83.3	94.8
Full-time	62.6	81.4
Part-time	19.6	9.0
Unknown	1.1	4.3
Unemployed	16.7	5.2

Source: George A. Pownall, "Employment Problems of Released Offenders," Report to U.S. Department of Labor (GPO, 1969), table 9, p. 49.

Employment and Parole Success

The employment problem is a serious one not only for the obvious reasons but also because there is a clear relationship between success in employment and success on parole. This is not to say that one causes the other, but perhaps only that the same characteristics that lead to steady work patterns also lead the individual to refrain from crime.

The author of a study of parolees and mandatory releasees concluded that unemployment was a major factor contributing to violations.[60] A Massachusetts study showed that parole success (defined as not having parole revoked) was related to both stability and quality of employment (see table 7-3).[61] On the other hand, a study conducted in Minnesota at about the same period covering groups of similar size revealed *no* significant relationship between parole adjustment and employment (using

tion, Manpower Research Monograph no. 28 (GPO, 1973), pp. 21–24; and George A. Pownall, "Employment Problems of Released Offenders," Report to U.S. Department of Labor (1969; processed), pp. 1–2, 8–18.

60. Pownall, *Employment Problems*, p. 18.

61. See the commentary on this study in Cook, "The Correctional Carrot," pp. 33–47. It must be noted again that parole violations are not a satisfactory criterion of failure because revocation decisions may be subject to bureaucratic pressure and caprice. Violations are *one* indication of parole failure, however, and in the absence of more refined measures of success, studies using them are cited in this book.

Table 7-3. *Parole Success and Characteristics of Employment,*
Two Samples of Massachusetts Parolees, 1959

	Sample I		Sample II	
Employment status	Number	Percent successful	Number	Percent successful
Completely unemployed during first three months on parole	12	8	5	20
No unemployment	91	58	44	52
Employment experience reasonably good, but some unemployment	70	39	48	44
Employment experience good— steady employment	81	58	55	58
No job required any skill	104	30	89	40
At least one job involved semi- skilled work	78	60	36	64

Source: Robert Evans, Jr., "The Labor Market and Parole Success," *Journal of Human Resources*, vol. 3 (Spring 1968), p. 207.

the dimensions time employed, time unemployed, and number of jobs held).[62]

A more recent analysis by the federal Bureau of Prisons shows first that persons who were employed for more than 25 percent of the two-year period *before* commitment to prison have a success rate of 72 percent;[63] those who were employed for a lower percentage of that period had a success rate of 60 percent.[64] Turning to employment after release, the same study shows that success rates correlate positively with the length of time on a job (see table 7-4).

Barriers to Employment

Despite this demonstrated relationship of jobholding to parole success, efforts to help put parolees to work are seriously blocked by restrictive laws and policies. Three prime examples of these barriers are licensing restrictions, civil service rules and practices, and bonding requirements. These obstacles, based on the need to protect the public, greatly limit the

62. McRae and others, *A Study of Community Parole Orientation*, pp. 18–19.

63. The success rate is the percentage of the group who were *not* recidivists during the two-year period following release to the community. "Recidivism is defined as parole revocation, or any new sentence of 60 days or more, including probation." U.S. Bureau of Prisons, "Success and Failure of Federal Offenders Released in 1970" (January 1974; processed), p. 1.

64. Ibid., p. 24.

Table 7-4. *Parole Performance of Federal Offenders*[a] *and Longest Time on a Job after Release, 1970*

Percent

	Parole performance		
Longest time on a job	Success[b]	Failure	Unknown
No job	45	41	14
One year or less	56	32	12
Two years or less	58	27	15
Three years or less	66	22	12
Four years or less	67	19	14
More than four years	78	12	10
Total	61	27	12

Source: U.S. Bureau of Prisons, "Success and Failure of Federal Offenders Released in 1970" (January 1974; processed), table 41, p. 68.
  a. N = 1,491.
  b. As defined in n. 63 above.

choices that can be made by parolees and by those trying to help them get satisfactory jobs. Fortunately, all three obstacles are now under systematic attack.

Licensing. In nearly all states, a parolee who wants to be a barber, a beautician, or a practical nurse will either be denied the license necessary to engage in such an occupation or will have to prove his or her "good moral character." If he wants to work in a bar or restaurant where alcoholic drinks are sold, he will encounter restrictions in ten states. And so it goes: chauffeur, plumber, physical therapist, teacher, tree surgeon, dry cleaner, midwife, funeral director—there are lists pages long of occupations for which a license may be denied if the applicant has committed a criminal offense or be made conditional upon "good moral character."[65] A comprehensive study by the American Bar Association (ABA) found "1,948 separate [state] statutory provisions that affect the licensing of persons with an arrest or conviction record," an average of 39 for each state. The ABA says that literally millions of people are potentially affected.[66]

65. James W. Hunt, James E. Bowers, and Neal Miller, *Laws, Licenses, and the Offender's Right to Work* (Washington, D.C.: American Bar Association, National Clearinghouse on Offender Employment Restrictions, 1973), pp. 5–12, A-1–A-13. For other useful analyses, see *The Invisible Prison: An Analysis of Barriers to Inmate Training and Post-Release Employment in New York and Maine* (New York: RCA Institutes, 1972); and Brian Bomberger, "Rehabilitation and Occupational Licensing: A Conflict of Interests," *William and Mary Law Review*, vol. 13 (Summer 1972), pp. 794–823.
66. Hunt, Bowers, and Miller, *Laws, Licenses*, p. 8.

Understandable caution lies behind the welter of inhibiting statutes. One would hesitate to license a person with a series of assault convictions to work with a straight razor, or a habitually fraudulent lawyer to practice his profession. Nevertheless many of the laws are so inflexibly worded and administered that they block the employment of deserving exoffenders who are unlikely to commit crimes—particularly if they are gainfully employed. Licensing agencies have been known to consider arrest records not followed by convictions, criminal records that have been officially expunged, and convictions for crimes unrelated to the occupation.

The ABA's National Clearinghouse on Offender Employment Restrictions has not only analyzed the various laws but has published guidelines for a variety of remedial steps, among them a model state law limiting the extent to which criminal records should be considered in disqualifying persons for "permits, registrations, certificates or licenses" to engage in certain occupations; examples of court decisions that invalidate unreasonable restrictions; examples of attorneys general's opinions that limit the discretion of licensing agencies.[67]

Public Employment Requirements. Governments are natural employers for exoffenders to turn to. About 14.2 million persons (17 percent of the employed civilian labor force) hold government jobs.[68] The U.S. Department of Labor administers a variety of grants to finance jobs in state and local government for unemployed and underemployed groups in the population. And governments are always under political and civic pressures to be the ideal employers. Nevertheless, an authoritative professional study found that exoffenders face formidable obstacles to getting jobs with governments.[69]

They are asked about arrest records, even arrests that do not end in conviction. They either do not have the right to have their criminal records expunged or, where they have it, do not know about this right. Laws requiring records of juvenile crime to be kept confidential are not observed. Most civil service laws use language that can be used (and is used) to

67. Ibid., pp. 13–16 and apps. A–F. See also American Bar Association, National Clearinghouse on Offender Employment Restrictions, *Removing Offender Employment Restrictions: A Handbook on Remedial Legislation and Other Techniques for Alleviating Formal Employment Restrictions Confronting Ex-Offenders* (Washington, D.C., 1973).

68. *Monthly Labor Review*, vol. 98 (August 1975), tables 1 and 8, pp. 67 and 73.

69. See Herbert S. Miller *The Closed Door: The Effect of a Criminal Record on Employment with State and Local Public Agencies* (Georgetown University Law Center, 1972), pp. 4–10.

exclude offenders with criminal records. Job applicants are not advised that a criminal record does not automatically disqualify them, and probation and parole officers do not or cannot initiate action to expunge criminal records. Most jurisdictions do not issue guidelines on how to process applicants who have criminal records. Exoffenders are also handicapped by: long delays between time of application and time of selection for the job; unrealistically high requirements for some jobs, such as high school graduation, a long apprenticeship, or extensive prior experience; and not being informed of, or allowed to take, civil service tests while in prison.

Such findings are sometimes disputed by the argument that public-service employers should maintain a high standard. No one can deny that; the answer is that the standard should not be unrelated to the job to be filled, nor ignore the fact that the applicant may be ready to lead a law-abiding life, nor force him onto the relief rolls or back into crime.

Bonding. One of the parolees interviewed in the present study said that he had lined up a job as a deliveryman for a furniture company but could not be hired because he could not be bonded. His experience is shared by many exoffenders elsewhere. The U.S. Department of Labor describes the problem in this way: "Many jobs require bonding. However, the employer may state that his bonding company will not cover persons with questionable records. . . . Other employers will insist on a bond even though the job involved has not heretofore been covered; that is, they would refuse to employ on that job an individual with a questionable record unless he is bonded."[70]

Both aspects of the problem have been solved through a federally funded bonding assistance program. Either the employer or the applicant may apply to the local state employment service office for coverage. To get it the applicant must be qualified for the job and not commercially bondable.[71] From June 1966 through July 1974, 6,655 bonds were issued under the program (225 persons were bonded more than once).[72] Only 295 claims were submitted, of which 128 have been paid; the average claim paid was about $1,000.[73] The default rate (claims paid per 100 bondees) was under 2 percent, and the loss ratio (ratio of dollars paid in

70. U.S. Department of Labor, Manpower Administration, *The Federal Bonding Program: Questions and Answers* (GPO, 1971), Q. 6.

71. Ibid.

72. Contract Research Corp., "An Analysis of the Federal Bonding Program: Summary" (Belmont, Mass.: CRC, September 1975; processed), p. 33.

73. Ibid., "Vol. II: Program Analysis," p. 53.

claims to premiums paid) was somewhat lower than that for comparable activities in the bonding industry generally.[74]

Attacking the Barriers

Of these three obstacles, the bonding problem has been the easiest to attack. Restrictive licensing and employment laws and practices, including those in the public sector, are much more difficult. They require legislative action, and state legislatures may be slow to act, first because of the pressure of more urgent business, and second, because they are responsive to occupational pressure groups who may want to keep up standards and restrict the entry of exoffenders to their fields.[75]

Nevertheless, the ABA has clearly shown what needs to be done and has even supplied a model state law and other how-to-do-it instructions.[76] Its National Clearinghouse on Offender Employment Restrictions also publishes brochures to report progress and to spread the gospel of hiring exoffenders, with titles such as "What You Can Do To Expand Job Opportunities for Ex-Offenders," "The Offender as a Manpower Resource," "Expanding Government Job Opportunities for Ex-Offenders," and "Developing Jobs for Parolees." The clearinghouse also publishes the "Offender Employment Review," a newsletter that chronicles progress with such headlines as, "Four More States Lift Automatic Restrictions on Licensing, Three Cover Public Employment," and "Hawaii Passes Nation's First Measure Prohibiting Discrimination Against Ex-Convicts by Private Employers." It also summarizes pertinent court decisions and executive actions and describes local job-finding programs for exoffenders.

In varying degrees public agencies are struggling with the civil service employment problem. The U.S. Civil Service Commission has adopted positive policies on hiring offenders both for regular jobs and on work-release arrangements.[77] Another example is the intensive effort by the Office of Employment Development of the District of Columbia correc-

74. Ibid., "Summary," p. 34.

75. One legal student writes that it would be both feasible and desirable to enact federal legislation to sweep aside state laws that require or permit employment discrimination based on criminal records. Barry Portnoy, "Employment of Former Criminals," *Cornell Law Review*, vol. 55 (January 1970), pp. 306–20. This idea raises questions of constitutional interpretation, legislative wisdom, and political feasibility, and there is as yet no support for it in the literature. It is nevertheless an idea whose time could conceivably come.

76. See nn. 65 and 67 above.

77. U.S. Civil Service Commission, *Employment of the Rehabilitated Offender in*

tions department to encourage other D.C. departments to hire offenders. More than 150 inmates and parolees were hired over three years to renovate public housing units.[78] Such activities not only remove technical obstacles but also encourage more favorable attitudes on the part of employers and the public generally, as well as parolees, for employment of exoffenders.

More Subtle Barriers

Better attitudes are certainly needed, for changes in laws and rules can only partly correct for the reluctance of an employer to hire an exconvict. If he knows the applicant is a parolee he may come up with all sorts of reasons for not hiring him—wrong training, wrong experience, the presence of other better qualified applicants. If he does not know about the applicant's criminal record at first he can find out about it by probing in the interview or by checking into the applicant's background. Some parolees make no secret of their records when they look for jobs, despite their fear of rejection. Others hide their histories, hoping that the employer will not probe deeply yet knowing and fearing that they can be discharged for falsifying their application forms. In our interviews with parole officers we found no consistency in the advice they give parolees on this point. Some strongly urge openness; others accept the parolee's concealment of his past and cooperate in keeping the employer in the dark. The Citizens' Inquiry study in New York also found that some parole officers advised parolees "not to disclose their criminal record or parole status to a prospective employer unless it was specifically requested."[79] Likewise, the *Washington Post* found District of Columbia parole officers concealing parolees' criminal records from prospective employers.[80] Such dilemmas may diminish, though never disappear, as nondiscrimination in employment is more and more accepted.

Another difficulty is the parolee's inexperience and insecurity in the mechanics of applying for work: filling out blanks, being interviewed,

---

the *Federal Service* (GPO, 1968); and CSC, "Employment of Public Offenders," *Federal Personnel Manual* (GPO, 1969), pp. 306-23–306-27.

78. National Capital Housing Authority and D.C. Department of Corrections, "Community Rehabilitation Project" (n.d.; processed), p. 2.

79. Citizens' Inquiry on Parole and Criminal Justice, *Prison without Walls: Report on New York Parole* (Praeger, 1975), pp. 88–89.

80. Jane Seaberry, *Washington Post*, Sept. 29, 1975.

taking tests. The mere act of filling out an application, John Irwin writes, is a formal act of laying oneself open to the close scrutiny of conventional judges. This scrutiny usually makes the ex-convict feel embarrassed or guilty. One parolee reported to me his feelings about job hunting and filling out applications:

"Man, I just never've been able to go through that job-hunting scene. I don't know how to ask for a job. I feel shitty standing there asking some broad about a job. Then she hits me with a long application and I'm really in trouble. I just can't fill out one of them. Most of the questions I can't answer because they haven't got anything to do with me or my life or I can't remember. They just weren't written for a guy like me. They were written for some guy who went to work right out of high school and only held two jobs before this one. I get to that part about former employment and I got to pass. Last place I just wrote across that space that I would explain all that when they talked to me."[81]

But despite all these kinds of obstacles, a large majority of parolees do get jobs. They face continuing problems, however, in the low status and low pay of the jobs they get and the length of time they stay employed.

The First Job after Release

Parolees, as noted earlier, may have specific jobs lined up before they are released or they may be paroled in the belief that they can get a job. It would certainly be desirable for the parolee to have a job ready for him, but this is not realistic in many cases. The job may be a phony or a "can opener" (a job that "withstands investigation but exists only for purposes of the parole plan"[82]). None of the parole boards covered in this study except Georgia, however, required a promised job as a condition of parole. Obviously it is hard to look for a job while still in prison; the New York Citizens' Inquiry study tells of convicts writing dozens of letters to employers whose names and addresses were found in the yellow pages.[83] A prisoner is more likely to line up a job through family, friends, or former employers, sources mentioned frequently in interviews and parole board hearings. The Pownall study found that such sources accounted for 80 percent of prearranged jobs in its sample of releasees in Baltimore and Philadelphia.[84]

When the same researcher looked more broadly at releasees' first jobs

81. John Irwin, *The Felon* (Prentice-Hall, 1970), p. 135.
82. Citizens' Inquiry, *Prison without Walls*, p. 84.
83. Ibid.
84. Pownall, *Employment Problems*, p. 137.

(not merely the prearranged jobs), he discovered that 57 percent of the releasees found jobs through family, friends, or former employers; 22 percent through their own efforts; 6 percent through the probation [parole] office or prison personnel; 9 percent through the state employment service; and 6 percent through other sources.[85]

Fewer than 20 percent of these releasees started on white-collar or skilled jobs, with 25 percent each in operative, service, or unskilled positions.[86] The jobs were low paying: a median of $65 per week at a time (1965) when the federal minimum wage was $1.25 an hour (or $50 for a forty-hour week), and average earnings for nonagricultural workers were $95.[87]

How long do parolees stay on their first jobs? One parole officer told us: "Eight out of ten parolees blow their first jobs." The Pownall study found a median duration of four months;[88] this is confirmed by other research showing releasees leaving their first jobs in five weeks, three months,[89] and "less than two months."[90]

Unstable Job Histories

The problem is not just with the first job. The typical parolee, relatively unskilled and unenterprising, has a spotty work history. Several of the parolees we interviewed had worked at "drop-off jobs," that is, they were casual laborers waiting at a designated street corner for employers such as contractors or scavengers.

Parolees interviewed in one part of the Pownall study worked a median of 7.6 months on their longest jobs between release and the interview and 5.2 months on the last job before the interview.[91] Of those who had been on parole (or supervised mandatory release) for one year or more, 2 percent had held no jobs; 17 percent had held one job; 19 percent, two jobs; 20 percent, three jobs; 8 percent, four jobs; 15 percent, five jobs; and 19 percent, six or more jobs.[92] They did make more money than the $65

85. Ibid., pp. 149–50.

86. Ibid., p. 148.

87. Ibid., p. 151; Monthly Labor Review, vol. 97 (August 1974), p. 113.

88. Pownall, Employment Problems, p. 155.

89. Rovner-Pieczenik, A Review of Manpower Projects, p. 63.

90. Robert Evans, Jr., "The Labor Market and Parole Success," Journal of Human Resources, vol. 3 (Spring 1968), p. 204.

91. Pownall, Employment Problems, p. 155.

92. Ibid., p. 170.

median for the first job—$83 on the longest job and $87 on the last job.[93] A later study, also of federal releasees, showed that over half of the group analyzed had not kept a job for a whole year.[94]

Many reasons can be given for such instability: the state of the local labor market, lack of training for the jobs available, the intermittent nature of many service jobs and semiskilled or unskilled blue-collar jobs, and the institutional obstacles discussed earlier. There are also personal, non-job-related reasons, as in several examples cited by Pownall showing deeply ingrained patterns of instability in both employment and life-style.[95] The author hypothesizes that the reason released inmates do not hang on to jobs even though they are trained for them and the pay is reasonable is "lack of a supportive subculture."[96] He suggests that if the offender's cultural environment is not supportive and he lacks motivation for achievement and mobility,

training and assistance will probably be ineffective. Former inmates will be unemployed or will work only sporadically on part-time, low-level jobs and thus become likely candidates for return to criminal behavior. If change is to take place in these groups, either the subcultural frame of reference must be changed or the individual moved to a different and supportive subculture. It is not easy to move a man from one environment to another; however, work release programs and community release centers have made this possible in some cases.[97]

In this connection a correctional psychologist warns that " 'steadiness' can be misleading in its apparent promise for reducing recidivism. It may postpone but probably will not prevent further delinquency. While a small steady income may ease some pressures, and regular work attendance may reduce the free time in which delinquency might occur, there is evidence that these do not offset the influence of other, more potent factors."[98] He cites exposure to criminal behavior and environmental stresses as crucial factors and points out that "steady employment in a marginal occupation may tend to confirm an offender's view that there is no future in legitimate work and lead him back to crime."[99] This is why some community agencies have emphasized personal counseling and therapy ses-

93. Ibid., p. 151.
94. U.S. Bureau of Prisons, "Success and Failure of Federal Offenders," pp. 25–26.
95. Pownall, *Employment Problems*, pp. 218–26.
96. Ibid., pp. 238–43.
97. Ibid., p. 243.
98. Clyde E. Sullivan, "Changes in Corrections: Show or Substance?" *Manpower*, vol. 3 (January 1971), pp. 5–6.
99. Ibid., p. 6.

sions along with employment assistance (some examples are given later in this chapter).

The Job-Finding Effort

Meanwhile, help is needed on the job front. There is much help available, but there will never be enough; the variables are too numerous, the human mechanism too delicate, too beset by problems, to justify a prediction of success. Nonetheless, there is some encouragement to be found in the concern and effort being devoted to the job problem. Special attempts are being made to train, counsel, refer, and place exoffenders that are not being made for other persons who need employment assistance. This may seem to constitute a paradox in public priorities: why are we devoting more emphasis to helping the sinner than the merely unfortunate? Justifications for this run deep in our theological heritage, as well as in the practical hopes of preventing future crime. Hence jobs for parolees are being developed or sought by a great variety of individuals and institutions.[100]

Parole Officers. As already noted, most jobs are found by the parolee himself or by friends, family, or former employers; parole officers have decided they can devote very little time to this activity. In some cases officers are rationalizing their own inability to provide this service. A more charitable explanation is their own belief that the parolee needs to work toward independence by finding his own job; the parole officer's role is to encourage him and tell him about sources of jobs. Though some parolees will reject even this, having been disillusioned about any government or community help by their experiences with police, prosecutors, and prisons, most will welcome leads.

Nevertheless, in the governments studied here some parole officers do develop job opportunities and refer their parolees, sometimes even escorting them personally to interviews. The parole officers usually try to line up a few cooperative employers to whom they send parolees—a hotel in the Washington, D.C., area, a beer factory in Colorado, a meat processing plant in Wisconsin, a crate and veneer company in Georgia. Such employers are usually known to and used by all parole officers, but an occasional officer practices what they call the "hip pocket system"—that is, not telling others about the employers he uses.

100. Employment on work release, when the offender is still in the custody of correctional authorities, is discussed above, pp. 140–44.

In addition, parole officers are usually provided with a list of employers or employment offices and, in some jurisdictions, a job development service. The District of Columbia, for example, maintains an Office of Employment Development in its Department of Corrections. Job opportunities are sought not only for parolees but also for probationers, work releasees, and arrestees released on bail. Reports of this office show that in an average year about 60 percent of their clients are placed in jobs, but this dropped to 40 percent in 1974 because of economic conditions. Failures have been running a little under 15 percent of referrals (failures include parolees referred who do not follow through to get jobs, who do not report for work, or who reject counseling and placement services).[101] The director of the division says that some parole officers use his services much more than others and (a familiar complaint) that a big problem is the tendency of parolees to jump from job to job.

Other examples of job help were encountered in field research:

—A "job bank" of opportunities staffed by two half-time VISTA volunteers (both exoffenders) in a field parole office in California. Since then the state has started a program to match job opportunities and qualifications of releasees by computer.

—Job referral services, mostly through other community agencies, from a regional community services office of the federal Bureau of Prisons.

—Assignment of a Wisconsin parole officer to community liaison work, particularly with the local office of the National Alliance of Businessmen, on job-finding matters; his supervisory case load was reduced to make this work possible.

State Employment Services. The offices of the various state employment services are natural choices for referring exoffenders to jobs. After all, the offenders are state charges, and it is in the states' interest to have them become productive (or at least noncriminal) members of society. This does not mean that employment service staff will necessarily be zealous in referring parolees to employers or that employers will be in a receptive mood. Parole officers interviewed for this study said that the effectiveness of employment services in getting parolees into jobs depends on the attitudes of individual employment counselors, on their relationships with individual parole officers, and on how persuasive they are in dealing with employers.

In short, the situation has called for special efforts, and the U.S. De-

101. Data from interview and internal reports of D.C. Department of Corrections, Employment Development Division.

partment of Labor made one for two years in five states in its Model Ex-
Offender Program (MEP).[102] Special grants were made to finance staff
acting as job developers–counselors–coaches stationed at prisons. The
MEP staff either accompanied their clients to job interviews or directed
them to specific employers. The former method was more satisfactory
both because it made more impression on employers and because it helped
compensate for the lack of self-confidence shown by many exoffenders.
But despite this special effort, adverse labor market conditions resulted in
disappointing progress. Ironically enough, it was difficult to put exoffenders on the staffs of the state MEP projects because of the inflexibility of
civil service rules and procedures.[103]

When the Department of Labor evaluated the program it found that
39 percent of MEP clients had been placed in "permanent" jobs (initial
placements only); clients earned between $2.15 and $2.40 per hour;[104] the
cost per placement was $361; and recidivism was lower than expected.[105]
This pilot program showed that some progress could be made through a
special effort, but now the special effort is over. Field visits conducted
in the present study, a year after MEP ended, revealed no special services
offered by the state employment offices, though they continue to refer
qualified exoffenders to employers in the course of regular operations.

New model employment programs are now being sponsored by ten
states and Puerto Rico, with financing by the U.S. Department of Labor.
They include employability development units inside prisons and offender
placement units in large urban areas.[106] Other kinds of job-finding efforts
have been made under various types of sponsorship, some examples of
which appear later in this chapter.[107]

Organizing Business Employers. Community employment programs
have been urging businessmen to commit some jobs for the employment

102. The years were 1970–72; the states were Arizona, Georgia, Massachusetts,
Oklahoma, and Pennsylvania. The program served probationers and mandatory releasees as well as parolees. Much of the information in this section is drawn from
internal evaluative reports of the Office of Policy, Evaluation, and Research, Manpower
Administration, U.S. Department of Labor.

103. See discussion of barriers to public employment, pp. 153–54.

104. In those years average hourly earnings (nonagricultural) ranged from $3.22
to $3.67. *Monthly Labor Review*, vol. 98 (August 1975), p. 77.

105. From internal Department of Labor reports.

106. "Grants Fund Diversion, Ex-Offenders Job Aid," *Criminal Justice Newsletter*,
vol. 6 (Dec. 8, 1975), p. 3.

107. For examples of special employment programs aided by the U.S. Law Enforcement Assistance Administration, see Joseph F. Cunningham, "Jobs for the Ex-
Offender," *Case and Comment*, vol. 77 (1972), pp. 19–23.

of exoffenders as well as to lower the discriminatory barriers discussed earlier. In New York City a unified approach is being attempted by the Alliance for a Safer New York, a group made up largely of rehabilitative agencies, but also including the city's Chamber of Commerce, the Equitable Life Assurance Society, and several large labor unions.[108] One member of the alliance, the New York City Urban Coalition, has published a directory of services and programs for former prisoners and guidance material on regaining their citizen's rights.

A nationwide effort to get businesses to hire exoffenders is being pressed by the National Alliance of Businessmen (NAB) with the aid of a U.S. Department of Labor grant. Started in 1973, the program involves 137 metropolitan offices of the NAB; by July 1974, over 6,000 persons had been placed.[109] A new effort within the NAB program is a series of governor's conferences, in which a state governor invites leading businessmen to a one-day meeting on developing jobs for exoffenders. These and other initiatives are resulting in an increasing acceptance by business leaders of the values of hiring and training exconvicts.[110]

Concentrated Assistance Projects

Parolees may also have access to other special helping facilities. Some are nonresidential and some are halfway houses of one type or another. Some are temporary and experimental; some are long-term. All supply a coordinated group of services. There are several hundred of these organizations in the United States, financed by government or philanthropic grants, but a few examples will illustrate the kinds of assistance they can provide.

108. "The Employment Problems of Ex-Offenders" (a Presentation [for business leaders] sponsored by Senator Jacob K. Javits, the Alliance for a Safer New York, and the Edna McConnell Clark Foundation) (New York: The Fry Consulting Group, n.d.; processed); also "Statement of David F. Linowes, Chairman, Committee on City Affairs, New York Chamber of Commerce, before the Commission on Human Rights on the Employment Problems of Ex-Offenders" (May 24, 1972; processed).

109. Interview, Richard C. Wells, vice president, and John R. Armore, director, Ex-Offender Program, National Alliance of Businessmen, Washington, D.C., May 10, 1974. This figure includes probationers and work releasees as well as parolees.

110. Gopal C. Pati, "Ex-Offenders Make Good Employees," *Public Personnel Management*, vol. 2 (November–December 1973), pp. 424–28; and Pati, "Business Can Make Ex-Convicts Productive," *Harvard Business Review*, vol. 52 (May–June 1974), pp. 69–78.

Nonresidential Employment-Related Services

A pair of projects financed by the federal Law Enforcement Assistance Administration (LEAA) and managed by a contractor were set up to help parolees, work-releasees, and probationers: Project EXIT (Ex-offenders In Transition) in Maine and Project EXCEL (Ex-offender Coordinated Employment Lifeline) in Indiana. Both included prerelease orientation, intensive job development, and counseling. EXIT made 363 placements in its first year, EXCEL, 506.[111]

Projects like this have to keep running just to stand still, both because of the flow of new clients from the criminal justice system and because of the problems exoffenders tend to have with job instability. These figures are reported by EXCEL:

Of the 506 job placements that were made by EXCEL during its first year of operation, 236 (47%) were not active as of August 1, 1972. Of 236, 85 quit, 64 were fired, 33 were laid off and 24 did not show up for even their first day of work. The 236 . . . also include 8 individuals who graduated from their jobs without giving notice to their employers, 6 who graduated from a training program during the year and received other jobs, 4 individuals who walked out of the Indiana Work Release Center and therefore lost their jobs, and finally 6 individuals who after being placed in jobs lost them because they were arrested as a result of further trouble with the criminal justice system.[112]

Similar figures were reported for EXIT.[113]

There are numerous other such projects, all of them geared to job counseling, training, development, and placement. Like EXIT and EXCEL, they all have had to fight both the reluctance of employers to hire exoffenders and the tendency of their clients to be erratic in their work behavior. Some successes have been recorded, but in general the results were mixed.[114]

It is customary for all types of these concentrated assistance projects

111. Palmer-Paulson Associates, *Analysis '72* (Chicago: Palmer-Paulson Associates, Inc., 1973), pp. 7, 16; Palmer-Paulson, *EXCEL in Indiana* (1973).

112. Palmer-Paulson, *Analysis '72*, p. 16.

113. Ibid., pp. 16–17.

114. Examples include: Project DEVELOP in New York (see Leonard R. Witt, "Final Report on Project DEVELOP" [New York State Division of Parole, n.d.; processed], pp. 39–42); the Concentrated Employment Program in Baltimore (see Emil Michael Aun, "Staying Free Is a Job," *Manpower*, vol. 3 [January 1971], pp. 8–13); the Minneapolis Rehabilitation project (see Ericson and Moberg, "The Rehabilitation of Parolees"); and Job Therapy, Inc., in Washington state (see "What Is Job Therapy, Inc.?" [brochure; n.d.]; and Arthur Gordon, "They Go to Prison on Purpose," *Reader's Digest*, vol. 97 [August 1970], pp. 147–52).

to employ exoffenders, a sensible and desirable policy. In addition, some exoffenders have formed their own assistance organizations, qualified for criminal justice grants, and gone into business. Three such groups were encountered in our field research: EMPLOY-EX and the Colorado Pinto Project, both in Denver, and EFEC (Efforts from Ex-Convicts) in Washington, D.C. All three are focused on job finding and offer much the same range of services—counseling, training, placement—as the other community projects.[115]

Such exoffender groups have some important advantages. They make some worthwhile jobs available to exoffenders, they have proved their ability to gain community support and cooperation, and they obviously relate well to their clients and are more likely to be listened to than are less compatible counselors. They do well, as one federal official remarked, if they add administrative ability and leadership to these other advantages.

Halfway Houses for Parolees

The term halfway house has various meanings. It may be a "halfway-in house," meaning a shelter or crashpad for runaways or other ill-adjusted but not-yet-criminal youths. The term may also mean "halfway-out"—a residence for work releasees, an improvement over prison life but still a form of incarceration. Parolees who have a "demonstrated need for closer control and more concentrated supportive assistance than can be offered through regular supervision" may also benefit from living in such an institution.[116]

Four halfway houses used by parolees as well as other types of offenders were visited in the course of our field research.[117] In all such projects parolees are only partly living in the free community. Even in the program with the most freedom they are in a government-sponsored institution,

115. See "EFEC Expansion Project: Final Report to Office of Criminal Justice Plans and Analysis" (April 1974; processed), p. 9.

116. U.S. Bureau of Prisons, *The Residential Center: Corrections in the Community* (GPO, 1971), p. 2. For more detailed guidance on planning and management, see John M. McCartt and Thomas J. Mangogna, *Guidelines and Standards for Halfway Houses and Residential Treatment Centers* (U.S. Department of Justice, Law Enforcement Assistance Administration, 1973); Richard L. Rachin, "So You Want to Open a Halfway House," *Federal Probation*, vol. 36 (March 1972), pp. 30–37; and U.S. Comptroller General, *Federal Guidance Needed.*

117. They were Prep House in Sacramento, Macon Transitional Center in Georgia, Crittenden Community Center in Oakland, California, and Project SAFE in Madison, Wisconsin. Three halfway houses for work releasees in Atlanta, Denver, and Los Angeles were also visited.

subject to rules, and under scrutiny. In the others they are mixed in with work-releasees (who are still technically in prison) in facilities where a custody-comes-first attitude has to prevail. It is arguable whether this is good for parolees. The few evaluative studies made of halfway houses indicate either that they have no effect on recidivism or that they actually show an increase.[118]

A parolee is not likely to be in a halfway house unless he has already had trouble making it outside. He needs shelter, guidance, a little control, but will this help him learn independent living? The answer is yes in some cases, no in others. His association with work-releasees, who are under greater control, can also be either good or bad. Certainly the staff must place constant emphasis upon self-determination and independence of action. The outcome probably depends on the individual personality, and it is all too doubtful that either the parole officer or the halfway house director has the time or skill to give the parolee the best kind of guidance.

Comprehensive Multiservice Projects

Every community project mentioned so far has more than one goal and offers more than one kind of service. Some facilities go much further: their avowed purpose is to meet the many and diverse needs of different kinds of offenders.

Reachout Today, for example, is a Minneapolis project offering both youthful and adult offenders six kinds of service: "Hotline . . . Crisis Intervention"—advice and help at any hour to head off crises; "Alternatives" —preparation of an agreement concerning activities during probation and preparation of parole plans; "Education and employment"—counseling and referral; "Chemical Dependency Counseling"—which supports the first three; "Detached Workers"—referral of clients to other community agencies, and expediting of needed services from them; "Living Learning Center"—a therapeutic community/halfway house.[119]

Other projects in San Diego[120] and Louisville, Kentucky,[121] both coali-

118. Letter to the author from Robert Martinson, Dec. 17, 1974. One study of a California halfway house for problem parolees and probationers may yield significant results, but early research resulted in a "too soon to say" conclusion. See California Council on Criminal Justice, *Evaluation of Crime Control Programs in California: A Review* (Sacramento, April 1973), pp. 113–17.

119. "Reachout Today" (Minneapolis, n.d.)

120. See California Council, *Evaluation of Crime Control Programs*, pp. 119–23.

121. See James L. Hurd, Jack L. Fevurly, and Elgin L. Crull, "Organized against Crime: A Full-Service Clearinghouse," *Federal Probation*, vol. 38 (December 1974), pp. 16–20.

tions of several cooperating agencies, offer the same sorts of services. Again, results have been mixed.

Volunteer Aid

Parolees may need different kinds of advice and guidance than they can get from their parole officers or the various kinds of community facilities just discussed. Their problems are multiple and difficult, and they lack, in many cases, the competence, enterprise, and perseverance to find help on their own. This has led to the creation of volunteer organizations in which citizens befriend and help parolees on a one-to-one basis.

In a typical case the volunteer visits the offender several times while he is still in prison. He makes friends; listens to the inmate's troubles; may get him a magazine or a hobby kit; helps him understand parole and work-release rules; and may initiate some job-finding contacts. As a friend, but a disinterested friend (he has no "angle," no axe to grind, no power over his "client"), the volunteer can provide a kind of support and give a kind of advice that neither the parole officer nor the inmate's relatives can give. Many volunteers also have professional backgrounds that are helpful—bankers, nurses, social scientists, small businessmen, teachers. They are trained by their organizations to work cooperatively with jailers and parole officers, to understand correctional procedures, and to observe rules.

Examples of organizations providing such services include: the American Bar Association's National Volunteer Parole Aide Program, in which attorneys are encouraged to help offenders, but not to give legal advice;[122] Job Therapy, Inc., of Washington State;[123] Offender Aid and Restoration of Virginia;[124] and Amicus, Inc., of Minneapolis.[125] Like other types of assistance projects discussed earlier, these organizations cannot be appraised with any confidence because their statistical reporting was not designed with rigorous evaluation in mind.[126]

122. *The Parole Release* (bulletin of the National Volunteer Parole Aide Program, American Bar Association, Washington, D.C.), various issues.

123. See n. 114 above. See also Donald Thornton, "Citizens Assisting Convicts," *Washington Post*, Oct. 7, 1973.

124. "A History of OAR of Virginia" (n.d.; processed). For evaluative comments, see "OAR Volunteer Program Gets Positive Review," *Criminal Justice Newsletter*, vol. 7 (Jan. 5, 1976), p. 5. The author of this book serves as an OAR volunteer.

125. Barbara West and Frank Sweeney, "Amicus, Inc.: An Evaluation" (Minneapolis: Minnesota Center for Sociological Research, September 1974; processed).

126. A systematic evaluation of Job Therapy, Inc., recognizes this difficulty in re-

Evaluation and Alternatives

Parole assistance is a complex, ill-organized group of services: some public, some private; some intended only for parolees, some for all ex-offenders, some for any citizens in need; some permanent, some expiring with the grants that spawned them. Multiple services are needed to deal with the multiple problems of parolees, and the examples just cited convey an impression of the scope and approach of community service facilities. Unfortunately, the situation is still far from satisfactory; there is no clear evidence that such services meet the needs of exoffenders in their localities or that their work has any significant relationship to the reduction of recidivism. Nevertheless, in the absence of any more comprehensive program, efforts to help parolees should certainly continue and efforts to evaluate their success should be refined.

The Parole Officer as Helper

To return to the parole officer, he can be expected to give little effective assistance, for two main reasons. First, he is the parolee's overseer and adversary, the symbol to his client of a policing society, and he is avoided or misled by the parolees most likely to get into trouble. "Any attempt at a viable social work relationship between officers and parolees is handicapped because of the non-voluntary relationship between staff and client."[127] Second, it isn't practical. Chapter 6 has shown how little time the parole officer can devote to each parolee for *any* purpose. Further, the time he can give may not be at the hour when it is needed. Elliot Studt's seven-year Parole Action Study emphasized the unrealism of expecting the parole officer to help when difficulties arise:

When the parolee does experience some emergency situation in connection with which he would like the advice or help of the agent, he quite often finds it difficult to reach the agent [parole officer]; and because of the agent's working conditions, there is often a lapse of time before the agent responds. In consequence, when the agent does get to the parolee in response to a call, the problem is frequently already resolved, less urgent for the parolee, or has

---

porting results that are encouraging but vulnerable to methodological challenge. Alfred Gordon Lawyer, "The Effects of Social Attention on Recidivism," *Journal of Volunteers with Delinquents*, vol. 1 (Spring 1972), pp. 2–21 and appendix.

127. Robert E. Wolin, "After Release: The Parolee in Society," *St. John's Law Review*, vol. 48 (October 1973), p. 17.

escalated into big trouble requiring crisis measures rather than the step by step problem solving possible when the situation was still fluid and uncrystallized. Parole is a 24-hour a day, seven days a week, matter for the parolee; the agent's availability is not co-extensive with the status he is managing. . . .[128]

This situation results in uneven work:

Given such conditions for agent-parolee interaction, it is not surprising that the outstanding impression about helping activities in parole, gained through weeks of observation, was one of sporadic effort. There was a notable lack of concentration of such activities within the work week of any given agent. The process for bringing together identified need with specific problem-solving resources seemed very haphazard, with much depending on the parolee's willingness to reveal a problem and make a request, much on the agent's availability at the time of parolee readiness, and still more on the agent's capacity to produce an appropriate and effective response . . . *Regardless of the agent's skill and conscientiousness the strains in the conditions governing the helping interaction seemed to be toward ad hoc, reactive behavior on the part of the agent and sporadic use of help by the parolee.*[129]

We have also noted that the parole officer is judged by his superiors on a number of bureaucratic criteria, and that these are more likely to influence his decisions on how to use his time than are the parolee's needs for help.

Success Factors

It has been stated that success on parole (though variously and unsatisfactorily measured) is associated with age, with employment, and with supportive family relationships. This is not to say that such factors necessarily *cause* parole success, though they may. It may only mean that an offender who is ready to succeed on parole may also be mature, work steadily, and stay in touch with his family. As the final chapter indicates, there is real need for more rigorous experimentation in assisting exoffenders so that future programs can be better designed to meet their needs. But both our present knowledge and our lack of knowledge of what works argue for offering as wide a range of readily available services as possible. The parolee who is ready to make it can take whatever help he needs; the parolee who is not ready—who is unstable, deceptive, fearful, angry, dependent—needs all kinds of help to keep him out of trouble as long as possible. Perhaps the assistance he gets will help him get a foot on the ladder in his climb to a crime-free way of life.

128. Studt, *Surveillance and Service*, p. 111.
129. Ibid., pp. 111–12 (emphasis added).

Criteria for Services

To achieve these purposes, aid to parolees should meet these criteria:

Be *known*. The parolee must know where to go, or where to find out where to go.

Be *open for business*. Problems arise at 4:00 A.M., and guidance or temporary remedies must be available around the clock.

Be *reachable*—located near clients or with provision for transportation.

Be *comprehensive*. Whatever the difficulty—money, drugs or alcohol, family problems—a remedial service should exist.

Be *trusted*. The parolee must feel that he will not be punished or threatened when he reveals a problem.

Be *voluntary*. The offender has been coerced and told what to do for long enough: forced treatment is unlikely to be effective treatment. In the free community he must make his own choices, and compelling his participation will delay his rehabilitation.[130]

These standards will be difficult to meet if government and community agencies continue to provide specialized services during a standard workday, tied to a coercive relationship, parole supervision. They can be achieved if public policies are changed and if agencies and foundations that make financial grants provide appropriate incentives.

130. The case for self-determination has been strongly made in recent articles by a sociology professor and a supervising probation officer and by a federal judge. See Alexander B. Smith and Louis Berlin, "Self-Determination in Welfare and Corrections: Is There a Limit?" *Federal Probation*, vol. 38 (December 1974), pp. 3–7; Lawrence W. Pierce, "Rehabilitation in Corrections: A Reassessment," *Federal Probation*, vol. 38 (June 1974), pp. 14–19. See also Citizens' Inquiry, *Prison without Walls*, p. 179.

CHAPTER EIGHT

How Good Is Parole?

EARLIER CHAPTERS have raised doubts about how much sense there is in the process of parole. The hearing and decision procedures have been shown to be on the whole cursory, unreliable, demeaning, and of questionable efficacy. Parole surveillance has been shown to produce an unsatisfactory human relationship without proven effect. Parole revocation, influenced by bureaucratic considerations, is an unfair process. Parole assistance, impaired by its linkage with surveillance and revocation, may do some good, but there is little evidence to this effect. But because release, surveillance, and assistance are late interventions in a person's criminal history, parole can be only partially blamed or credited for outcomes—principally the degree of recidivism—that have a complex of causes. So it is difficult to evaluate the effectiveness of parole by itself.

What to Evaluate?

Any evaluation must begin by reviewing the goals of parole. The first and most frequently cited are to protect society and to help the parolee.[1] This means protecting society from crime and helping the parolee toward a crime-free life, in short, to reduce criminal behavior. No one could quarrel with this goal, but efforts to achieve it are based on the theories of incapacitation and rehabilitation, with their consequent difficulties and costs: preventive incarceration of prisoners who might not return to crime and the errors, waste motion, and false hopes of "treatment" programs.

There are other purposes, as the Standards and Goals Commission showed: fairness to the offender, appropriateness of punishment, and support of other parts of the criminal justice system.[2] The first two rest on the retribution theory, or "just deserts" concept. The last is less a purpose than a fact of life: parole authorities, police, and correctional officials obviously have to cooperate because they deal with the same people. In practice,

1. See chap. 1, pp. 1–2.
2. See chap. 1, p. 2.

parole authorities are guided by a mixture of these often-conflicting purposes. This results in failure to achieve any of them to a satisfactory degree, an inevitable difficulty but one that could be lessened by a greater effort to order priorities.

The confusion of purpose that pervades theories of crime and imprisonment is also present in the rationales underlying parole. Our examination of the parole process has shown that these theories, long reflected in laws and court decisions, are untenable in practice. The three main theories are:

Grace. This expresses the idea that the parolee could be imprisoned for his full sentence and that the government lets him out as a privilege, which can be readily withdrawn. The theory ignores the impracticality, both financially and humanly, of keeping all offenders in prison.[3] Courts are now perceptibly moving toward treating parolees as if they have a *right* not to be deprived of their liberty without due process.

Contract-consent. Here the government bargains with the offender, releasing him in return for his agreement to be bound by parole conditions. It is, of course, no bargain: "The convict cannot determine the conditions of his release; and his consent cannot affect it."[4]

Custody. This idea denies that the parolee is at liberty; he is in the custody of officers of the government. But

few courts, if any, are prepared to adhere to that theory for all parole problems. The result has been to recognize the parolee's liberty for some purposes, and to deny it for others. For instance, if the parolee commits another crime while on parole, the parolee will be found at liberty in order to permit prosecution under the laws of another sovereign.[5]

... The confused application of the theory of custody reflects the basic illogic of holding that a man can be at liberty while being in custody.[6]

The fact that parole supervision is actually exercised for only a few minutes a month exposes the custody theory as palpably nonsensical.

Measures and Methods for Evaluation

The primary problem in evaluating parole systems is to find measures and methods that show the extent to which parolees refrain from criminal

3. Michael Gottesman and Lewis J. Hecker, "Parole: A Critique of Its Legal Foundations and Conditions," *New York University Law Review*, vol. 38 (June 1963), pp. 703–07.

4. Ibid., p. 709.

5. Ibid., p. 713.

6. Ibid., p. 720.

behavior as a result of what happens in the parole system. The criterion of criminal behavior is necessary to keep us from confusing the reform of criminals with any success they may have in work, school, marriage, personal habits, and other areas that may be generally thought of as part of success on parole. Community agencies and parole officers can, on occasion, take credit for aiding parolees to become more satisfactorily employed, better educated, more solvent, and better family people. These are gratifying human achievements, but the emphasis of parole success must be on staying out of trouble. An exoffender can be unemployed, ignorant, promiscuous, and drunk but still a success as far as the criminal justice system is concerned if he commits no crime.

Recidivism: How to Count It?

Since criminal behavior is the principal concern, the main criterion has to be recidivism, defined as a tendency to relapse into a previous condition or mode of behavior, specifically criminal behavior. However, recidivism can mean many things and can be based on various factors, which helps explain why recidivism rates vary from such figures as 80 percent down to 5 percent. The figure arrived at depends upon how one counts three things: the event (arrest, conviction, parole revocation), the duration of the period in which the measurement is made, and the seriousness of the behavior to be counted.[7] A fairly typical recidivism analysis is based on reimprisonment within one or two years, either after conviction of a felony or after parole revocation because of a technical violation.

THE EVENT. Arrests are used in some studies as indicators of criminal behavior: "If he was arrested he was up to something," so the thinking goes. However, their use as a reliable measure assumes more consistency in police performance than really exists. One community arrests more people on suspicion than another. There are times when police sweep the streets; other times when they turn away. There are also, of course, enormous variations from one police officer to another. Arrests, if faithfully reported, may overstate crime when not followed by charges, indictment, and conviction. Yet they may not be faithfully reported. One scholarly analysis points to gross inaccuracies and underreporting.[8] A study by the U.S. Gen-

7. National Advisory Commission on Criminal Justice Standards and Goals, *Corrections* (GPO, 1973), p. 512.

8. Susan Bradley Long, "Evaluating Correctional Research: Estimation and Implications of Measurement Error in Arrest Data" (M.A. thesis, University of Washington, 1972).

eral Accounting Office also found that arrests resulting in return to prison in one state were underreported by 66 percent.[9] There is no assurance that overarresting and underreporting cancel each other out, only a disquieting awareness of a lot of ambiguity in the figures.

Reimprisonment figures are normally reliable and accurate. The problem with them as a measure of parole success, as discussed in chapter 6, is the inclusion of parole revocations for reasons other than convictions. If a parolee is reincarcerated for chronic insolence, for traffic violations, or on suspicion of having committed a crime for which he could not be convicted, he has not necessarily relapsed into criminal behavior. To argue that he has, as many a parole officer does, is to apply a different standard of proof to the parolee than to other persons.[10] Another problem, also discussed in chapter 6, is the responsiveness of parole violation rates to individual caprice and bureaucratic pressures—another instance of criminal injustice.[11]

This leads into the use of convictions as a measure, a gauge that is faulty but fair. It is faulty because a person who committed a crime may be acquitted for reasons of insufficient evidence, weak prosecution, technical flaws, or an eccentric jury, or because an innocent person may plead guilty in a plea bargaining situation. It is fair because the courtroom is where society sits in judgment on a defendant and where he enjoys due process protections; only conviction *proves* him a criminal. A government criminologist interviewed in this study disagrees, arguing that arrests and revocations are more reliable indicators of criminal behavior than are convictions. He contends that the parolee was arrested or his parole was revoked because he was doing something illegal, yet he may not be convicted in court. The answer is, of course, that he may *not* have done something illegal. So all three measures are subject to uncertainty, error, and possible manipulation. Conviction, however, is the most careful, responsible, and equitable measure.

9. Cited in an internal evaluative report of the Office of Policy Evaluation and Research, Manpower Administration, U.S. Department of Labor, concerning the "Model Employment Program" mentioned in chapter 7.

10. In a recent case a state supreme court said the standard should be different. A parolee was acquitted of assault charges in a criminal prosecution, but the court upheld use of the same evidence to revoke his parole, holding that there was a difference in burden of proof. *Standlee* v. *Smith*, Washington Supreme Court, Jan. 31, 1974, *Prison Law Reporter*, vol. 3 (July 1974), pp. 216–18.

11. See also James O. Robison, "Unraveling Delinquency: Caseworker Orientation and Client Characterization" (D.Crim. dissertation, University of California, Berkeley, 1971), esp. pp. 105–09.

DURATION. How long is a noncriminal? That is, does a parolee have to stay free of crime for the rest of his life to be counted a success? This would be as unreasonable as holding a physician responsible for a patient's life-long health after two years of examination and treatment. The one-year or two-year postrelease period used in some studies is based both on a wish to keep the study or tabulation within manageable limits and on the frequent finding that parolees are more likely to fail (however this is defined) in the first and second years under supervision. The former reason one can sympathize with yet deplore. The latter tends to be true but is greatly over-emphasized in typical recidivism studies because of some technical statistical traps.[12] There is both practicality and merit in the recommendation of the Standards and Goals Commission that recidivism be measured "for three years after release of the offender from all correctional supervision."[13]

SERIOUSNESS. This is the third dimension of recidivism—the degree, intensity, or severity of criminal behavior. How bad must behavior be to be counted as criminal for this purpose? Is a parolee a recidivist if he engages in a tavern brawl; if he drives into a lamppost; if he has been missing for two months? The answers vary from one government to another and from one researcher to another. The severity is usually defined and measured by the penalties imposed. California, for example, in its work unit program lists jail sentences of less than ninety days and misdemeanor probations under "favorable parole outcomes." Missing parolees who have been at large less than six months are in the same category.[14] Similarly, the Moberg-Ericson recidivism outcome index counts as a "marginal success" a parolee who gets a jail sentence of ninety days or less or a fine of between $25 and $100. It counts an absconder who is wanted for a misdemeanor as a "marginal failure."[15] This use of penalties to measure seriousness is sim-

12. Notably the failure to analyze the proportion of parole violators among total offenders in a specified period of time following release. See John E. Berecochea, Alfred N. Himelson, and Donald E. Miller, "The Risk of Failure during the Early Parole Period: A Methodological Note," *Journal of Criminal Law, Criminology and Police Science*, vol. 63 (March 1972), pp. 93–97.

13. National Advisory Commission, *Corrections*, pp. 512–13, 528–29; and *Criminal Justice System* (GPO, 1973), pp. 93–94. Less meritorious, for reasons cited above, is the commission's companion recommendation that technical violations be included in the measure.

14. California Department of Corrections, Parole and Community Services Division, *A Report to the Legislature on the Work Unit Parole Program* (Sacramento, 1971), p. 19.

15. David O. Moberg and Richard C. Ericson, "A New Recidivism Outcome Index," *Federal Probation*, vol. 36 (June 1972), pp. 53–54. For other helpful discussions of recidivism criteria, see W. O. Jenkins, *Prolegomena to the Measurement and*

ple, understandable, and widely used. It is based, however, on the questionable assumption that the punishment always fits the crime. The discussion of sentencing in chapter 2 raised doubts on this point. The problem for parole evaluation is insoluble short of reform of criminal codes and sentencing practices, and there are at present no alternatives.

There is no easy way to simplify the complex human issues in measuring seriousness. For example, a parolee who is convicted of a misdemeanor and serves two months in the county jail can certainly be said to have relapsed into criminal behavior. Suppose, however, that he is paroled in 1970, then serves time in jail for the misdemeanor in that same year, but stays out of trouble for the next three years. Would he not then be considered a success?

How Useful Is Recidivism?

Whoever evaluates parole picks his own measures of success or failure, whether or not he uses the word recidivism. On the basis of the present analysis, the most defensible indicators of a return to criminal behavior would be conviction of a new felony, of a misdemeanor punishable by ninety days or more imprisonment, or of more than one misdemeanor whose penalties add up to 90 days or more; all this to apply within three years after release. The ninety-day figure is arbitrary. The longer the sentence for an offense, the easier it is to justify a definition of criminality for the offense; a shorter sentence means a harsher definition. Other criteria of recidivism can be used, and some may be more sensitive than others to the impact of treatment on offenders.[16] Whatever the criteria, they should be specifically defined and consistently applied.

What about absconders? It can be argued that they are not necessarily engaged in crime but may have had urgent and confidential personal reasons for going elsewhere, possibly including the discomfort of being under

---

Assessment of Human Behavior (Montgomery, Ala.: Rehabilitation Research Foundation, Experimental Manpower Laboratory for Corrections, August 1971), esp. pp. 7–8; and A. D. Witherspoon, E. K. deValera, and W. O. Jenkins, *The Law Encounter Severity Scale (LESS): A Criterion for Criminal Behavior and Recidivism* (Experimental Manpower Laboratory for Corrections, August 1973). See also Clarence C. Sherwood, "The Testability of Correctional Goals," in Joint Commission on Correctional Manpower and Training, *Research in Correctional Rehabilitation* (December 1967), pp. 42–50.

16. Letter to the author from Prof. Daniel Glaser, Jan. 8, 1975.

supervision. The contrary argument is that they would not disappear unless they were concealing something illegal or improper. Without evidence pointing one way or the other all one can do is count absconders separately.

The question of who is a recidivist may simply be avoided, as in the statistics of the National Council on Crime and Delinquency's Uniform Parole Reports. They set forth the number and percentage of parolees who have been continued on parole, returned to prison as technical violators, recommitted to prison with new major convictions, or absconded. The reader must draw his own conclusions.

Readers of this study may have wondered how many parolees are committing crimes that the authorities do not know about. After all, at least twice as many crimes occur as are reported;[17] some of them are surely committed by parolees. After an original and elaborate mathematical analysis, David Greenberg concludes that released prisoners on the average will commit between 0.5 and 3.33 index offenses (the seven major crimes reported to the FBI) per year.[18] Using an alternate method of computation, he estimates 2.0 such crimes per parolee per year.[19] These are uncomfortable figures, although Greenberg shows that they have little effect on overall crime rates.[20] In any event, conclusions can be based only on the basis of what is *known* about parolees' behavior.

Whether or not the word is used, recidivism is a useful measure of parole, or of prisons' efforts to rehabilitate, or of any other aspect of criminal justice *only* under carefully defined conditions. It is almost meaningless to know that 50 percent of the felons paroled in a state in 1972 were rearrested or that 40 percent were returned to prison without having more specific information. It is also misleading to compare such figures with, say, 60 percent rearrested or 50 percent reimprisoned in another state. There may be great differences in police practices, the characteristics of inmates released, parole revocation policies, and many other variables.

17. President's Commission on Law Enforcement and the Administration of Justice, *Task Force Report. Crime and Its Impact: An Assessment* (GPO, 1967), p. 17; also U.S. Law Enforcement Assistance Administration, National Criminal Justice Information and Statistics Service, *Crime in the Nation's Five Largest Cities: Advance Report* (GPO, April 1974), p. 1.

18. It should be remembered that not all index offenses are heinous. They include larceny-theft and auto theft, both of which may involve articles of modest value.

19. David F. Greenberg, "The Incapacitative Effect of Imprisonment," *Law and Society Review*, vol. 9 (Summer 1975), pp. 541–80.

20. Ibid., pp. 569–72.

Likewise, citizens may be either comforted or alarmed by the federal bureau of prisons' finding that "over 67 percent of federal offenders released in 1970 were not recidivists during the two year period following release";[21] or the Uniform Parole Reports figure that about 73 percent of parolees nationwide had neither returned to prison nor absconded after two years.[22] Such percentages are useful only as they are compared to something else, and are related to specific objectives.

Parole Evaluation Studies

Parole release decision making can be and has been evaluated by comparing the recidivism of parolees with that of mandatory releasees (prisoners who have completed their terms minus good time and who, in some states, are placed under the supervision of parole officers). Such research should show how "correct" the board was in its release decisions compared with the nondecisional release of the other group. The board would be considered "wrong" when a parolee commits a crime or possibly disappears. (The board can always defend itself, however: "Even though he went wrong after release, we were right in not releasing him earlier."[23])

Parole versus Mandatory Release

Such research is sure to show that parolees do better than mandatory releasees if the parole board applies the predictive data discussed in chapter 4—that is, if it paroles inmates with characteristics that correlate with measures of success on parole. The parolees may do better yet if the board carefully denies parole for any inmate about whose chances of success they are dubious.

The analysis will also reveal how the board was "wrong" in the opposite way, by keeping in prisoners who would probably have made it on the outside and who eventually do so on mandatory release. Here again the conclusion is not beyond doubt. It can be argued that the offenders needed to stay in prison until they achieved a successful level of rehabilitation, though this is a weak argument in view of research findings on the ineffec-

21. U.S. Bureau of Prisons, "Success and Failure of Federal Offenders Released in 1970" (GPO, January 1974; processed), p. 1.

22. P. 106 above.

23. Peter B. Hoffman, "Mandatory Release: A Measure of Type II Error," *Criminology*, vol. 11 (February 1974), p. 543.

tiveness of prison rehabilitation programs. It can also be argued that an unknown number of crimes was prevented by detaining the prisoners.

Research of this general type, though lacking some of its elements, was conducted by Peter B. Hoffman in New York State. He studied all adult male offenders under indeterminate sentences for robbery, burglary, or manslaughter originally released by parole or mandatory release during 1968 (1,135 in number). Each individual was followed up after one year and classified in one of these categories: no violation of parole or canceled violations; technical violation or absconding; or new arrest. Hoffman's results on parole outcome by type of release show:[24]

Status	Percent of parolees	Percent of mandatory releasees
No violations or canceled violations	74	53
Technical violation or absconding	12	19
New arrest	14	28

Two important findings are clear: parolees do better; yet a majority of mandatory releasees "completed the first year of supervision without delinquency."[25]

Hoffman later computed ratios of "Type I errors" (a parole board releasing a man who fails) to "Type II errors" (failing to release a man who succeeds) for each of the types of crimes studied. For example sixty-seven paroled robbers (with no narcotics history) were delinquent on parole, but fifty-one robbers who came out on mandatory release were not delinquent. Thus the ratio is 1.3:1, or 1.3 let-them-out mistakes to every 1 keep-them-in mistake. Hoffman says that a higher proportion of inmates released by parole tends to increase the number of parole violators but decrease the number of Type II errors. Such an analysis can be made on a crime-by-crime basis as an aid to policy making by parole boards.[26]

This is original and helpful research, but it is questionable to rely upon arrests and technical violations as measures since they are subject to personal and bureaucratic caprice and to local variations. The researcher can assume that the bureaucratic factor will apply equally to parolees and mandatory releasees, but the California and Iowa studies discussed above[27] call this assumption into question. It must be recognized that the parole bureaucracy *can* rig recidivism rates.

24. Ibid., p. 549.
25. Ibid., p. 547.
26. Ibid., pp. 547–53.
27. See pp. 116–17.

Evaluating Parole Supervision

To assess the effectiveness of the policing and assistance functions of parole officers, additional controlled studies are needed. The research should:

1. Randomly select two significantly large, comparable groups of prisoners (call them A and B) selected for parole release in the same jurisdiction in the same time period, comprising, say, all male adult felons paroled in a medium-large state in a year.

2. Give Group A the normal surveillance and service provided by the parole system. Give Group B no surveillance at all but provide information about government and community agencies prepared to assist them with problems of jobs, housing, finance, or personal problems. Their use of such agencies would be entirely voluntary. An alternative approach could be to permit Group B to come to the parole staff (or a special part of the staff) on a voluntary basis for counseling and referral.

3. Determine, over a period of three years, the proportion of each group convicted of new felonies or of misdemeanors punishable by ninety days or more incarceration. (Other time periods or measures could be substituted.)

How to count absconders is a problem in such research. In the control group they have to be considered as one type of failure in parole supervision. Members of Group B, however, are not required to stay in touch. Any requirements for reporting in or notifying of change of address would have an element of compulsion or monitoring. The only solution is to report the number of Group A absconders as a separate category. For Group B only evidence of serious criminal behavior would be considered.

To my knowledge, there is no completed research that compares parole supervision with nonsupervision in this way. The University of Connecticut Law School, however, is making a study of two hundred felons given early releases from prison by court order. They will not be subjected to parole supervision but will have assistance made available to them on a voluntary basis from counselors of the Department of Corrections.[28]

A completed study in California is helpful and relevant, although it lacks some of the features suggested above. This analysis covered three groups of male felons, all of whom were discharged from parole super-

28. "CT to Monitor 200 Inmates Freed by Court Order," *Criminal Justice Newsletter*, vol. 5 (Sept. 23, 1974), p. 4.

vision during the months of July through October 1971: 341 men released from prison on parole a year earlier and discharged from parole because they had completed the year without arrests or abscondings; 413 men paroled earlier and discharged after two years of parole supervision uninterrupted by any suspensions; 143 men discharged from parole because their sentences had expired.[29] The three groups were followed for a year to find out if they had any known criminal involvement.[30]

The results showed that of the total of 897 offenders only 42, or 4.7 percent, had unfavorable outcomes. There were no significant differences among the three groups except that the sentence-expired men had fewer clean records, the most arrests, and the most short-term jailings—none of these being counted as unfavorable outcomes.[31] The outcomes also were unrelated to the offenders' backgrounds, type of parole supervision, past records, use of narcotics, or the violence or nonviolence of their offenses.[32]

The outstandingly significant result is that an offender who neither absconded from parole nor was arrested for one year while on parole had a very high probability of staying out of difficulty with the law for the next year after discharge.[33] It may be argued that this demonstrates the effectiveness of parole supervision, but the authors of this analysis say:

On a somewhat more conjectural level and in order to avoid an incorrect inference from this presentation, there is nothing in this study (or any other known study) which would preclude the discharge from parole of those who do *not* meet the criterion of remaining arrest-free during their first year on parole. *Indeed, nothing in this (or any other known) study indicates that parole supervision is effective in controlling criminal behavior of the parolee.* Rather, the data provided in this and other studies indicate that parolees who remain free of criminal involvement for a year (or more) are not likely to subsequently become criminally involved, be they continued on parole or discharged.[34]

Useful as this study is, it unfortunately does not permit a direct com-

29. Dorothy R. Jaman, Lawrence A. Bennett, and John E. Berecochea, *Early Discharge From Parole: Policy, Practice, and Outcome*, California Department of Corrections, Research Report no. 51 (Sacramento, April 1974), pp. 1, 19.

30. Outcomes were considered favorable if there was no difficulty or booking by authorities; if there was release after arrest, fine, bail forfeited, misdemeanor probation, jail term of less than ninety days, or jail all suspended. Unfavorable categories included jail sentence of ninety days or more, felony probation, death in commission of a crime, or commitment to prison or to the California Rehabilitation Center. Ibid., p. 19.

31. Ibid., pp. 22–25.

32. Ibid., p. 29.

33. Ibid., p. 31. In interpreting this study one should keep in mind that arrests are *not* considered to be proof of criminal behavior.

34. Ibid., p. 33 (emphasis added).

parison of offenders under parole supervision with offenders set entirely free. More such comparative studies are needed.

Cost Considerations

Believers in parole are accustomed to point out how much less it costs to keep an offender on parole than in prison. The figures bear this out emphatically, as table 8-1 shows. The differences between prison and parole costs are impressive, but it would be a mistake to treat them as pure

Table 8-1. *Prison and Parole Costs, Selected States and Years*

Year	Government	Cost per man per day (dollars)		Prison/parole ratio
		Prison	Parole	
1966	Average of 49 states, District of Columbia, and Puerto Rico	5.24	0.88	6:1
1971	Massachusetts	20.00	0.85	24:1
1972	Maine	12.80	0.81	16:1
1973	Georgia	8.45	0.95	9:1
1973	Wisconsin	18.60	1.48	13:1

Sources: Average, Michael J. Hindelang and others, *Sourcebook of Criminal Justice Statistics* (U.S. Law Enforcement Assistance Administration, August 1973), pp. 123, 425. Massachusetts, Massachusetts Department of Correction, "Some Statistics Relevant to the Two-Thirds Parole Law" (February 1972; processed), p. 2. Maine, Palmer-Paulson Associates, *Analysis '72* (Chicago: Palmer-Paulson Associates, Inc., 1973), p. 29. Georgia, author's correspondence with Georgia Department of Offender Rehabilitation. Wisconsin, field interviews.

savings. The sources of these figures do not say how they are computed, but it is probable that gross annual operating costs are divided by the number of offenders. Many components of the costs of prisons will continue even if some offenders are paroled and not replaced. Appreciable savings are not realized unless the prison population is so reduced that an institution is closed, a wing emptied, or staff laid off. Even then the savings may (and probably should) be diverted to some means of making prison life more tolerable or constructive, or to community alternatives to imprisonment.[35]

35. For a technical discussion of the relationship of prison costs (including capital costs) to inmate population, see Michael Block, "Costs, Scale Economies, and other Economic Concepts: A Case Study" (Washington, D.C.: American Bar Association, 1975). See also Carl W. Nelson, "Cost-Benefit Analysis and Alternatives to Incarceration," *Federal Probation*, vol. 39 (December 1975), pp. 45–50.

There are clearly other cost factors in parole outside of the prison and parole bureaucracies. A job-related analysis of costs in Maine points out that 141 paroled prisoners earned over $120,000 in a nine-month period and paid nearly $14,000 in federal and state taxes on these wages.[36] The costs of keeping these men in prison ($269,478), plus unknown costs of welfare payments to their families, are contrasted with the costs of parole supervision ($17,000), less the $14,000 in paid-in taxes.[37] But this is a sketchy analysis, based on questionable assumptions. Furthermore, the average wage earned was $95 a month, which will not take many people off welfare. A similar report from Ohio says that "3,000 Ohio men and women who completed their parole in 1972 earned $13.7 million in wages that year, of which $2.7 million reverted to the public in state and federal taxes. It would have cost $9 million per year to keep these 300 people in prison where they would have accomplished little or no productive labor for the community and paid no taxes."[38]

Such statements suggest only part of the relative advantages and expenses of parole as compared to imprisonment. In the literature consulted for this study there were no professional cost-benefit analyses of these factors. Such studies have been made of pretrial diversion[39] and of probation,[40] and could well be made of the discharge of parolees from supervision; this has been done in a small way in the California parole discharge study.[41]

Sophisticated analysis of the costs and benefits of incarceration and its alternatives is beyond the scope of the present study. It is obviously cheaper to parole rather than to imprison, to discharge rather than to supervise—unless these alternatives can be proved to result in increased crime that is more costly than the punishments and remedies of the correctional system. Cost-benefit research will throw more light on the entire problem.

36. Palmer-Paulson, *Analysis '72*, pp. 28–29.
37. Ibid.
38. *The Parole Release* (bulletin of the National Volunteer Parole Aide Program, American Bar Association, Washington, D.C.) (July 1973), p. 3.
39. John F. Holahan, *A Benefit-Cost Analysis of Project Crossroads* (National Committee for Children and Youth, December 1970).
40. Janice Holve, "An Evaluation of the Effects on State and Local Costs of the California Probation Subsidy Program" (University of California, Davis, Center on Administration of Criminal Justice, March 1972; processed); Robert Lee Fraizer and others, "Incarceration and Adult Felon Probation in Texas: A Cost Comparison," *Criminal Justice Monograph*, vol. 4 (1973), Sam Houston State University.
41. Jaman, Bennett, and Berecochea, *Early Discharge*, pp. 25–26.

Even without such research, supporters of the parole system argue that it would work better if more money were allotted to it. This would buy more help for overburdened parole board members and lower case loads for parole officers. This is a traditional solution offered for many problems of governmental management: if something works poorly, spend more on it. The solution will not work here. The problems of parole, as we have frequently urged, are problems of logic, concepts, acculturation, goals, and methods, not of resources. Tripling the budgets, even if this were politically feasible, will not solve the problems.[42]

Should Parole Continue?

Rationality and human values, as well as crime statistics and dollar costs, must enter into any final evaluation of parole. Defenders and critics alike soon find that figures are not enough and that ethical and political values have a strong influence on policy choices. In this respect the question of whether to continue the present institutions and practices of parole is like other difficult questions of public policy—whether to maintain, for example, foreign military assistance or agricultural and maritime subsidies. The evidence is never all in and the outcome never beyond doubt, but policy choices must nonetheless be made.

The information and reasoning presented in this book point to a new and different model of parole, which can be considered and tested in whole or in part by governments where it is possible politically. The elements of the model, and the reasons for proposing them, have been delineated in earlier chapters, but a final summarization is in order.

Release without Parole

Some favorable things can be said about the work of parole boards. First, they release some offenders from the destructive environment of prison earlier than would otherwise be possible. Second, if they use prediction data they are more likely to release persons who will succeed (that is, stay out of crime) in the community than persons who will not.

42. Increased budgets *would* permit the employment of more parole officers, so that more supervisory time could be devoted to parolees. The case load studies cited in chapter 6 and the constraints and difficulties presented in chapters 5 and 6 strongly suggest that there would be no payoff from such an expenditure.

There is more to be said on the other side. First, the parole board is in effect an important participant in the sentencing process, but under conditions where the offender has less assistance and protection than he had in court. Second, the board's rationale for ending or continuing incarceration is often unclear and varies from one inmate to another. Prisoner A is denied parole because he "hasn't been punished enough yet for a crime of such seriousness" (retribution); or "what happens to him must be an example to others" (deterrence). Prisoner B is told "we'll see you again next year; meanwhile stay out of trouble and work on that bricklaying course" (rehabilitation). Prisoner C is deferred because "he looks to me like someone all ready to commit another assault" (incapacitation). Third, boards release some prisoners on the basis of equally unclear or conflicting standards.

In fact, parole boards are trying to do something that is impossible: predict the future behavior of human beings. They are doing some things that are not valid: basing decisions on the belief that prison training or therapy are effective. They are doing other things that are unjust: keeping people in prison because they may do something bad when they get out. These efforts should be abandoned if there is a better alternative.

MODIFIED SENTENCING DISCRETION. The most equitable and logical alternative involves changes much broader in scope than the parole system. Changes are needed in the philosophy of punishment and the discretion to set sentences. The major rationale for imprisonment, when it is used,[43] should be an appropriate punishment for the crime—the theory of retribution. The other purposes of incarceration are ethically wrong or not practical to implement. Deterrence is a valid objective, but data on the deterrent effect of prison terms are inconclusive, and this goal cannot stand alone. Incapacitation involves predictive restraint, a policy to be avoided on grounds of fairness. Rehabilitation within the correctional system is a myth.[44] The principle of fair punishment, however, is generally recognized in our society as valid and practical. Relying on it as the primary basis for imprisonment should make sentencing judgments less difficult and more consistent.

43. Alternatives to the incarceration of accused or convicted persons—pre-trial release, probation, work or study release, and others—would of course continue to be used as appropriate.

44. In addition to references previously cited on this subject, see Robert W. Kastenmeier and Howard C. Eglit, "Parole Release Decision-Making: Rehabilitation, Expertise, and the Demise of Mythology," American University Law Review, vol. 22 (Spring 1973), pp. 477–525.

The system of administering justice that follows from these considerations would have these features:[45]

• Sentences should be set only by judges.

• Standard penalties should be specified for each crime. They could be determined initially by choosing a period close to the median time actually served for the crime by offenders in recent years. This would mean that the term set by the judge would be shorter than it is now.

• Judges' discretion should be limited to modest variations on the standard penalties, based on the circumstances of the offense and the offender's past record.

• Parole boards should be abolished, as offenders will serve the full sentence imposed. If there are extraordinary reasons for releasing prisoners before the end of their terms, they can be pardoned.

Such a plan has several advantages. It places responsibility for sentencing in one place, the court, avoiding the disparities, injustices, and inefficiency that result from the present division between courts and parole boards. The plan also provides a clear rationale for sentencing, thus preventing unjust discrepancies, yet it also permits some use of judgment to allow for differences in the histories of offenders and the circumstances of crimes.

One question sure to be raised about this plan is: How is society to be protected from the dangerous offender who is "likely" to commit a violent crime after he is released? One answer is that the repeat offender will get a longer sentence. A second answer is that if he continues to attack or rob people in prison he will be considered to have committed a new crime and will be punished by more incarceration. He cannot, however, be imprisoned indefinitely unless he receives a life sentence. Use of such a heavy penalty can be justified only for the most heinous crimes, and even that

45. See pp. 76–80. See also Andrew von Hirsch, *Doing Justice: The Choice of Punishments*, Report of the Committee for the Study of Incarceration (Hill and Wang, 1976), esp. pp. 98–106, 124–31. For other studies advocating an end to the indeterminate sentence, and consequently to parole boards' sentencing function, see Richard A. McGee, "A New Look at Sentencing: Part I," *Federal Probation*, vol. 38 (June 1974), pp. 3–8, and "Part II" (September 1974), pp. 3–11; Fred Cohen, "Parole: A New Approach for Lawyers" (Washington, D.C.: American Bar Association, Resource Center on Correctional Law and Correctional Services, 1973; processed); *A Program for Prison Reform*, Final Report of the Annual Chief Justice Earl Warren Conference on Advocacy in the United States (Cambridge, Mass.: Roscoe Pound–American Trial Lawyers Foundation, 1972); *Toward a New Corrections Policy: Two Declarations of Principles* (Columbus, Ohio: The Academy for Contemporary Problems, 1974); Citizens' Inquiry on Parole and Criminal Justice, *Prison without Walls: Report on New York Parole* (Praeger, 1975), pp. 178–80.

punishment can be mitigated by use of the chief executive's power to pardon.[46]

OBSTACLES. The main roadblock to putting such a plan into effect is that it would be politically difficult, if not impossible. Abolition of parole release would be opposed by judges who do not want their discretion reduced or criminal penalties shortened; by parole board members and staffs who want to keep their jobs; by prison officials who value parole consideration as a means of controlling the behavior of inmates and the size of the prison population; and by those political leaders and community groups who want penalties to be at least as severe as they are now. The proposal would be denounced in many quarters as being "soft on crime," albeit unjustifiably.

The ambivalent attitude of the general public—reacting punitively and yet believing in the rehabilitation of prisoners—has been pointed out earlier.[47] More recent research among executive and legislative leaders in three states shows that "strong majorities endorsed rehabilitation as the fundamental goal of correction and rejected the goals of correction and punishment. . . . A discrepancy was noted between the progressive ideological position of the elites and their views on how individual offenders should be handled. This may mean that some of the support for progressive changes may be eroded when it reaches the level of the individual offender."[48] It is doubtful that legislative bodies will want to, even if they could, overpower the political and emotional objections to this kind of reform of sentencing. The response of the New York, Illinois, and Connecticut legislatures to the reforms recommended in those states can be watched for clues.

OTHER ALTERNATIVES. This hard-to-enact plan, combining imposition of definite sentences and abolition of parole release, is also favored by the Committee for the Study of Incarceration, as noted above. Other critics of sentencing and parole favor other alternatives.

---

46. The proposal publicized by the governor of Illinois says "a life sentence would be life; that is, no time off for good behavior, no parole board to reduce the sentence. A variation would permit an appellate court to re-sentence the convict after a specific term of years (say fifteen or twenty years has been served." "News from the Office of the Governor," Feb. 18, 1975, p. 1). The Illinois proposal derives from proposals in David Fogel, *We Are the Living Proof: The Justice Model for Corrections* (W. H. Anderson Co., 1975), esp. pp. 203–04, 245–60.

47. Pp. 19–20, 68–70.

48. Peter H. Rossi and Richard A. Berk, "The Politics of State Corrections Reforms" (abstract), *Crime and Delinquency Literature*, vol. 7 (March 1975), pp. 37–38.

1. Richard McGee would abolish indeterminate sentences and parole release. He would create a "sentence review division of the court of appeals" to establish sentencing guidelines, receive reports of all sentences, and review all sentences over a two-year period with power to increase or decrease them.[49] This proposal would also be hard to put into effect. It calls for an unprecedented amount of reporting and detailed review within the judicial branch. It also raises the unnerving possibility of the review court's being able to increase the punishment of an already-sentenced offender. Its rationale for punishment is apparently a mixture of rehabilitation and retribution. Revision of sentences, particularly upward, would run counter to long judicial tradition and generate opposition accordingly.

2. Judge Constance Motley would also have definite but short sentences and hence limited judicial discretion. The length of the sentence would depend upon the seriousness of the crime and the number of previous convictions. She would keep parole boards but use them only for release for "compelling humanitarian reasons."[50] This proposal would also tend to reduce sentencing disparities but would encounter hearty opposition because it downgrades the responsibilities of both judges and parole boards.

3. The authors of the Yale Law School study, although objecting to the present overlap of sentencing responsibilities between the federal courts and the U.S. Board of Parole, assume "that parole decisionmaking will continue basically in its present form." They urge that courts be guided by something like the USPB guidelines and "articulate the reason for imposing a given sentence."[51] Thus, this plan would do nothing about the overlap, but there would presumably be more logic and consistency in sentencing. This is certainly meritorious, but the uncertainties of the indeterminate sentence and the inequities of the present USPB system would remain.

4. The New York Citizens' Inquiry study, although preferring to abolish parole, sets forth "transitional recommendations," including several due process provisions and shifting the burden of proof so that the parole board would have to show why the offender should *not* be released.[52]

49. McGee, "A New Look at Sentencing: Part II," pp. 7–10.
50. Constance Baker Motley, " 'Law and Order' and the Criminal Justice System," *Journal of Criminal Law and Criminology*, vol. 64 (September 1973), pp. 267–68.
51. William J. Genego, Peter D. Goldberger, and Vicki C. Jackson, "Parole Release Decision Making and the Sentencing Process," *Yale Law Journal*, vol. 84 (March 1975), pp. 899–900.
52. Citizens' Inquiry, *Prison without Walls*, pp. 179–81.

Due process in parole proceedings is clearly desirable; the shift in burden of proof, however, reduces but does not eliminate the tendency toward preventive imprisonment.

Thus objections can be raised to each of these proposals, as well as to the stronger measure recommended here. But the strongest objections of all should be directed at the present system, politically realistic though it may be. Criminal offenders are sentenced by a chaotically irrational decision-making system (if it is a system), and the sentences are then reduced (or not reduced) by another equally erratic process, parole release.

An End to Policing

Parole surveillance, like parole release, has some positive features. There are doubtless parolees who are deterred from criminal behavior by the knowledge that their parole officers may see them unexpectedly, that they must report in periodically, that their statements can be checked, and that even minor misdemeanors can be grounds for reimprisonment. Occasionally parole officers catch parolees doing things that might well lead to new felonies if not stopped. Some parolees who have never had enough guidance respond constructively to firm direction by a parole officer; they may be more likely to get jobs, take courses, or accept therapy because the parole officer insists on it. These possible benefits are based upon a superficially attractive rationale: society is safer because the parolee is being watched. The parolee, otherwise awash in his unaccustomed liberty, is having his fitness for freedom tested.[53]

In practice, this is, in most cases, nonsense. The parole officer cannot possibly and does not actually keep an eye on the parolee. He is likely to learn of misbehavior only when somebody informs on the parolee or when he is picked up by police. The parolee who responds cooperatively to surveillance is making it anyway; the parolee who is up to no good can easily avoid or deceive the parole officer.

When the parolee does violate his parole agreement he faces a different standard of trial and punishment than other citizens do. Post-*Morrissey* revocation hearings, both preliminary and evidentiary, are inadequate proceedings by normal criminal justice standards. The parolee, usually unrepresented, is in a hopelessly weak position to advance favorable evidence and to attack the government's evidence. He may be returned to the peni-

53. Norval Morris and Gordon Hawkins, "Attica Revisited: The Prospect for Prison Reform," *Arizona Law Review*, vol. 14 (1972), p. 759.

tentiary as a parole violator for an offense for which he could not be convicted in court. He may also be sent back to serve many months for an offense that might normally call for a week in jail or a $50 fine.[54]

There are no research findings that prove the efficacy of parole supervision. Any studies that try to do so by citing the number of parole violations discovered should be rejected out of hand: parole staffs can arbitrarily raise or lower the number of violations reported. Research does show that parolees who have stayed out of trouble continue to do so when discharged. Further research in this area has been proposed earlier in this chapter.

Finally, parole surveillance causes intense psychological stress to its objects, as Studt has found.[55] The parolee, dispirited, disoriented, resentful, rubbed raw by prison, now must accept policing from yet another official of the society and government that have punished him.

The alternative is plain: abolish supervision of the releasee. Don't visit his job or his home or his tavern; don't make him come in to the office or write in. Leave him alone, except for making help available. If he gets drunk or fights or drives a car into a tree, deal with him as you would with any other person who does such things. If he commits a burglary or robbery, proceed with arraignment, indictment, trial, and punishment, with due attention to his previous record.

Help—And More of It

Arguing that the releasee should get the same sort of justice as other citizens does not mean that he should get the same help in the community as other citizens. He needs more help because of the fear and suspicion that other citizens harbor toward exoffenders. The possibility that he will return to crime if his needs are not met argues for the provision of timely, accessible, and comprehensive assistance.

Such help has presumably been available from parole officers. We have seen that they sometimes give useful aid but that the strain of the relationship and their heavy case loads put severe limits on their effectiveness as helpers. The parolee is in many cases reluctant to ask the parole officer for help, and when he does ask for help the parole officer may not be available.

The typical large community to which a releasee returns has employ-

54. One study by Martinson, a reanalysis of data from one phase of the California Special Intensive Parole Unit experiment, does suggest that a policy of severity in returning parole violators to prison does have a deterrent effect. See p. 15, n. 35, above. Other tests of this relationship are needed.

55. See pp. 100 and 132 above.

ment and social service facilities available to all persons in need, plus others solely for offenders. The former may or may not meet the specialized and urgent needs of parolees. There may be overlaps or gaps in service because of the differing histories, objectives, and budgets of the agencies (see the standards recommended in chapter 7).

Any community with a substantial population of offenders and exoffenders (pretrial divertees, probationers, work-releasees, parolees, mandatory releasees) needs to take inventory of its facilities, both public and private, and then plan to provide the services that are wanting. Such an assessment should be required by the state criminal justice planning agency and carried out by the local government criminal justice coordinating council, if there is one—otherwise by whatever planning staff is available. An inventory might reveal, for example, unmet needs for middle-of-the-night crisis counseling, job-finding help for releasees with professional qualifications, low-interest emergency credit, temporary housing for evictees, or outpatient psychiatric therapy. Financial help could then be systematically channeled for these services, to the extent possible under federal and state grants, as well as privately through community funds. It would be even more appropriate to reallott for this purpose at least part of the state funds now being used for parole release and policing functions.

The inventory should also consider whether a central reentry facility is needed for exoffenders. The releasee would go there first, on a voluntary basis, be interviewed about all of his problems of community adjustment and then referred to other agencies that could help him. Some may feel that since the offender is free, he should be held responsible for making his own way without anyone looking over his shoulder. But if there is no compulsion on the offender to accept assistance, it is probable that he can benefit from guidance from a source that is familiar with offenders' problems and with the community's institutions. Such a referral service could be staffed by properly qualified and motivated exparole officers, who would be available when parole supervision is abolished.

This review of parole is written at a time when criminal codes, the processes of justice, and the functioning of bureaucracies are under continuing scrutiny. Remedial steps in any of these areas could profit from taking account of the findings here. The fact that parole processes abound in unfulfilled promises, waste motion, injustice, and deception should be added impetus to change. Alternatives to the present system must be found that are humane and honest as well as prudent.

Selected Bibliography

Law Enforcement and Criminal Justice

National Advisory Commission on Criminal Justice Standards and Goals. *Criminal Justice System*. Washington, D.C.: Government Printing Office, 1973.
——. *A National Strategy to Reduce Crime*. Washington, D.C.: Government Printing Office, 1973.
President's Commission on Law Enforcement and the Administration of Justice. *The Challenge of Crime in a Free Society*. Washington, D.C.: Government Printing Office, 1967.

Theories of Imprisonment

Andenaes, Johannes. *Punishment and Deterrence*. Ann Arbor: University of Michigan Press, 1974.
Antunes, George, and A. Lee Hunt. "The Deterrent Impact of Criminal Sanctions: Some Implications for Criminal Justice Policy," *Journal of Urban Law*, vol. 51 (November 1973).
Knutden, Richard D. *Crime in a Complex Society*. Homewood, Ill.: Dorsey Press, 1970.
Mabbott, J. D. "Punishment," in Frederick A. Olafson, ed., *Justice and Social Policy*. Englewood Cliffs, N.J.: Prentice-Hall, 1961.
Packer, Herbert L. *The Limits of the Criminal Sanction*. Stanford: Stanford University Press, 1968.
Wilson, James Q. "If Every Criminal *Knew* He Would Be Punished if Caught," *New York Times Magazine*, Jan. 28, 1973.
von Hirsch, Andrew. *Doing Justice: The Choice of Punishments*. Report of the Committee for the Study of Incarceration. New York: Hill and Wang, 1976.
Zimring, Franklin E., and Gordon J. Hawkins. *Deterrence: The Legal Threat in Crime Control*. Chicago: University of Chicago Press, 1973.

Prisons

Goffman, Erving. *Asylums: Essays on the Social Situation of Mental Patients and Other Inmates*. Garden City, N.Y.: Doubleday, 1961.

Haney, Craig, Curtis Banks, and Phillip Zimbardo. "Interpersonal Dynamics in a Simulated Prison." Processed. Stanford: Stanford University, n.d.

Minton, Robert J., Jr., ed. *Inside: Prison American Style*. New York: Random House, 1971.

Morris, Norval. *The Future of Imprisonment*. Chicago: University of Chicago Press, 1974.

Nagel, William G. *The New Red Barn: A Critical Look at the Modern American Prison*. New York: Walker and Co., 1973.

New York State Special Commission on Attica. *Attica: The Official Report*. New York: Bantam, 1972.

Orland, Leonard. *Prisons: Houses of Darkness*. Riverside, N.J.: Free Press, 1975.

Rothman, David J. "Prisons, Asylums, and Other Decaying Institutions," *Public Interest*, no. 26 (Winter 1972).

Sentencing

American Law Institute. "Model Penal Code." Preliminary official draft, May 1962. Excerpts in *Judicature*, vol. 57 (October 1973).

Council of Judges, National Council on Crime and Delinquency. "Model Sentencing Act, Second Edition," *Crime and Delinquency*, vol. 181 (October 1972).

Dawson, Robert O. *Sentencing: The Decision as to Type, Length, and Conditions of Sentence*. Boston: Little, Brown, 1969.

Frankel, Marvin E. *Criminal Sentences: Law Without Order*. New York: Hill and Wang, 1973.

Gresens, James W. "The Indeterminate Sentence: Judicial Intervention in the Correctional Process," *Buffalo Law Review*, vol. 21 (Spring 1972).

Hand, Richard C., and Richard G. Singer. *Sentencing Computation Laws and Practice: A Preliminary Survey*, Washington, D.C.: American Bar Association, Resource Center on Correctional Law and Legal Services, 1974.

McGee, Richard A. "A New Look at Sentencing," *Federal Probation*, vol. 38 (June and September 1974).

Walker, Nigel. *Sentencing in a Rational Society*. New York: Basic Books, 1971.

Zumwalt, William James. "The Anarchy of Sentencing in the Federal Courts," *Judicature*, vol. 57 (October 1973).

Corrections

American Correctional Association. *Manual of Correctional Standards*. Washington, D.C.: ACA, 1966.

Grant, Walter Mathews, and others. "Special Project: The Collateral Consequences of a Criminal Conviction," *Vanderbilt Law Review*, vol. 23 (1970).

Irwin, John. *The Felon*. Englewood Cliffs, N.J.: Prentice-Hall, 1970.

National Advisory Commission on Criminal Justice Standards and Goals. *Corrections.* Washington, D.C.: Government Printing Office, 1973.

President's Commission on Law Enforcement and the Administration of Justice. *Task Force Report: Corrections.* Washington, D.C.: Government Printing Office, 1967.

A *Program for Prison Reform.* Final Report of The Annual Chief Justice Earl Warren Conference on Advocacy in the United States. Cambridge, Mass.: Roscoe Pound–American Trial Lawyers Foundation, 1972.

Work Release

Johnson, Elmer H. "Report on an Innovation: State Work Release Programs," *Crime and Delinquency,* vol. 16 (October 1970).

Root, Lawrence S. "State Work Release Programs: An Analysis of Operational Policies," *Federal Probation,* vol. 37 (December 1973).

Parole

Carter, Robert M., and Leslie J. Wilkins, eds. *Probation and Parole: Selected Readings.* New York: John Wiley and Sons, 1970.

Citizens' Inquiry on Parole and Criminal Justice. *Prison without Walls: Report on New York Parole.* New York: Praeger, 1975.

Dressler, David. *Theory and Practice of Probation and Parole.* New York: Columbia University Press, 1969.

O'Leary, Vincent, and Joan Nuffield. *The Organization of Parole Systems in the United States.* Hackensack, N.J.: National Council on Crime and Delinquency, 1972.

Parker, William. *Parole: Origins, Development, Current Practices, and Statutes,* American Correctional Association, Parole Corrections Project, Resource Document no. 1. College Park, Md.: ACA, 1975.

Parole Decision Making

American Correctional Association. *The Mutual Agreement Program: A Planned Change in Correctional Service Delivery.* Parole Corrections Project, Resource Document no. 3. College Park, Md.: ACA, 1973.

————. *Proceedings: Second National Workshop on Corrections and Parole Administration.* Parole Corrections Project, Resource Document no. 4. College Park, Md.: ACA, 1974.

Dawson, Robert O. "The Decision to Grant or Deny Parole: A Study of Parole Criteria in Law and Practice," *Washington University Law Quarterly* (June 1966).

De Gosten, Lucille K., and Peter B. Hoffman. "Administrative Review of Parole Selection and Revocation Decisions." Processed. Washington, D.C.: United States Board of Parole Research Unit, January 1974.

Genego, William J., Peter D. Goldberger, and Vicki C. Jackson. "Parole Release Decision Making and the Sentencing Process," *Yale Law Journal*, vol. 84 (March 1975).

Jenkins, W. O., and others. *The Measurement and Prediction of Criminal Behavior and Recidivism: The Environmental Deprivation Scale (EDS) and the Maladaptive Behavior Record (MBR)*. Elmore, Ala.: Rehabilitation Research Foundation, Experimental Manpower Laboratory for Corrections, 1973.

Kastenmeier, Robert W., and Howard C. Eglit, "Parole Release Decision-Making: Rehabilitation, Expertise, and the Demise of Mythology," *American University Law Review*, vol. 22 (Spring 1973).

National Council on Crime and Delinquency. *Parole Decision-Making Reports*. Davis, Calif.: NCCD Research Center, 1972–73.

Scott, Joseph E. "The Use of Discretion in Determining the Severity of Punishment for Incarcerated Offenders," *The Journal of Criminal Law and Criminology*, vol. 65 (1974).

von Hirsch, Andrew. "Prediction of Criminal Conduct and Preventive Confinement of Convicted Persons," *Buffalo Law Review*, vol. 21 (Spring 1972).

Due Process

Bronstein, Alvin J. "Due Process at Parole Hearings or Playing God Without Rules." Conference on Corrections and Due Process, Working Paper. Processed. Columbus, Ohio: The Academy for Contemporary Problems, 1974.

"Comment. Due Process: The Right to Counsel in Parole Release Hearings," *Iowa Law Review*, vol. 54 (1968).

Davis, Kenneth Culp. *Discretionary Justice*. Urbana: University of Illinois Press, 1971.

Gottesman, Michael, and Lewis J. Hecker. "Parole: A Critique of Legal Foundations and Conditions," *New York University Law Review*, vol. 38 (June 1963).

Johnson, Phillip E. "Federal Parole Procedures: Report in Support of Recommendation 72-3," in *Recommendations and Reports of the Administrative Conference of the United States*, vol. 2 (July 1, 1970–Dec. 31, 1972).

Resource Center on Correctional Law and Legal Services and the Editors of *Prison Law Reporter*. *Prisoners' Legal Rights: A Bibliography of Cases and Articles*. 2nd ed. Seattle: American Bar Association, 1974.

Parole Surveillance and Revocation

Carter, Robert M., Daniel Glaser, and E. Kim Nelson. "Probation and Parole Supervision: The Dilemma of Caseload Size." Processed. Washington, D.C.: Administrative Office of the U.S. Courts, Probation Division, February 1973.

Council of State Governments. *Handbook on Interstate Crime Control*. Rev. ed. Chicago: CSG, 1966.

Neithercutt, M. G., and Don M. Gottfredson. "Caseload Size Variation and
    Difference in Probation/Parole Performance." Processed. Administrative
    Office of the U.S. Courts, Probation Division, 1973.
Resource Center on Correctional Law and Legal Services, Commission on
    Correctional Facilities and Services. *Survey of Parole Conditions in the
    United States.* Washington, D.C.: American Bar Association, 1973.
————. *Survey of Parole Revocation Procedures: State Parole Board Compli-
    ance with Morrissey v. Brewer.* Washington, D.C.: American Bar Associ-
    ation, 1973.
Robison, James O. "Unraveling Delinquency: Caseworker Orientation and
    Client Characterization." D.Crim. dissertation, University of California,
    Berkeley, 1971.
Studt, Elliot. *Surveillance and Service In Parole: A Report of the Parole Action
    Study.* Los Angeles: University of California, Institute of Government and
    Public Affairs, 1972.
Takagi, Paul Takao. "Evaluation Systems and Adaptations in a Formal Or-
    ganization: A Case Study of a Parole Agency." Ph.D. dissertation, Stanford
    University, 1967.

The Parolee in the Community

Erickson, Rosemary J., and others. *Paroled but Not Free: Ex-Offenders Look
    at What They Need to Make It Outside.* New York: Behavioral Publica-
    tions, 1973.
Ericson, Richard C., and David O. Moberg. *The Rehabilitation of Parolees.*
    Minneapolis: Minneapolis Rehabilitation Center, 1967.
McRae, William, and others. "A Study of Community Parole Orientation."
    Processed. St. Paul: Minnesota Department of Corrections, 1969.
Studt, Elliot. *Reintegration of the Offender into the Community.* Criminal
    Justice Monograph. Washington, D.C.: U.S. Law Enforcement Assistance
    Administration, June 1973.

Employment Problems

American Bar Association. National Clearinghouse on Offender Employment
    Restrictions. *Removing Offender Employment Restrictions.* Washington,
    D.C.: ABA, 1973.
Bromberger, Brian. "Rehabilitation and Occupational Licensing: A Conflict
    of Interests," *William and Mary Law Review,* vol. 13 (1972).
Cunningham, Joseph F. "Jobs for the Ex-Offender," *Case and Comment,* vol.
    77 (January–February 1972).
Hunt, James W., James E. Bowers, and Neal Miller. *Laws, Licenses and the
    Offender's Right to Work.* Washington, D.C.: American Bar Association,
    National Clearinghouse on Offender Employment Restrictions, 1973.
Miller, Herbert S. *The Closed Door: The Effect of a Criminal Record on
    Employment with State and Public Agencies.* Washington, D.C.: George-

town University Law Center, 1972 [distributed by National Technical Information Service, U.S. Department of Commerce].

Pownall, George A. "Employment Problems of Released Prisoners." Processed. Washington, D.C.: U.S. Department of Labor, Manpower Administration, 1969.

Taggart, Robert. *The Prison of Unemployment: Manpower Programs for Offenders*. Baltimore: Johns Hopkins University Press, 1972.

Subsidies

Dightman, Cameron R., and Donald R. Johns. "The Adult Correction Release Stipend Program in Washington," *State Government*, vol. 47 (Winter 1974).

Lenihan, Kenneth J. *The Financial Resources of Released Prisoners*. Washington, D.C.: Bureau of Social Science Research, Inc., 1974.

Scientific Analysis Corporation. *Direct Financial Assistance to Parolees Project*. San Francisco: The California Council on Criminal Justice, 1973.

Parole Administration and Staffing

Bentel, David Joseph. "Parole Officer: An Examination of the Occupational Career of California Parole Agents." D.Crim. dissertation, University of California, Berkeley, 1970.

Dembo, Richard. "Orientation and Activities of the Parole Officer," *Criminology*, vol. 10 (August 1972).

Federal Judicial Center. "Probation Time Study." Processed. Washington, D.C., 1973.

Palmer, Ted B. "Matching Worker and Client in Corrections," *Social Work*, vol. 18 (March 1973).

Research and Evaluation of Parole and Related Functions

Berecochea, John E., Alfred N. Himelson, and Donald E. Miller. "The Risk of Failure During the Early Parole Period: A Methodological Note," *Journal of Criminal Law and Police Science*, vol. 63 (March 1972).

Berecochea, John E., Dorothy R. Jaman, and Welton A. Jones. *Time Served in Prison and Parole Outcome: An Experimental Study*. Sacramento: California Department of Corrections, Research Division, 1973.

Bernstein, Ilene Nagel, and Howard E. Freeman. *Academic and Entrepreneurial Research*. New York: Russell Sage Foundation, 1975.

Chapman, Jeffrey I., and Carl W. Nelson. *A Handbook of Cost-Benefit Techniques and Applications*. American Bar Association, Correctional Economics Center, 1975.

Citizens' Inquiry on Parole and Criminal Justice. *Prison without Walls: Report on New York Parole*. New York: Praeger, 1974.

Eichman, Charles J. *The Impact of the Gideon Decision upon Crime and*

Sentencing in Florida: A Study of Recidivism and Sociocultural Change. Tallahassee: Florida Division of Corrections, 1966.

Evans, Robert, Jr. "The Labor Market and Parole Success," *The Journal of Human Resources,* vol. 3 (Spring 1968).

Glaser, Daniel. *The Effectiveness of a Prison and Parole System.* Indianapolis: Bobbs-Merrill, 1969.

—————. *Routinizing Evaluation: Getting Feedback on Effectiveness of Crime and Delinquency Programs.* Rockville, Md.: National Institute of Mental Health, Center for Studies of Crime and Delinquency, 1973.

Greenberg, David F. "The Incapacitative Effect of Imprisonment," *Law and Society Review,* vol. 9 (Summer 1975).

Gottfredson, Don M., and others. *Four Thousand Lifetimes: A Study of Time Served and Parole Outcomes.* Davis, Calif.: National Council on Crime and Delinquency, 1973.

Hawkins, Keith Owen. "Parole Selection: The American Experience." Ph.D. dissertation, University of Cambridge, 1971.

Hoffman, Peter B. "Mandatory Release: A Measure of Type II Error," *Criminology,* vol. 11 (February 1974).

Holt, Norman, and Donald Miller. *Explorations in Inmate-Family Relationships.* California Department of Corrections, Research Division, Report no. 46. Sacramento, 1972.

Jaman, Dorothy R., Lawrence A. Bennett, and John E. Berecochea. *Early Discharge from Parole: Policy, Practice, and Outcome.* California Department of Corrections, Research Division, Report no. 51. Sacramento, April 1974.

Kassebaum, Gene, David A. Ward, and Daniel M. Wilner. *Prison Treatment and Parole Survival: An Empirical Assessment.* New York: Wiley, 1971.

Lipton, Douglas S., Robert Martinson, and Judith Wilks. *The Effectiveness of Correctional Treatment: A Survey of Treatment Evaluation Studies.* New York: Praeger, 1975.

Messinger, Sheldon L. "Strategies of Control." Ph.D. dissertation, University of California, Los Angeles, 1969.

Moberg, David O., and Richard C. Ericson. "A New Recidivism Outcome Index," *Federal Probation,* vol. 36 (June 1972).

Robison, James O., and others. *By the Standard of His Rehabilitation.* California Department of Corrections, Research Division, Report no. 39. Sacramento, 1971.

Toliver, Lawrence J. *A Tradition of Abuse: Parole in South Carolina.* Columbia, S.C.: South Carolina Council on Human Relations, Inc., 1973.

U.S. Bureau of Prisons. "Success and Failure of Federal Offenders Released in 1970." Processed. Washington, D.C., 1974.

von Hirsch, Andrew. *Doing Justice: A Rationale for Criminal Sentencing,* Report of the Committee for the Study of Incarceration. New York: Hill and Wang, 1976.

Waller, Irvin. *Men Released from Prison.* Toronto and Buffalo: University of Toronto Press in association with the Centre of Criminology, 1974.

Index

ABA. *See* American Bar Association
Abadinsky, Howard, 111n
Absconders: number of, 179; parole revocation for, 108–09; problem of categorizing, 176, 177, 180
ACA. *See* American Correctional Association
Adams, Stuart, 128n, 142n, 143
Administrative Conference of the United States, 71, 75
Agus, Bertrand, 135n
Alabama, work-release program, 143
Alcohol use, effect on parolees' success, 51–52
Allen, Thomas E., 135n
Alliance for a Safer New York, 163
American Bar Association (ABA), 70n; on licensing of persons with criminal records, 152; National Clearinghouse on Offender Employment Restrictions, 153, 155; National Volunteer Aide Program, 167; survey of parole conditions, 83–84
American Civil Liberties Union, 74–75
American Correctional Association (ACA), 8n; on mutual agreement programming, 66; on parole board standards, 29, 44
American Friends Service Committee, 78
Andenaes, Johannes, 9n
Antunes, George, 10n
Ares, Charles E., 140n
Arizona, mutual agreement programming, 66
Armore, John R., 163n
Armstrong, K. E., 8n
Attica, 14
Aun, Emil Michael, 164n

Bailey, William C., 10n
Beccaria, Cesare, 9
Becker, Gary, 7n
Behavior: effect of punishment on, 9; prison, 53–55
Beless, Donald W., 94n

Bennett, James V., 14n
Bennett, Lawrence A., 121n, 122n, 181n, 183n
Bennett, Pamela A., 94n
Bentel, David Joseph, 89n
Bentham, Jeremy, 9
Berecochea, John E., 121n, 175n, 181n, 183n
Berk, Richard A., 187n
Berlin, Louis, 170n
Bixby, F. Lovell, 24n
Block, Michael, 182n
Blumstein, Alfred, 9n
Bomberger, Brian, 152n
Bonding, of exoffenders, 154
Boucher, Richard J., 53n
Bowers, James E., 152n
Bowers, William J., 10n
Bradford v. *Weinstein*, 72n
Braswell, Michael, 144n
Brewster, Kingman, 13n
Bronstein, Alvin J., 75n
Buckley, Marie, 136n
Bureau of Social Science Research, 148
Busher, Walter H., 141n

California: direct financial assistance to parolees, 147; evaluation study of parolee surveillance, 180–81; mutual agreement programming, 67; parole action study, 100, 102; parolee behavior study, 133–34; short-term return program, 110; study of parolees' success, 52, 54; work-release program, 142; Work Unit Parole Program, 85, 128, 175
California Adult Authority, 32n, 54; effect of public opinion on decision of, 69; factors influencing decisions, 54, 60; financial assistance to parolees, 146; hearings, 33n, 38; members, 29; parole conditions, 83; parole revocation process, 114, 116
California parole board. *See* California Adult Authority; California Youth Authority

California Youth Authority, 61–62, 86
Canter, Barbara, 143n
Cargan, Leonard, 23n
Carter, Robert M., 50n, 86n, 116n, 128, 129n, 140n
Chaiklin, Harris, 136n
Chambliss, William J., 11n
Childs v. *U.S. Board of Parole*, 72n
Citizens' Inquiry on Parole and Criminal Justice (New York State), 39n, 48n, 96n, 101n, 170n, 186n; recommendations for due process, 188; recommendations for sentencing, 79; study of parolee employment, 156
Clements, Raymond D., 95n
Coates, Mary A., 23n
Cohen, Fred, 186n
Cohen, Jacqueline, 9n
Colorado: job placement projects, 165; preparole release center, 136
Colorado parole board: factors influencing decisions of, 60; notification of parole denial by, 74; revocation process, 114; selection of members, 29
Commensurate deserts principle. *See* Retribution
Community: activities of, as alternatives to prison, 140; assessment of prisoners' needs by, 191; job assistance to parolees, 163–65; multiservice projects for parolees, 166–68; parolees' reentry into, 137, 190; work-release programs, 140–44
Conditional release. *See* Mandatory release
Conroy, Patricia, 115n
Cook, Philip J., 149n, 150n
Cook v. *Whiteside*, 72n
Cost, of parole, 182–84
Council of State Governments, 123, 124
Counseling: community services for, 164–65, 166–67; at parole board hearings, 37; by parole officers, 156, 160–61; by parole officer aides, 94; prerelease, 136
Court decisions: on parolees' right to counsel, 114; on prison practices, 14; on reasons for parole denial, 72; on search of parolees' homes, 101
Crime: effect of incapacitative imprisonment on, 13, 185; punishment to deter, 9–11, 185; retribution for, 8–9, 77, 185; victimless, 9n
Criminal justice system, 2–3
Criminal punishment, 2; rationales for, 8–11

Crull, Elgin L., 166n
Cunningham, Joseph F., 162n

Dash, Leon, 99n
Davis, Kenneth Culp, 71
Dawson, Robert O., 48n, 59, 71n
Death penalty, 10n
DeFrancis, Paul, 144n
DeGostin, Lucille K., 24n
Dembo, Richard, 93n, 116n, 130, 131, 132
Deterrence of crime: effect of sentence on, 10–11; parole and, 185; punishment for, 9
DeValera, E. K., 176n
Diamond, Bernard L., 53n
Diaz et al. v. *Ward et al.*, 101n
Dightman, Cameron R., 147n
Disclosure of information, 74–75
District of Columbia: job placement program, 161, 165; prisoner furloughs, 144
District of Columbia parole board, 29, 33n; effect of public opinion on decisions of, 69; factors influencing decisions of, 60; hearings, 33n; members, 29; recommendations for work-release, 141; revocation process, 114
Dressler, David, 56n
Drug use, effect on parolees' success, 51–52
Due process, 39; in parole release decisions, 70–74, 188–89; in parole revocations, 105, 112, 113
Dunbar, Ellen Russell, 67n

Education programs, for prisoners, 14, 55. *See also* Vocational training
Edwards, Paul G., 144n
Eglit, Howard C., 185n
Eldridge, William B., 23n
Empey, LaMar T., 12n
Employment for parolees, 149; business groups' approach to, 162–63; as condition of parole, 157–58; effect of bonding on, 154; effect of licensing restrictions on, 152–53; effect on parole success, 150–51; efforts to remove obstacles to, 155–56; instability of, 157–59; model program for, 162; placement projects for, 164–65; requirements for public, 153–54; role of parole officer in, 156, 160–61; state employment service for, 161
Erickson, Rosemary J., 139n, 145n
Ericson, Richard C., 138n, 139n, 164n, 175

Erskine, Hazel, 20n
Esseltyn, T. C., 143n
Evaluation of parole, 5–6; methods for, 172–78; related to goals of parole, 171–72; studies of, 178–82. See also Hearings, parole board, evaluation; Recidivism; Surveillance, effectiveness of
Evans, Robert, Jr., 158n
Evjen, Victor H., 51n

Faber, M. A., 10n
Federal Judicial Center, 125, 128
Fevurly, Jack L., 166n
Fogel, David, 187n
Frankel, Marvin E., 23, 24n, 77
Fraizer, Robert Lee, 183n
Freed, Daniel J., 140n
Furloughs, prisoner, 144–45

Gagnon v. Scarpelli, 114n
Gallup poll. See Public opinion polls
Garabedian, Peter G., 68n
Garofalo, Ralph F., 53n
Gaylin, Willard, 23n
Genego, William J., 66n, 76n, 188n
Georgia: combined parole-probation staff, 124; parole officer case load, 126; pilot project for parolees, 138
Georgia parole board, 47; factors influencing decisions of, 57; interviewing of prisoners by, 33n; revocation process, 112, 114; written reasons for parole denial, 74
Gettinger, Steve, 66n
Gibbons, Don C., 68n
Gilman, David, 39n, 70n
Glaser, Daniel, 2n, 7n, 11n, 15n, 53n, 56n, 86n, 128, 129n, 132n, 176n
Glendinning, Sara, 143n
Goffman, Erving, 16, 17n
Goldberger, Peter D., 66n, 188n
Gordon, Arthur, 164n
Gordon, David M., 7n
Gottesman, Michael, 1n, 172n
Gottfredson, Don M., 43n, 55n, 61n, 62n, 86n, 128
Grant, Walter Matthews, 82n
Gresens, James W., 21n
Griggs, Bertram S., 139n
Greenberg, David F., 11n, 13n, 177

Halfway houses: for parolees, 165–66; for work-release program participants, 141
Hand, Richard C., 21n
Hawkins, Gordon J., 11n, 189n
Hawkins, Keith Owen, 30, 48n, 53, 60, 61
Hayner, Norman S., 51n

Hearings, parole board, 33; caseworker's role in, 40–41; counseling efforts at, 37; evaluation of, 42–44; proceedings, 34–37; protection of parolees' rights at, 39–40; reaction of prisoners to, 41–42; time spent on, 38–39
Hecker, Lewis J., 1n, 172n
Himelson, Alfred N., 175n
Hindelang, Michael J., 19n
Hoffman, Peter B., 24n, 43n, 54n, 56n, 62n, 178n, 179
Holahan, John F., 183n
Holt, Harmon, 136n
Holt, Norman, 52n, 134n, 148n
Holt v. Sarver, 14n
Holve, Janice, 183n
Hudson, Joe, 140n
Hunt, A. Lee, 10n
Hunt, James W., 152n
Hurd, James L., 166n

Incapacitative imprisonment, 11, 185; effect on crime rate, 13; explanation of concept, 11–12; protection of public by, 12
Inciardi, James A., 52n
Interstate Compact for the Supervision of Parolees and Probationers, 123
Irwin, John, 132n, 157

Jackson, George, 14n
Jackson, Vicki C., 66n, 188n
Jaman, Dorothy R., 54n, 121n, 181n, 183n
Javits, Jacob K., 163n
Jenkins, W. O., 175n, 176n
Johns, Donald R., 147n
Johnson, Elmer H., 140n, 141n, 143n
Johnson, Phillip E., 28n, 71
Johnston, James M., 9n
Johnston, Norman, 128n
Jones, Joseph F., 68n
Judges, sentencing, 20–25, 77, 186
Jury, sentencing, 23–24

Kassebaum, Gene, 15n
Kastenmeier, Robert W., 185n
Keith-Lucas, Alan, 69n
Kenefick, Donald, 53n
King v. United States, 72n
Kirkham, George L., 143n
Knudten, Richard D., 7n
Kobrin, Solomon, 10n
Kolodny, Steve E., 55n
Kotch, Kenneth E., 140n
Kozol, Harry L., 53n

Landman v. *Royster,* 14n
Law Enforcement Assistance Administration, 5; job placement projects, 164; National Institute of Law Enforcement and Criminal Justice, 23n
Lawyer, Alfred Gordon, 168n
Legislation, proposed for sentencing, 24
Lenihan, Kenneth J., 145n, 146n, 148n
Levi, Edward H., 79n
Lewis, Morgan V., 15n
Licensing, effect on parolee employment, 152–53
Linowes, David F., 163n
Lipton, Douglas, 15n
Logan, Charles H., 11n
Long, Susan Bradley, 173n
Looney, Francis B., 10n
Louisiana, parole discharge, 120n

Mabbott, J. D., 8n
McArthur, Virginia, 143n
McCartt, John M., 165n
McCune, Gary R., 139n
McGee, Richard A., 25n, 186n, 188
McKee, John M., 144n
Macnaughton-Smith, P., 50n
McRae, William F., 136n
Mandatory release, 4; parole versus, 178–79; surveillance accompanying, 122
Mandatory sentencing, 10n
Mangogna, Thomas J., 165n
Mannheim, Hermann, 50n
MAP. *See* Mutual agreement programming
Martin, William L., 23n
Martinson, Robert, 15n, 129, 166n, 190n
Massachusetts, study on parole employment, 150
Mattina, Joseph S., 23n
Mead, George H., 8n
Megathalin, Susi, 126n
Merton, Robert K., 8n
Messinger, Sheldon L., 18n, 130
Meyer, Lawrence, 19n
Milan, Michael A., 144n
Miller, Donald, 52n, 148n
Miller, Donald E., 175n
Miller, Herbert S., 153n
Miller, Michael J., 149n
Miller, Neal, 152n
Minnesota, prisoner furloughs, 144; study on parolee employment, 150
Minton, Robert J., Jr., 14n, 42n
Mitford, Jessica, 14n, 38
Moberg, David O., 138n, 139n, 164n, 175
Model Exoffender Program, 162
Moreland, Roy, 25n

Morris, Albert, 11n
Morris, Norval, 12n, 143n, 189n
Morrissey v. *Brewer,* 112, 113, 114, 118
Motley, Constance Baker, 24n, 25n, 188
Mutual agreement programming (MAP), 66–68

Nagal, Stuart, 14n
Nagel, William G., 15n
National Advisory Commission on Criminal Justice and Goals, 2, 16n, 140n; emphasis on community-based corrections, 139; on parole goals, 171; on parole officer performance, 127; on reasons for parole denial, 72; recommendations on recidivism, 175; on short-term jailings during parole, 106
National Alliance of Businessmen, 163
National Council on Crime and Delinquency (NCCD), 12; on furlough success rates, 145; on parole results, 106; research on parole board decisions, 61–62; study of parolees' success, 53–54; study of parole revocation, 117, 119; study of state parole boards, 29–30, 33, 38, 39
Neil, Thomas C., 126n
Neithercutt, M. G., 86n, 118n, 128
Nelson, Carl W., 182n
Nelson, E. Kim, 86n, 128, 129n
Newman, Donald J., 70n
New York City, efforts to employ exoffenders, 163
New York City Legal Aid Society, 115n
New York City Urban Coalition, 163
New York State parole board, 57n; factors influencing decisions of, 53, 60
New York State Special Commission on Attica, 39n
Nixon, Richard M., 10n
North Carolina, work-release program, 143
Nuffield, Joan, 26n, 27n, 28n, 29n, 31n, 33n, 38n, 39n, 44n, 87n, 108n, 111n, 113n, 119n, 120n, 122n

O'Connor, Gerald, 16n
Oelsner, Lesley, 22n
Ohlin, Lloyd E., 12n, 50n, 116n, 131n
Olafson, Frederick A., 8n
O'Leary, Vincent, 26n, 27n, 28n, 29n, 31n, 33n, 38n, 39n, 44n, 53n, 56n, 87n, 108n, 111n, 113n, 119n, 120n, 122n, 133n
Openness principle, 71

Packer, Herbert L., 8n
Painter, James A., 52n

Palmer, Ted B., 86n

Pappenfort, Donnell M., 116n, 131n

Parker, William, 1n, 2n, 22n, 28n, 29n, 31n, 35n, 83n

Parnas, Raymond I., 13n

Parole: basic concepts of, 1; compared with mandatory release, 178–79; conditions of, 82–84; contract, 66–68; cost of, 182–84; duration of, 120; effect of employment on, 150–51; effect of prison needs on, 26; eligibility for, 21–22; factors influencing readiness for, 53–55, 57; factors influencing success of, 169; functions of, 1–2, 4; goals of, 2–3, 171; prisoners' reactions to deferred, 45–46; reasons for denial of, 72, 74; results of, 179; sentencing reform as alternative to, 185–87, 188; theories of, 171; variations in discharge requirements, 120–21; violations of, 104, 133. See also Evaluation of parole; revocation of parole

Parole boards: balloting by, 57; effect of public opinion on, 20, 69; evaluation of, 184–85; factors influencing decisions of, 7, 48–50, 59–60, 68–70; functions of supporting staff, 32; political influence on, 3, 68–70; proposed abolition of, 186, 187, 188; qualifications of, 28–30; relation to correctional institution, 26–27; revocation decisions, 115–16; salaries, 32; standards for decisions, 47–48, 70–72; state laws on selection of, 29; term of office, 31. See also Hearings, parole board

Parolee: anxieties of, 135–36; criteria for aid to, 170; financial assistance to, 146–49; matching parole officer to, 85–86; needs of, 138–39, 145–46; number of, 1; out-of-state, 122–24; parole officer's relations with, 101–03, 124, 137–38, 168–69, 190; predicting success of, 50–57; reaction to parole surveillance, 81–82, 100–01; short-term jailings of, 105–06; volunteer aid for, 167. See also Community; Employment for parolees; Surveillance, parole

Parole officer: advice on employment by, 156, 160–61; advisability of arming, 111–12; aides for, 93–95; arrests by, 111; bureaucratic pressures on, 88–89, 116–17, 130; case load, 84, 88, 126–29, 133; combined probation and, 87–88, 124; correctional department supervision of, 86–87; factors influencing performance of, 128–32; job experi-

ence, 93; matching parolee to, 85–86; parolee's relations with, 101–03, 124, 137–38, 168–69, 190; personal background, 89; qualifications, 90; role in revocation hearings, 115, 116; salary, 90; training, 93; use of working hours, 125–27

Parsons, Talcott, 8n

Partridge, Anthony, 23n

Pati, Gopal C., 163n

Phillips, Llad, 10n

Pierce, Lawrence W., 170n

Pilcher, William S., 94n

Pincoffs, Edmund L., 9n

Piven, Herman, 116n, 131n

Plea bargaining, 20, 21, 23

Portnoy, Barry, 155n

Powers, Sanger B., 15n

Pownall, George A., 17n, 150n, 157, 158, 159

President's Commission on Law Enforcement (1967), 128, 139

Prisoners: educating and training, 14, 17, 18; number of, 9n; protection of rights at parole board hearings, 39–40; reaction to deferred parole, 45–46; reaction to parole board hearing, 41–42; rehabilitation of, 13–19; working conditions of, 17

Prisons, 2, 3; distortion of society in, 16; public opinion poll on function of, 19; reform of, 14, 15–16

Probation: combined staff for parole and, 87–88, 124; federal organization of, 88–89; time spent on supervision during, 126

Project DEVELOP, 164n

Project EXCEL, 164

Project EXIT, 164

Prus, Robert Charles, 117n, 130

Public employment, for exoffenders, 153–54

Public opinion polls: on function of prisons, 19; on imprisonment, 68; on rehabilitation, 20; on sentencing, 19

Punishment. See Criminal punishment

Quinn, John P., 70n

Rachin, Richard L., 165n

Rankin, Anne, 140n

Recidivism: criteria of, 173–76; definition of, 173; effect of financial assistance on, 147, 148; effect of prerelease counseling on, 136; parole to reduce, 2, 135; problems in measuring, 173–76; rate of, 85, 177, 178; rehabilitation to reduce, 15

Reese, Charlotte, 28n
Reform: prison, 14, 15–16; sentencing, 24–25, 77–79, 185–87, 188
Rehabilitation, 4, 13, 187; failure of, 15, 18, 185; methods used in, 14; progress in, as criteria for release, 54; psychological problems influencing, 16; public opinion poll on, 20; structural problems influencing, 17–18
Renteria, Rudy, 136n
Resource Center on Correctional Law and Legal Services, 82n, 113n, 114n
Retribution, 8–9, 77, 185
Revocation of parole, 4; for absconding, 108–09; abuses in, 109–10; automatic, 108; disparities in standards for, 117–18; due process for, 105, 112, 113; effect of bureaucratic pressures on, 116–17, 130, 132; hearing for, 113–15; in lieu of prosecution, 107, 109; for new crimes committed, 106-07; reparole after, 118–20; short-term imprisonment as alternative to, 110–11; violation leading to, 104, 105
Risley, Henry B., 66n
Robinson, Paul H., 106n
Robison, James O., 53n, 67n, 68n, 116n, 117n, 130, 174n
Robison, Margo N., 121n
Rockefeller, Nelson, 10n
Root, Lawrence S., 141n, 142n, 144n
Rosenfeld, Anne H., 67n
Rossi, Peter H., 187n
Rothman, David J., 17n
Rottenberg, Simon, 7n, 10n
Rovner-Pieczenik, Roberta, 149n, 158n
Rubin, Sol, 70n
Rudoff, Alvin, 143n
Ryan, Ellen Jo, 94n

Salem, Richard G., 10n
Savitz, Leonard, 128n
Schwitzgebel, Ralph, 101n
Scott, Joseph E., 59–60, 94n
Scott, Ronald J., 16n
Seaberry, Jane, 156n
Seiler, Fanny, 29n
Senate Subcommittee on Criminal Laws and Procedures, 23n
Sentencing: as alternative to parole, 185–87, 188; crime deterrence and, 10–11; definite, 187, 188; disparities in, 22–23; guidelines for, 188; indeterminate, 21, 74, 77, 188; by judges, 20–23, 77, 186; by jury, 23–24; mandatory, 10n; presumptive, 77–78; proposed changes

in, 24–25, 77–79, 185–87, 188; public opinion polls on, 19; retribution and, 77; suspended, 22
Serrill, Michael S., 15n
Sherwood, Clarence C., 176n
Shin, H. Joo, 24n
Singer, Neil M., 17n, 140n
Singer, Richard G., 17n, 21n
Skolnick, Jerome H., 82n
Smith, Alexander B., 170n
Smith, Gerald W., 53n
Smith, Robert R., 144n
Smith, Ronald W., 10n
Standards and Goals Commission. See National Advisory Commission on Criminal Justice Standards and Goals
Standlee v. Smith, 107n, 174n
Stanley, David T., 130n
Stanton, John M., 51n, 57n
Studt, Elliot, 9n, 81n, 100, 102, 130, 132n, 137, 168, 169n, 190
Study-release programs, 144
Sturmthal, Joan, 140n
Sturz, Herbert, 140n
Sullivan, Clyde E., 159n
Supervision. See Surveillance, parolee
Surveillance, parolee, 4; effectiveness of, 95, 101, 122, 132–34, 180–81, 189; parolee's reaction to, 81–82, 100–01; proposed abolition of, 189–90; through personal contacts and visits, 96–99; time spent on, 126
Swanson, Richard W., 141n
Sweeney, Frank, 167n
Sykes, Gresham, 7n, 17n

Taggart, Robert, 149n
Takagi, Paul Takao, 104n, 116n, 117n, 127n, 130
Thomas, Charles W., 17n
Thorton, Donald, 167n
Tittle, Charles R., 11n
Toby, Jackson, 8n
Tullock, Gordon, 11n

United States ex rel. Johnson v. Chairman, 72n
University of Connecticut Law School, 180
U.S. Bureau of Prisons, 19; on inmate release funds, 145; on parolee employment, 151
U.S. Civil Service Commission, 155
U.S. Department of Justice, 27–28
U.S. Department of Labor: on bonding of exoffenders, 154; Model Exoffender Program, 162

U.S. Parole Board: combined parole-probation staff, 124; on disclosure of information, 75; members, 29; proposed independence from Justice Department, 27–28; revocation process, 114

Viano, Emilio, 11n, 142n
Violations of parole, 104, 105, 133
Virginia, furloughs for prisoners, 144
Vocational training, prison, 17, 18
von Hirsch, Andrew, 8n, 56n, 77n, 186n

Wald, Patricia M., 140n
Walker, Nigel, 23n, 25n
Ward, David A., 15n, 50n
Washington State, financial assistance to parolees, 147
Washington State Board of Prison Terms and Paroles, 57n
Wayson, Billy L., 7n
Weisman Steven R., 89n
Wells, Richard C., 163n
Wenk, Ernest A., 53n
West, Barbara, 167n
West Virginia parole board, 29
Wicker, Tom, 14n
Wilkins, Leslie T., 43n, 50n, 116n

Wilks, Judith, 15n
Wilner, Daniel M., 15n
Wilson, James Q., 7n, 23n, 24n
Wisconsin: combined parole-probation staff, 124; mutual agreement programming, 67; short-term jailings during parole, 105–06
Wisconsin parole board: effect of public opinion on decisions of, 60; factors influencing decisions of, 60; interviewing of prisoners by, 33n; members' qualifications, 34; notification of parole denial, 74; parole conditions, 83; revocation process, 112, 114
Witherspoon, A. D., 176n
Witt, Leonard R., 164n
Wolfgang, Marvin E., 128n
Wolin, Robert E., 102n, 168n
Wool, Robert, 34n, 40n, 63n
Work-release programs, 140–44

Yale Law School, study of sentencing process, 76–77, 188

Ziegler, Max, 122n
Zimring, Franklin E., 11n
Zumwalt, William James, 22n, 23n, 24n, 25n